Keene On Chess

ABOUT THE AUTHOR

Grandmaster Raymond Keene, multiple tournament winner, and former British Champion, is the world's most prolific chess writer, with more than 100 books to his credit including *World Champion Combinations* (with Eric Schiller) for Cardoza Publishing. Considered one of the strongest players in the world and one of the top theoreticians, Keene is well known for his work organizing world championships, his many best-selling chess titles, and for his co-authorship with World Champion Garry Kasparov and Eric Schiller on *Batsford Chess Openings* - the all-time best-selling reference work on chess openings.

Keene was the first British player to achieve a FIDE Grandmaster norm, was a member of eight Olympic chess teams, was a medal winner in the chess Olympiad, and was awarded the title Officer of the British Empire, by Queen Elizabeth II for his services to chess. He is the chess correspondent for the Spectator, London (since 1977), and Thames Television (since 1986), and writes the London Times daily chess column.

Keene On Chess

GM Raymond Keene

CARDOZA PUBLISHING

CARDOZA PUBLISHING CHESS TITLES

Our philosophy is to bring you the best quality chess books from the top authors and authorities in the chess world, featuring *words* (as opposed to hieroglyphics), *clear explanations* (as opposed to gibberish), *quality presentations* (as opposed to books simply slapped together), and *authoritative information*. And all this at reasonable prices.

First Edition

Library of Congress Catalogue Card No: 98-71031
ISBN: 1-58042-008-7

TABLE OF CONTENTS

INTRODUCTION
A Complete Chess Education in One Volume!

WHAT YOU WILL LEARN

In this book I have sought to cover all aspects of chess, from learning the basic moves, strategies and tactics, via simple endgames, to chess heroes and heroines of the past and the present, as well as the most outstanding games.

This is my personal choice of what is important. It is based on decades of writing chess columns, plus over 100 books, as well as articles for specialist chess magazines in over fifteen countries, including the USA, Australia, Germany, Spain, Holland and the Philippines. Over this time, I have come to develop a feeling for what my readers really want to know, what truly motivates them to pick up the chessboard and follow what I have written.

By reading further you will discover everything you ever wanted to know about chess in the covers of just one book. Your play will improve but you will also be able to astound your friends, colleagues and club members with your newfound knowledge about the entire tradition and intellectual riches of the world's greatest game!

HOW TO PLAY CHESS
All You Need to Know to Start Playing Chess

'It is always best to start at the Beginning'
- The Wizard of Oz

SIMPLIFIED CHESS NOTATION

Chess is a war game. Just as in a real war a general preparing for combat will scrutinize the field of battle and will examine closely the mobility and fighting capacity of every unit under his command, so we shall begin our study of chess with a thorough survey of the chessboard and pieces. The chess-player's battleground is an 8 x 8 square board.

The board looks like this:

Black's side

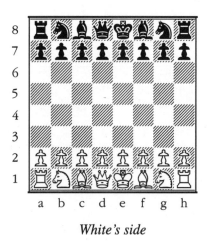

White's side

Two players will sit on opposite sides of the board. In representing this 3-dimensional situation in a 2-dimensional diagram the convention, which applies to chess books in general, is that White's side of the board is the bottom of the diagram and Black's is the top. Another accepted convention is that each player has a white square in his or her right hand corner.

Columns of squares stretching from White's side of the board to Black's are called **files**. Rows of squares stretching across the board are called **ranks**. Looking from White's side of the board, let us assign a letter to each of the files from left to right: a, b, c, d, e, f, g, h, and numbers to each of the ranks: 1, 2, 3, 4, 5, 6, 7, 8. Each square on the board has a unique designation - namely, the intersection of the symbols representing the file and the rank on which it stands. Thus the squares indicated by Roman numerals I-V are respectively, d1, f3, b4, e7, and h6.

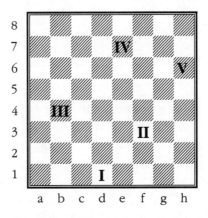

The labelling system outlined above forms the basis for the simplified modern notation. Well the chessboard is still empty, so let us enlarge our horizons by marshalling our forces for inspection. Each player controls an army consisting of sixteen units. Opposing forces are distinguished by different colors, normally White (W) and Black (B). These armies consist of:

eight *pawns*:	W pawn	♙	B pawn	♟
two *rooks*:	W rook	♖	B rook	♜
two *knights*:	W knight	♘	B knight	♞
two *bishops*:	W bishop	♗	B bishop	♝
one *queen*:	W queen	♕	B queen	♛
one *king*:	W king	♔	B king	♚

The letter symbols for each of the different kinds of chess piece are as follows:

K for king
Q for queen
B for bishop
N for knight
R for rook

Note that it is a convention that no special symbol is used for pawn moves!

At the start of the game these chessmen are set up as follows:

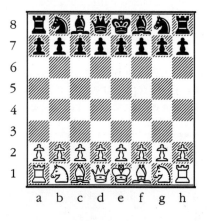

Let us look at the starting position more carefully. The pawns, line up on the second and seventh ranks; the rooks on a1, h1, a8 and h8, are commonly referred to as Castles and the horse-like pieces on b1, g1, b8 and g8 are the knights; and the mitre shaped pieces on c1, f1, c8 and f8 are the bishops.

This brings us neatly to the two key pieces, the queens on d1 and d8 and the kings on e1 and e8. The queen is the most powerful piece on the board, worth two rooks, or two knights and a bishop, while the king, although restricted in its movement, is the prime object of your own attack.

Note also that, except for the queen and king, the positions of the pieces are symmetrical. A simple rule to remember for where the queen and king get placed is this: *the queen starts on a square of her own color*. Thus, the White queen starts on d1, a white square, and the Black queen starts on d8, a black square.

The eight units on each side which are not pawns are called **pieces**, and a further distinction is also made: rooks and queens are called **major pieces**, while bishops and knights are called **minor pieces**. One more definition: the left half of the board is called the **queenside** (Q-side) and the right half is called the **kingside** (K-side).

BASICS OF CHESS

The players move alternately, with the player of the White pieces hereafter simply called **'White'** having the first move and the player of the Black pieces, **'Black'**, having the next move. A move consists of the transfer of a friendly unit from one square to another, according to specified rules. Such a move may involve the capture of an opposing unit, which is then removed from the board and takes no further part in the game.

The ultimate objective of each side is to capture the enemy king, and the game ends when the king of one side is threatened with capture and has no legal move which avoids this fate. Such a situation is known as **checkmate** and, of course, victory goes to the side who has checkmated the opposing king.

Not all games continue as far as checkmate: in many cases a player will surrender gracefully, that is, **resign**, long before the end because he or she can see that his or her opponent has an overwhelming superiority in either position or material (extra pieces) and that further resistance would be futile. In tournament games, which are played to the clock, it is also possible to forfeit the game by exceeding the time limit.

Also a game may be drawn for any one of a variety of reasons: by **attrition**, when there is insufficient material (pieces) left for either side to inflict checkmate, or because the side whose turn it is to move has run out of legal moves (**stalemate**), by three-fold repetition of the same position, or because a certain number of moves elapse without substantial alteration to the position (the **50 move' rule**), or even simply by agreement between the players. We shall discuss the possible outcomes of a game more fully later.

1. In the starting position one possible move for White is to advance the pawn from c2 to c4 to produce the following diagram:

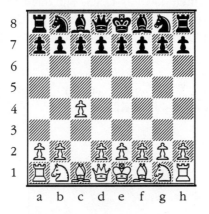

We would record this move as **1.c4.** White's pawn on c2 is, as we shall see, the only pawn which can reach c4, so there is no possible ambiguity about which pawn has moved. Black, in reply might choose to advance the pawn from e7 to e5.

Black has just moved

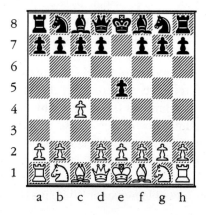

Black's move would be written down as **1...e5**. The three dots indicate that it is a Black move we are describing. But when we write down a sequence of White and Black moves together we shall omit the dots. The first two moves would be written as follows:

1.c4 e5.

2. In the following diagram, White's rook can, for example, reach f3. If White chose to move the rook to f3 we would write this as **Rf3**.

White to Play Rf3

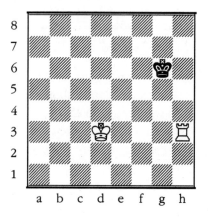

3. Sometimes, however, we shall need to be more precise. In the next diagram, both Black rooks can reach d2 in one move.

Both black rooks can reach d2

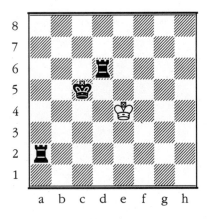

If the rook on d6 moved to d2 we should write this as **...Rdd2** while if the rook on a2 moved to d2 we would record it as **...Rad2.**

4. A piece captures an opposing piece by moving to the square on which the opposing piece is located. We have a special symbol to indicate a capture; a cross, **'x'**.

White to Play Rg8

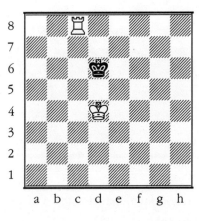

White to Play Rxg8

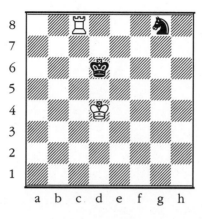

Thus in the former diagram White could move his rook from c8 to g8, written in our notation as **Rg8**. In the latter diagram, the same move is possible, but this time a Black knight is captured on g8, and so we would write the move as **Rxg8** instead. In either case, the resulting position would be the same:

After Rg8 or Rxg8

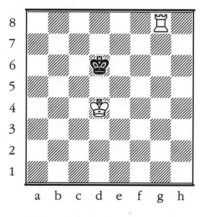

There are one or two other minor notational changes and special symbols connected with particular situations (checks, promotion, castling, en passant captures), but we shall defer consideration of these, until we have learned how the pieces actually move. Reading the moves is vitally important, so please review this important section if you are at all uncertain about this!

HOW THE PIECES MOVE - RELATIVE VALUES OF THE PIECES

It is a basic rule of chess that two units cannot occupy the same square simultaneously: when a unit moves to a square already occupied by an enemy man, a capture takes place, and the original resident is removed from the board. The capture of a unit belonging to one's own side is not permitted.

There is, however, a basic obligation to move; passing or losing a turn is not allowed in chess. It may happen that it is your turn to play and you find that every possible move leads to disaster, although your game would be perfectly defensible if your men were allowed to retain their present positions. Such situations occur with sufficient frequency for chess-players to have invented a special name for them. They are called **zugzwang** positions, 'zugzwang' being a German word meaning 'compulsion to move'. It is quite easy to construct positions in which both sides are in zugzwang and whoever has the move loses.

Another possibility is that the side whose turn it is to move has no legal moves; this is called *stalemate* and the game automatically terminates in a draw when a stalemate position is reached.

The coming sections will introduce the various pieces, examining the powers and limitations of each.

THE RELATIVE VALUE OF THE PIECES

Most chess games are decided through simple superiority of force. Either through good play or through the opponent's carelessness, one player will obtain a material advantage sufficient to determine the outcome of the game. Even at beginner's levels, the loss of a piece without compensation usually results in the loss of the game. Here is a 'point count' table to help you estimate the relative strengths of the pieces.

Pawn　 = 1 point
Knight = 3 points
Bishop = 3 points
Rook　 = 5 points
Queen = 9 points

Needless to say, the table gives no value for the king, since this piece can never be exchanged. If you like, the king is worth an infinite number of points. This point count table is in general, an honest reflection of the experience of chess players over the years.

Now I move on to examine in detail each individual piece, their special movements and their checkmating capacity.

THE KING - THE PARAMOUNT PIECE

The **king's** move is simple: one square in any direction. Diagram 13 shows three different king positions and the possible squares which the king can reach in one move from each location:

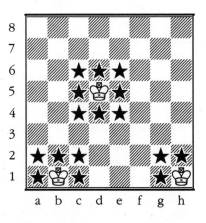

From a central square (d5) the king could move to any one of eight other squares indicated by a star in the diagram, namely c4, c5, c6, d4, d6, e4, e5, e6. A king on the edge of the board (b1) has five squares available - a1, a2, b2, c1, c2 - while a king in the corner (h1) is reduced to three - g1, g2, h2.

There is one exceptional case, called **castling**, in which the king moves two squares in one turn. Castling is a combination move of two pieces at once, so we shall postpone discussion of this case, until we know something about the rook, which is also involved in the castling operation. For the moment let us note a few obvious, but important, points:

1. In the following diagram, the king on f3 cannot move to either e2 or g2 because White units already occupy these squares, however, the king can move to f4, capturing the Black knight as it does so.

King Moves

2. The king is highly maneuverable, but is not a long-range piece - its sphere of influence

is confined to the adjacent squares. To attack enemy units, it must move up next to them, and if caught in an advanced position it can only retreat slowly. These factors combine to limit the usefulness of the king as an aggressive force; king safety must always be paramount. Remember, the object of the game for each player is to checkmate the enemy king!

Generally speaking, it is only in the later stages of the game (the endgame), when most of the pieces have been exchanged off through captures and the chance of snap checkmates is diminished, that the king emerges as a fighter; earlier on the risk of exposure is too great and the king's role tends to be defensive in character.

3. The activity of the king - measured by the number of possible moves it can make, or, equivalently, by the number of squares it controls - is diminished if it is placed on the edge of the board. We shall see this exploited repeatedly in elementary mating situations (king and queen against king, for instance) where the first stage in delivering the mate is to force the king to the edge where its freedom of action is reduced.

Check To The King

A king is said to be **in check** when it is threatened with capture by an opposing unit. A player, whose king is in check, has as his or her primary duty to avert the danger to the monarch, that is, to get out of check. If this is impossible, then **checkmate** has occurred, and the game is over. Royal suicide is prohibited - it is illegal to put one's own king in check. There are three ways of evading a check: by moving the king out of harm's way, by capturing the enemy man which delivers the check, or if the king is being attacked from a distance, by interposing a friendly unit to block the check. If more than one way of stopping a check is possible, the player may choose whichever move he or she thinks best.

If a player is in check and plays a move which fails to stop the check, then the move is illegal and must be retracted. To alert the opponent and avoid embarrassment, some players announce the fact that they have played a checking move by saying 'check' as they make the move. This practice is less common among masters, who are expected to notice such things for themselves. It is, however, customary to indicate a check when writing down a move; this is done by adding the symbol '+' at the end of the ordinary description of the move. Thus, the difference between the moves Qh5 and Qh5+ is that the latter attacks the enemy king while the former does not.

Note that if White is to move in the following diagram, he cannot play any of the moves 1.Kd5, 1.Ke5, and 1.Kf5, for after each of these moves the White king would be next to the Black king, and in reply, Black could capture White's king with his own. Hence, these three moves are illegal because they involve moving into check.

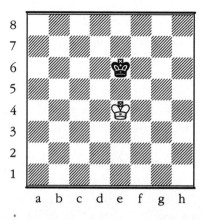

Two kings placed as in diagram 17 are said to be in **opposition**. In such a position which-ever side has the move cannot advance his own king any further and must maintain his king at its present location if he is to prevent the advance of the enemy monarch. Thus, it can be a disadvantage to have the move when the kings are in opposition. The player whose turn it is not to move is said to 'have the opposition'. As we shall see, the outcome of king and pawn end-ings sometimes hinges on which side can get the opposition.

STALEMATE

Stalemate occurs when one side has no legal moves at all, but has not been checkmated. This is a draw. We will observe various examples of this as we progress through the capacities of the different pieces.

THE QUEEN - HOW TO GIVE CHECKMATE
The Queen

The king is the most important piece on the chessboard, but the **queen** is the most power-ful. The queen is allowed to move through any number of empty squares along a rank, file or diagonal in a single move. It cannot turn corners, nor can it move through or on to a square already occupied by a friendly unit. It cannot move through a square occupied by an enemy man, although it can move on to such a square, capturing the hostile unit on that square.

Movements of the Queen

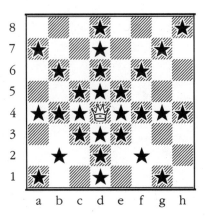

Power of the Queen

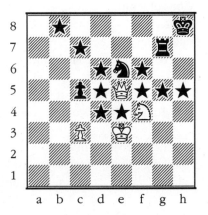

The former diagram shows a queen on d4 with an otherwise open board. In one move the queen can reach any one of the squares indicated by a star in the diagram, a total of 27 possible moves.

In the latter diagram White has 13 possible queen moves. The queen can move to any of the 10 empty squares marked with an star or could capture Black's pawn, knight or rook. Note that Black is not in check in the above diagram: White's queen is not attacking h8 because the Black rook is in the way.

In contrast to the king, the queen is very definitely a long-range piece capable of moving large distances rapidly. Part of its usefulness in attack derives from the fact that it can threaten two widely separated enemy units at once:

The Fork ...Qf2+

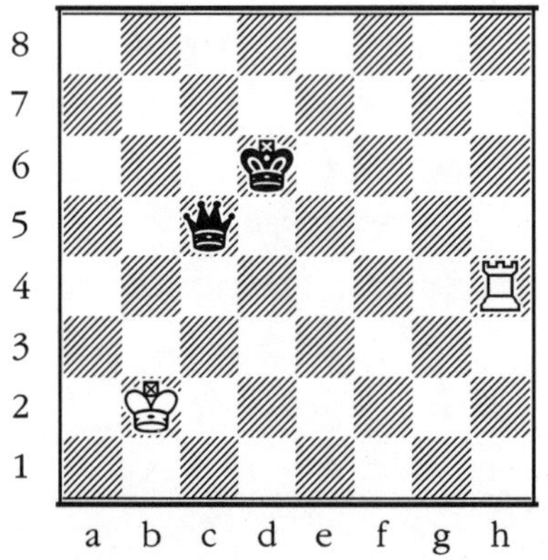

THE FORK

Black's best move in the previous diagram is 1...Qf2+ attacking both king and rook. White in reply must move his king to get out of check and then Black will capture White's rook on the next move. This is a simple example of an elementary tactical motif called the **fork** - a simultaneous threat against two (or more) enemy pieces. The astute reader will have noticed that in this diagram Black has two other forking possibilities, 1...Qb4+ and 1...Qd4+, but, as we shall verify when we come to study the rook's powers, both of these moves are bad for Black, since White's reply in either case would be to take Black's queen with his rook, rather than move his king.

In common with most of the other pieces, a queen placed in the center controls more squares than a queen placed on the edge. From a corner position the queen controls fewest squares of all. A well centralized queen can often exert a dominating influence over the whole board.

THE SKEWER

The **skewer** is illustrated in the following diagram. How does White, to move, win Black's queen?

White Plays Qh2+

White plays Qh2+. Black's king must move, then, as a result of the attack, White picks off the Black queen in the rear. In full, 1.Qh2+ Ke6; 2.Qxc7 and White wins on material.

Checkmate with King and Queen Against King

This is one of the most important checkmates, and it must be learned, otherwise many well-earned victories will escape you!

Mating with king and queen against king alone is, fortunately, an easy technical exercise. The way to solve a problem like this is to look first for a mating position and then seek a way to bring this position about. A few moments' study over a chessboard should convince the reader that there are plenty of mating positions, all of them in essence similar to one or the other of those shown in the following two diagrams.

Checkmate

Checkmate

In the former diagram, White's king is used to cover Black's flight squares on the seventh rank while his queen delivers the fatal lateral check. In the latter diagram, the queen covers all the escape squares single-handed; the function of White's king is merely to protect the queen.

The main feature to note about the previous two diagrams is that in both cases Black's king is trapped on the edge of the board. No mating positions exist with Black's king in the middle. Hence if we are faced with a fairly random configuration such as the above diagram and asked to deliver checkmate, our first task will be to drive Black's monarch towards the perimeter of the board like so: 1.Qb5 Ke6; 2.Qc6+ Ke7; 3.Kf5 Kd8 (3...Kf7; 4.Qd7+) 4.Qb7 Ke8; 5.Ke6 Kf8; 6.Qf7 mate.

THE PAWNS - SPECIAL RULES
The Pawns

For most of the game the **pawn's** role is uninspiring. The true cannon fodder of the army, the pawn's job is to secure and hold down territory or perhaps expend itself in an assault against the enemy positions. It is slow moving and vulnerable. When not in the immediate proximity of its fellows, it experiences great difficulty in defending itself and avoiding capture. Sometimes the pawns only seem to get in the way and restrict the scope of their own pieces.

But the chess-player's army is truly democratic; any pawn which survives long enough and advances far enough will suddenly find, as we shall see shortly, that it has been transformed into that most glorious of pieces - the queen.

The Soul of Chess

The eighteenth century master Andre Philidor said of pawns that they were the 'soul of chess', and he was not far from the truth. They add a much needed strategic element to what would otherwise be an almost purely tactical game. Piece configurations are fluid and can change rapidly. In contrast, pawn formations are relatively static and often remain stable for extended periods. You can build your whole game around them. Indeed, many more chess games are won through exploiting weaknesses in the enemy pawn structure, than through direct attacks against the opposing king.

We shall expand these strategic ideas at a later stage. First, we need to look at how the pawns actually move. The most basic characteristic of pawns is that they travel in only one direction - forward. When moving to an empty square pawns normally move one square forward at a time along the file. An exception is made if the pawn has not previously moved and is still on its starting position; then it may, for its initial move only, advance two squares along the file instead of one. It is not obliged to move two squares - this is only an extra option.

Pawns have a different action when capturing: they capture by moving one square diagonally. They cannot capture straight ahead.

The various types of pawn moves are illustrated in diagram 30:

Pawn Moves and Captures

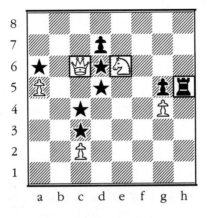

White's a-pawn has only one move: the basic one square forward. White's c-pawn is on its starting square (c2) and so has the choice of moving either one or two squares forward. White's g-pawn cannot move directly forward, since the square immediately ahead is blocked, but it can capture Black's rook by moving one square forward along the diagonal. Of the two black pawns, Black's g-pawn cannot move at all, while Black's d-pawn has four possible moves available: ...dxc6, ...dxe6, ...d6, and ...d5. The stars indicate the empty squares to which the pawns can advance, a box surrounding a square shows the captures possible.

Pawn Power

As the game progresses, the pawns will move farther down the board away from their home squares. When a White pawn reaches the 8th rank (or a Black pawn reaches the 1st rank) - the opponent's edge of the board - it has gone as far as it can go and runs out of normal moves. A transformation then takes place and the player who owns the pawn can replace it by any other type of piece he desires except a king.

This process is called **promotion** or, more popularly, **queening a pawn**, since in actual play one almost always chooses to promote to a queen. Subsequently, the promoted pawn behaves exactly as if it were an ordinary queen or whichever piece was chosen. Thus, it is theoretically possible for a player to have as many as nine queens on the board at the same time. There is no restriction on the number of pawns which a player can promote. The pawn is the only piece which promotes upon reaching the back rank.

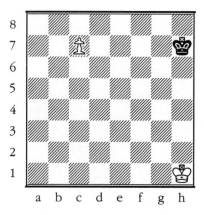

The pawn is on the seventh rank, just one step away from the eighth rank and promotion.

The pawn has advanced to the eighth rank. As part of the same move, the pawn has been removed from the board and a queen put in its place.

There is of course, a special notation for promotions. In the next diagram we see a position in which both sides are ready to promote pawns. White plays first and advances the pawn to d8 and promotes it to a queen. We write White's move as **1.d8=Q.** Then it is Black's turn and Black replies by capturing White's knight with the pawn. Black's pawn, too, has now reached its goal and is ready for promotion and Black also chooses a queen. Black's move would be written as **1...gxf1=Q.** After these two moves the position reached is shown in the second diagram.

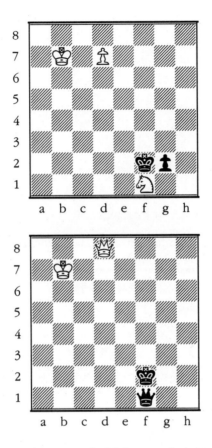

Underpromotion - promotion to rook, bishop, or knight - is rare in practical play, although it does provide a fruitful theme for composed studies. Note that a pawn must always be promoted to something. It cannot just sit there as a pawn. There might be times, when playing for stalemate, for example, when it would be advantageous to leave the pawn as a pawn, but the rules do not allow this.

Pawn Endgames

Each side starts with a complement of eight pawns and, although some will inevitably be exchanged or eliminated in the course of play, pawnless positions occur infrequently. When they do occur, they are usually much harder to win than positions with pawns. With no pawns left on the board, the general rule is that one side has to be massively ahead in material - a rook or two minor pieces up - in order to be able to force a victory.

With pawns left, the advantage of a single extra pawn is often a winning one, for this could later become the advantage of an extra queen.

In the ending of king and pawn against king the defending side usually has no hope unless he can control the pawn's queening square, but, when he can, drawing possibilities arise. The following diagram illustrates such a case.

The correct technique for White is to leave his pawn where it is for the moment and to drive Black's king away from d8 by advancing his own king. But this must be done carefully to avoid giving Black the opposition, which would spoil everything. The only move to win is 1.Kc5, e.g., 1...Kd7; 2.Kd5 Ke7; 3.Kc6 Kd8; 4.Kd6 Ke8; 5.Kc7. Success! Black no longer controls d8 and White is ready to advance his pawn. 5...Ke7; 6.d5 Ke8; 7.d6 Kf7; 8.d7 Ke6; 9.d8=Q and Black could resign.

Now return to the previous diagram and let us see what happens if White incautiously plays 1.Kd5 (the immediate 1.d5 leads to similar play) instead of 1.Kc5. Black would then reply 1...Kd7 (gaining the opposition) 2.Kc5 Kc7 and White can make no further progress with his king, so his only winning try must be to advance his pawn: 3.d5 Kd7; 4.d6 Kd8; 5.Kc6 Kc8; 6.d7+ Kd8 reaching the following diagram.

A Draw

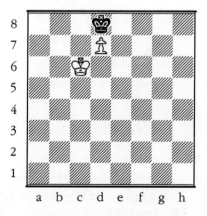

But what can White play now? If he moves his king away from the pawn, Black simply takes the pawn, 7...Kxd7, while if White plays 7.Kd6 - which is the only king move that protects the pawn - Black is in stalemate! Either way, the game must be drawn.

Always a Draw

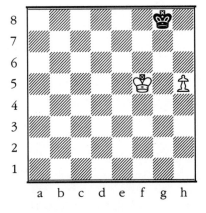

The rook's pawn always poses special difficulties in such endings. In this diagram Black draws, even though White can get the opposition, for he can never force black's king away from the queening square: 1.Kg6 Kh8; 2.Kh6 Kg8; 3.Kg6. Now we see the problem. White cannot out-flank Black's king because he has run out of board. 3...Kh8; 4.h6 Kg8; 5.h7+ Kh8; 6.Kh6 with the usual stalemate.

If there are additional pawns on the board, the task of the side with the extra pawn is usually much easier. The diagram below is typical.

White Wins

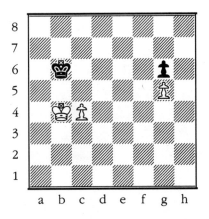

White no longer need concern himself that Black has the opposition - he can just march his king across the board and win Black's g-pawn: 1.c5+ Kc6; 2.Kc4 Kc7; 3.Kd4 Kc6; 4.Ke5 Kxc5; 5.Kf6 Kd6; 6.Kxg6 Ke7; 7.Kh7 and White's remaining pawn cannot be stopped from promoting to a queen, after which White wins as previously described.

A Special Case - En Passant

One special situation involving pawns can occur which I have not yet described - the **en passant** capture. The possibility of an en passant capture (referred to as **e.p.**) arises when a pawn on its starting square takes advantage of its initial move of two squares to bypass an enemy pawn which could have captured it - *if it had moved only one square forward.* A special rule then allows the opponent *on his next move only* to play the pawn capture as if the pawn had moved one square forward. The following three diagrams illustrate what happens. In the first, White plays 1.e4, bypassing Black's pawn on f4 which controls the intermediate square e3. Black in reply plays 1...fxe3 e.p. moving his pawn from f4 to e3 (second diagram) and removing White's pawn from the board. The resulting position is shown in the final diagram.

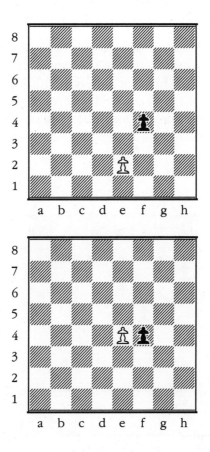

It is important to remember that the option to capture en passant must be exercised immediately or not at all. The en passant rule is not as arbitrary as it might at first appear. In earlier days, before the rules of chess had been completely codified, pawns were only allowed to move one square forward at a time in all positions. The initial double-square pawn move was introduced to speed up the game, but this innovation had one deleterious effect: it made it possible to use the double move to block a pawn position, so the en passant rule was adopted to prevent this happening.

Black to Play

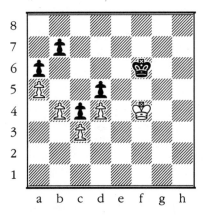

This diagram shows a position in which the possibility of an en passant capture changes the result of the game. Without the en passant rule Black, to move, could play 1...b5 and the game would be drawn. As it is, Black is in zugzwang; 1...b5 would be met by 2.axb6 e.p. and after a Black king move, White's king can penetrate, e.g. 1...Ke6; 2.Kg5 Ke7; 3.Kf5 Kd6; 4.Kf6 Kd7; 5.Ke5 Kc6; 6.Ke6 and Black can no longer defend the d-pawn.

THE ROOKS - HOW TO CASTLE
The Rook

Rooks move only along ranks and files - never along diagonals. In one move a rook can travel as many squares as it likes along a rank or file provided there is nothing blocking the path. As with the queen, a rook cannot move past a square occupied by another unit, and it captures in the usual way - by moving onto the square of the man it captures. The rook's action is illustrated in the following diagram:

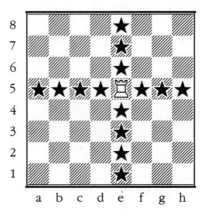

In this diagram the rook can reach any square marked with a star in a single move. Notice that, unlike the other pieces, the rook's activity is not necessarily reduced if it is positioned at or near the edge of the board - it still controls the same number of squares. In most positions, the critical factor determining whether or not a rook is actively placed is the presence (or absence) of open lines along which the rook can operate. Thus, in the next diagram, White's rook is hemmed in by pawns and is completely out of play, while Black's rook has the run of the board.

Rook Mobility

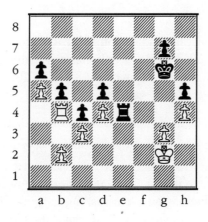

Checkmate with the Rook

Mating with king and rook against king is almost as easy as mating with king and queen against king. A typical mating sequence is shown in the next two diagrams. Again, as with the queen, the first step in the mating process is to push the opposing king to the edge of the board.

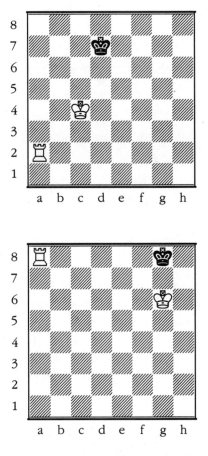

Checkmate

Thus, from the first diagram, play might continue: 1.Ra6 (cutting off the monarch from the center) 1...Ke7; 2.Kd5 Kf7 (2...Kd7 3.Ra7+ only hastens matters); 3.Re6 Kg7; 4.Ke5 Kf7; 5.Kf5 Kg7; 6.Re7+ Kf8; 7.Kf6 Kg8; 8.Ra7 Kh8 (or 8...Kf8 9 Ra8 mate) 9.Kg6 Kg8 and now 10.Ra8 mate brings us back to the latter diagram.

CASTLING

There is a special move involving the king and (either) rook called **castling**. Depending on whether the king's rook or queen's rook is used, we speak of **castling kingside** or **castling queenside**. This is the only move in which two pieces change position on the board simultaneously. There are severe limitations on when castling is legal. The most important requirements to be met, before the moves can be played, are that neither the king nor the rook involved may have made any previous moves (so both will be on their starting positions) and the squares between them must be vacant. The castling maneuver consists of moving the king two squares along the back rank towards the rook and then moving the rook to the square through which the king has passed. Thus, in the next two diagrams we see White before and after having castled kingside: the king moves from e1 to g1 and the king's rook from h1 to f1.

Before Castling Kingside

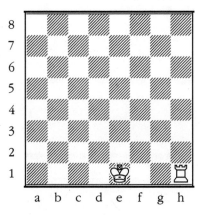

After Castling Kingside

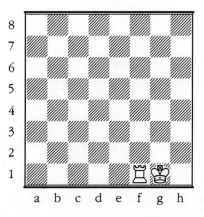

The analogous move with the queen's rook, queenside castling, is shown in the following two diagrams: White's king moves from e1 to c1 and his rook moves from a1 to d1. Black's castling mimics this, ...Ke8-g8 and ...Rh8-f8 for kingside castling, with ...Ke8-c8 and ...Ra8-d8 for queenside castling.

Before Queenside Castling

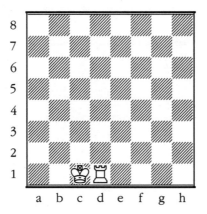

After Queenside Castling

Restrictions on Castling

There are two further conditions which must be satisfied before castling is possible:

1. The king may not castle if it is in check - but it regains the right to castle once the check has been removed, provided that the king has not moved in the meantime. Of course, it may not castle into check either.

2. Castling is prohibited if the square through which the king passes (i.e. the square on which the rook finishes) is under attack by an enemy unit.

It is possible to castle, even if the rook involved is threatened. Also, queenside castling is permitted even if the square b1 (or b8 in Black's case) is under fire, for this square is not one which the king crosses.

Naturally, we shall need special symbols in our notation to denote these castling moves. We designate kingside castling by 0-0 and queenside castling by 0-0-0. Thus, in the next diagram, Black has already played ...0-0 at some previous point in the game. White to move, may play 0-0 if he wishes, but 0-0-0 is illegal, since a Black rook covers d1, the square through which the king must pass.

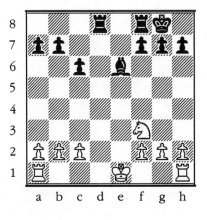

Benefits of Castling

The restriction that neither king nor rook have previously moved means that each side can castle at most once during a game. It also usually means that castling takes place at an early stage, if at all. Castling is often a most desirable move during the opening phase of the game, especially if the central pawns have been advanced, for it has the effect of bringing the king to a position of greater safety and at the same time allowing a rook to enter active service without delay.

THE BISHOPS - THE DOUBLE BISHOP MATE

Bishops move solely along diagonals. Their range of action is similar to the pieces previously studied - they move as many squares as they wish along one diagonal and must stop if they reach a square occupied by an enemy unit (which they may capture) or if blocked by a friendly unit.

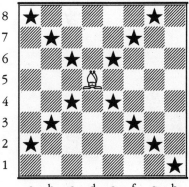

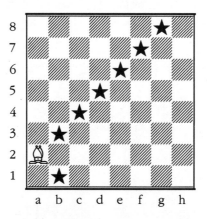

As we can see in the above two diagrams, where the bishop can reach in one move any one of the squares indicated by stars, the bishop is among those pieces which benefit from being placed near the center of the board where two useful diagonals can be controlled. Thus the bishop on d5 can reach 13 squares in a single move, while the bishop on a2 can reach only 7.

The most obvious and significant feature of the bishop's scope is that it is restricted to moving on squares of one color. Half the squares on the board will always remain immune from its attentions. In the starting position each side is given two bishops, one of which travels on light squares and the other on dark squares. Like bookends, these bishops function best as a pair. If one is exchanged off, a weakness may develop on the squares of the color it protected.

The next diagram provides a cautionary example: White to move played 1.Bxd5. Normally this exchange would be advantageous (a rook is more valuable than a bishop) but in this position it is suicidal because of the weak light squares which are created around White's king. Note that black still has his light square bishop on the board to exploit these weaknesses.

White to Play

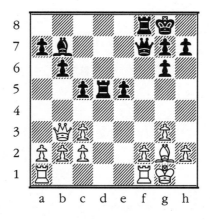

White was swiftly punished: after 1.Bxd5 there followed 1...Bxd5; 2.Qa4 Qf3 and White could not avoid being mated on g2.

THE PIN

A **pinned** piece is fettered to a more valuable piece behind it, but a piece pinned to the king is physically immobilized! I will exemplify this with a position which baffled many readers of my daily column in *The Times*.

White to Play

This position is from the game Leko-Lendwai, Erevan Olympiad 1996. 1.Bc6 wins, e.g. 1...Qxc6; 2.Qxf8 checkmate.

Many readers asked what about 1.Bc6 Rxd1+?

This is not possible as 1.Bc6 pins Black's d7 rook to the black king, and stops the rook from moving. The response 1...Rxd1+ (even though it will put White in check) is simply not an option. It is illegal, because it puts Black's own king in check!

In the ending, *bishops of opposite colors* are an important drawing factor. In the next diagram, although White is two pawns up, the opposite color polarity of the bishops ensures that Black will not lose.

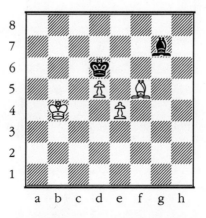

White has no control over the dark squares and hence no method of breaking up Black's blockade of e5 and d6 and advancing his pawns. To draw, Black simply shuffles his bishop back and forth along the a1 h8 diagonal.

Another unusual endgame position is shown in the next diagram. White to play. What should be the result?

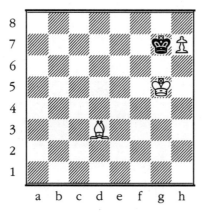

In spite of massive material advantage, the best White can achieve is stalemate, if Black keeps the king in touch with h8. The wing pawn is promoting on the wrong colored square for White's bishop.

Two Bishop Mate

Two bishops can mate a king rather easily. A typical mating position is shown in the next diagram.

Now start from the diagram below and see if you can reach it.

White to Play

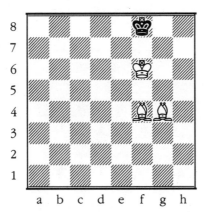

One line is 1.Bd7 Kg8; 2.Kg6 Kf8; 3.Bd6+ Kg8; 4.Be6+ Kh8; 5.Be5 mate.

THE KNIGHTS - LEAPING OVER OBSTACLES
The Knight

The move of the **knight** is rather crab-like: one square along a rank or file followed by one square along a diagonal. This is best illustrated by the diagram below: White's knight can reach any of the eight squares indicated by the stars.

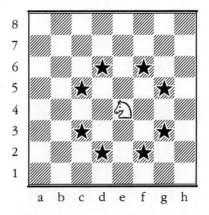

Near the edge of the board the knight has less mobility; for example, a knight on a1 can reach only the squares b3 or c2 in one move.

Compared to the other pieces the knight is ponderously slow. Three moves will not quite take it from one side of the board to the opposite side. But in compensation, it possesses one advantage not enjoyed by any other piece. Unlike the crab (but rather like the horse we use as a symbol) the knight can jump over intervening obstacles, whether enemy or friendly.

Thus, in the next diagram, White's knight on e4 could still get to the same eight squares, even if it were surrounded by a ring of pawns.

The Knight's Leap

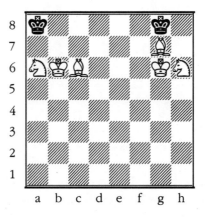

The general conclusion which may be drawn, is that in open positions with mobile pawns, the bishop is superior to the knight, while in closed positions, with fixed pawns the knight may be the master of the bishop. Bishops loath blocked positions; the agile knight enjoys maneuvering around pawn barriers. Both bishop and knight are normally inferior to a rook. A player who has a rook against his opponent's bishop or knight is said to have the advantage of the exchange. (The Russians say 'the advantage of quality' which is perhaps more descriptive.)

As a crude approximation, the advantage of the exchange is roughly equivalent in material terms to two pawns.

Checkmate with Bishop and Knight

Mating with bishop and knight against a lone king is nontrivial although it is always possible. The above diagram shows the mating positions, the salient feature of each being that Black's king must not only be on the edge of the board, but near a corner square of the same color as those used by the bishop. From an unfavorable starting position it may take as many as thirty-four moves to drive the king into such a corner and mate him.

It is not possible to deliver mate with two knights against king unless the opposition cooperates. There is a mating position but this can only be reached if Black plays inferior moves.

One of the difficulties is shown in the next diagram: White, to move, can force Black into the corner 1.Kg6 Kg8; 2.Nd7 Kh8; 3.Ne8 Kg8; 4.Nf6+ Kh8 but has no time for 5.Ne5 and 6.Nf7 mate because after 5.Ne5 the position is stalemate.

CLASHES BETWEEN CHAMPIONS

You now know how to read the moves of a chess game, how all the pieces move, what all the pieces are worth, and how to give checkmate. Armed with this knowledge, I now show you samples of play between former champions of the game - but before we see the greats in action, here are two pieces of preparatory information.

TWO QUICK CHECKMATES WITH THE QUEEN

1. Fool's Mate

The fastest known checkmate is called 'Fool's Mate' and goes like this: **1.f3 e5; 2.g4 Qh4 checkmate.**

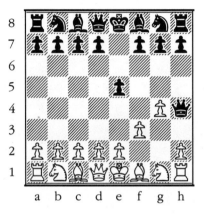

The reason for this name is obvious.

2. Scholar's Mate

This is more subtle, and you must know how to counter it, but it is unwise to try for it yourself against anyone but the weakest of beginners, since White's attack can easily be beaten off.

1.e4 e5; 2.Bc4 Bc5; 3.Qf3 Nc6; 4.Qxf7 checkmate

Scholar's Mate

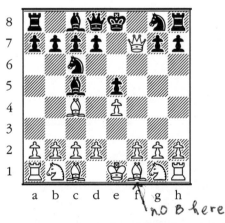

no B here

Naturally, Black's third move was very weak and failed to stop the threat to f7. By playing 3...Nf6, Black both develops a piece and easily blocks White's attack on f7.

One final word of caution: because the queen is the most valuable and powerful piece on the board, she is also uniquely susceptible to attack from enemy units of lesser worth. Usually the only defense to such threats is to retreat the queen to a position of greater safety, since the exchange of the queen for any other piece would confer a considerable material advantage on the opponent.

Beginners at chess often start their games in this way: at the earliest possible opportunity they will develop their queen to some imposing (but exposed) central square and then search around for some way to deliver a quick knockout punch to the enemy king. Against an experienced adversary, such a naive conception of strategy just accelerates defeat. The opponent merely sends out his minor pieces to harry the luckless queen, and her unhappy owner winds up having to waste several moves in bringing her back to shelter.

No general in real battle would send his best and least expendable troops on a mad charge against the enemy trenches; he would rather hold them in reserve until a break-through had been achieved by other means and only then use them to enlarge his advantage.

In the same way on the chessboard, one should deploy one's queen with great care and usually not commit her to action until weaknesses have appeared in the enemy camp, which her particular talents are capable of exploiting.

SOME EXTRA NOTATION

By now you should feel at home with the simplified modern notation system for chess moves, which we have been using. In subsequent parts of this book, I shall be looking at more complicated positions and I shall frequently wish to assign praise or blame to individual moves.

I now shall introduce some new symbols, with expressive, rather than descriptive, content.

!! means brilliant move
! means a strong move (usually also the best move)
!? means interesting or provocative move
?! means dubious move
? means weak move
?? means blunder

In Fool's Mate, White's second move gets "??", as does Black's third move in Scholar's Mate.

Here are some samples of how the new symbols are used:

RESHEVSKY VS. FISCHER
Palma 1970

Black to Play

This is a position from the game Reshevsky-Fischer, Palma 1970. It illustrates a tactical point frequently seen in positions where major pieces are active - the back rank mate. This can arise when the pawns in front of the castled king are unmoved and consequently the king has no flight squares on the second rank. Such is the case in the diagram and Bobby Fischer exploited this slight defect in White's formation by playing 1...Qf4! which threatens 2...Qxf1 mate - a back rank mate with the queen. White cannot reply by playing 2 Rxf4?? because this allows a back rank mate with the rook: 2...Re1+; 3.Rf1 Rxf1 mate.

White's best move after 1...Qf4 is just 2.Qb5! protecting the rook, after which the position is roughly equal. However, Reshevsky chose 2.Kg1?? (even Grandmasters make mistakes sometimes) and had to resign after 2...Qd4+; 3.Kh1 (or 3 Rf2 Re1 mate - a useful pin) 3...Qf2! since he must either lose a rook or allow mate; 4.Qb5 Re1.

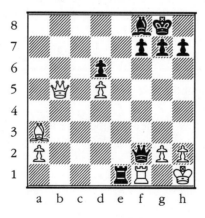

HOWARD STAUNTON - They Named the Pieces after Him!

Howard Staunton (1810-1874) is the only British player who can legitimately lay claim to being world champion. All the diagrams in this book are based on the pieces named after him, and the odds are that the chess set you are using is also a Staunton pattern set.

In Staunton's day, the world champion title was not officially recognised. However, by the time of his match victory over the French champion St. Amant at Paris in 1843, Staunton had not only laid the pattern for future championship matches but had also established himself as the strongest player of his day.

Staunton was a towering figure, a polymath who edited an entire edition of Shakespeare's plays, commenced a history of the public school system in Britain, wrote numerous books on chess, organized the first international chess tournament at London in 1851 and lent his name to the Staunton patent pieces which are now the standard in international play. Staunton was an archetypal symbol of the heights of Victorian imperial grandeur and optimism. Here is a superb example of Staunton's aesthetic play at its best.

One of the best exercises to improve your chess is to play through the moves of master games and think hard about the players' strategy and tactics.

STAUNTON VS. HORWITZ
London 1851
Dutch Defense

1.c4. Staunton's frequent use of 1.c4 earned it the name of 'English Opening'. **1...e6; 2.Nc3 f5; 3.g3 Nf6; 4.Bg2 c6.**

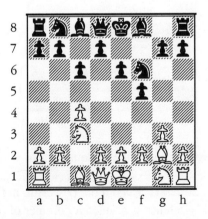

Horwitz, a German master from Berlin, has chosen an aggressive Dutch Defense set up against White's English Opening, but he soon compromises his position by interpreting the line in excessively passive fashion.

5.d3 Na6; 6.a3 Be7; 7.e3 0-0; 8.Nge2 Nc7; 9.0-0 d5; 10.b3. Staunton was fond of the double flank development of his bishop, known as 'fianchetto'. There can be no doubt, however, that this formation is somewhat time-consuming and Horwitz should now have seized his chance to exploit this by occupying the center with his pawns by 10...e5. **10...Qe8; 11.Bb2 Qf7; 12.Rc1 Bd7**. Black should still have played ...e5!

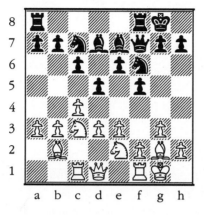

13.e4! This central thrust, all the stronger for being delayed, announces that White has won the battle of the opening. **13...fxe4; 14.dxe4 Rad8; 15.e5.** Black is driven back on all fronts. **15...Nfe8; 16.f4 dxc4; 17.bxc4 Bc5+; 18.Kh1 Be3; 19.Rb1.**

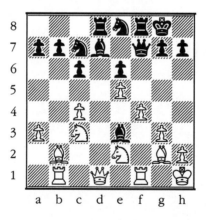

19...g6. An unnecessary weakening of the f6 square from which Staunton profits in dramatic fashion.

20.Qb3 Bc8; 21.Ne4 Bb6; 22.Rbd1. Even more powerful, in fact, would have been 22.c5 Ba5; 23.Nd6. As played, Black's defense is granted a glimmer of hope.

22...Na6; 23.Qc3 Rxd1; 24.Rxd1 Nc5; 25.Nd6 Qc7. An automatic reaction, neglecting the possible defense 25...Na4; 26.Nxf7 Nxc3 or 26 Qc2 Nxd6; 27.exd6 Nxb2 and although White has created a passed pawn, the exchanges and acquisition of the bishop pair would somewhat have eased Black's defensive task. Once Black has overlooked this hidden resource, Staunton crushes him with a few brisk strokes.

26.Qc2 Ng7; 27.g4.

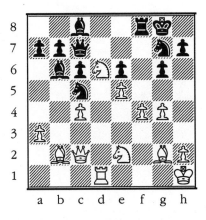

The prelude to the decisive attack, in which Staunton's pieces stream across to the right-hand side of the board to menace the black king. First of all, Staunton restricts the possibilities of Black's defensive knight on g7.

27...Qe7; 28.Bd4 Qc7; 29.a4 Na6; 30.c5 Ba5; 31.Qb3 b6; 32.Ne4 bxc5. If instead 32...Nxc5; 33.Bxc5 bxc5; 34.Nf6+ Kh8; 35.Qh3 Ne8; 36.Rd7! winning the black queen since 36...Bxd7 fails to 37 Qxh7 checkmate.

33.Nf6+ Kh8; 34.Qh3 Ne8; 35.Ba1.

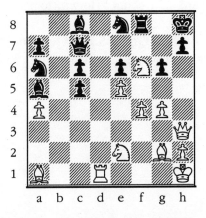

Staunton's deployment of his forces creates a wonderfully aesthetic impression, highlighted by this sweeping retreat of his bishop which is, nevertheless, still firmly targeted on the black king.

35...Nxf6; 36.exf6 Kg8; 37.Be5 Qb7; 38.Be4 Qf7.

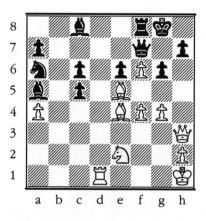

If Black can succeed in blockading the White passed pawn he may still survive, but Staunton's next brilliant stroke banishes such hopes.

39.Ng1! Another profound retreat which has the effect of substantially increasing the energy of the white knight. This piece is now free to maneuver via f3 to e5 or g5, thus causing havoc with the defensive units around the black king.

39...Bd8; 40.g5 Bb7; 41.Nf3 Re8; 42.Bd6. The coup de grace which puts the finishing touches to Staunton's encirclement of the entire black army. The threat of Ne5, trapping the black queen on almost a full board, now obliges Horwitz to make a desperate and futile sacrifice.

42...Bxf6; 43.gxf6 Qxf6; 44.Ng5 Qg7; 45.Be5 Qe7; 46.Bxg6. Black resigns. Black is hopelessly behind on material, and White's attack continues unabated!

CHESS TACTICS
Sharpen Your Skills For The Killer Blow

"The most usual of all tactical motifs is the weakness of a piece of little or no mobility. What is immobile must suffer violence. The light-winged bird will easily escape the huge dragon, but the firmly rooted big tree must remain where it is and may have to give up its leaves, its fruit, perhaps even its life." – Dr Emanuel Lasker, World Champion 1894-1921.

AN INTRODUCTION TO COMBINATIVE PLAY - MULTIPLE ATTACKS AND FORCING VARIATIONS

The tactical maneuvers which enliven chess games are called **combinations**. It is the combinational side of chess which exerts the most immediate appeal. The reader playing through games will almost certainly gain more pleasure from a game containing a well-conducted attack and culminating in a spectacular sacrifice, than from a positional game involving the exploitation of minute advantages in terrain, even though the latter may well contain the more profound ideas.

There is something about the nature of the sacrificial attack - the element of risk, perhaps, or our natural affinity with the 'underdog' which makes us rejoice in the triumph of the materially weaker side over the stronger. This strikes a chord of resonance within each of us.

Combinative ideas are to be found in every game of chess. Even if no actual combinations are played, they will still be found lurking 'in the notes', in the variations which the players have chosen to reject or bypass. Our strategic judgement must constantly be tempered by the tactical necessities of the position, and often we find that a positionally desirable continuation is unplayable because of a tactical refutation. The following diagram provides a simple example.

THE DOUBLE ATTACK

Black to Play

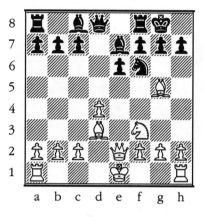

In the diagram position one of Black's difficulties is a lack of good squares for his *queen's* bishop. This piece is hemmed in by the e6-pawn and cannot develop actively at the moment. While searching for a way to remedy this state of affairs, Black might consider the move 1...b6, intending to follow up with 2...Bb7, developing the bishop on to the a8-h1 diagonal where it would be beautifully placed. Unfortunately for Black, this idea cannot be carried out, for White would reply to 1...b6?? by playing 2.Bxf6 Bxf6; 3.Qe4 with the decisive double threats of 4.Qxh7 mate and 4.Qxa8. Black is, therefore, forced to defend against checkmate, e.g. by 3...g6, when White wins a whole rook.

Various writers on chess have attempted to classify and analyze the nature of combinative play. Such a task is quite difficult, for in no aspect of the game is pure imagination and a gift for visualising unusual possibilities more important.

However, all combinations have as their essence some form of forcing double or multiple threat. *And these ideas and motifs can be named and learned!* For example, the combination which Black must avoid in the previous diagram has as its basis the fact that a White queen on e4 can fork the squares a8 and h7, creating a simultaneous attack on Black's king and rook. In the previous diagram the threats arose naturally from the geometry of the chessboard; in more complicated examples the side attacking must do some work to bring about a position in which all his threats operate together. Consider the following diagram.

DEFLECTION AND PIN

White to Play

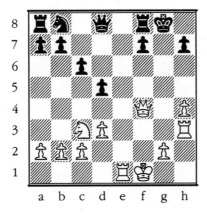

From the diagram, White won elegantly by 1.Rg3+ Kh8; 2.Qh6 (threatening 3.Qg7 mate) 2...Rg8; 3.Re8!!

Black to Play

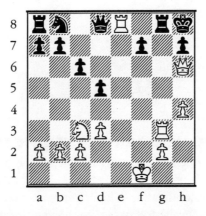

After this Black cannot avoid mate: 3...Rxe8; 4.Qg7 mate or 3...Qxe8; 4.Qf6+ Rg7; 5.Qxg7 mate. The key move 3.Re8 pins Black's rook and reactivates the threat of Qg7 mate, while the subsidiary threat of Qf6+ prevents Black from capturing the intruding rook with his queen.

The weakness in Black's position which White exploited by his combination may be thought of as stemming from the immobility of Black's queen and rook: the queen had to remain on the d8-h4 diagonal in order to guard f6 and, similarly, the rook was needed on the g-file to protect g7 and, thus, neither of them was really capable of moving to e8 to capture White's rook.

We are more likely to find a winning combination in a position where our pieces are mobile and actively placed. In contrast, if our pieces are passive and tied down to defense we are quite likely to have a combination inflicted upon us. If one side in a game enjoys an enormous advantage in mobility, then a combinative finale is almost inevitable.

Answers to the following puzzles can be found at the end of the section.

Puzzle 1:

In some combinations the double threat appears as two single threats on consecutive moves. The next diagram shows one such case. How did Black, to move, win material?

Black to Play

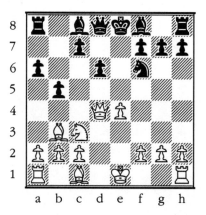

TACTICAL COMBINATIONS AGAINST THE UNCASTLED KING

Many combinations in the opening and early middlegame hinge on the relative insecurity of the king until it has castled. If one player falls behind in the race to develop, the other side may be able to exploit superior mobilization to launch an immediate attack, before the sluggard has a chance to catch up. Consider the following specimen of inferior opening play by Black: 1.e4 e5; 2.Nf3 d6; 3.Nc3 a6? (A totally wasted, non-developing move) 4.Bc4 Bg4? See the following diagram.

LEGALL'S TRAP

White to Play

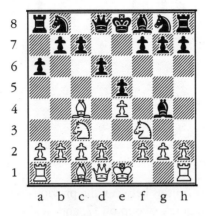

In just four moves Black has already reached a ghastly position! Not only did he lose a tempo by his futile third move, but his one developed piece is momentarily a weakness, since it is unprotected. At first glance it is not easy to see how White can exploit this, but closer study will reveal a surprising combination in which White uses mating threats to divert Black's attention while he attacks the loose bishop. The winning idea is 5.Nxe5!!, the main point of which is that the reply 5...Bxd1 is impossible because of 6.Bxf7+ Ke7; 7.Nd5 mate. Hence, Black has nothing better than 5...dxe5; 6.Qxg4 after which he has just lost a valuable central pawn without any compensation. Variations of this combination (known as Legall's mate, after a famous French master of the 18th century) form the basis of several well-known opening traps. It is not a particularly deep combination, but it is difficult to spot, because one automatically assumes that White's knight on f3 is pinned.

The best way for the reader to improve his or her own combinative skill is to play through collections of combinations. Some tactical combinations are truly original and brilliant, but many others share a common heritage for, not surprisingly, similar configurations of pieces tend to produce combinational ideas of a similar type. After a time you will be able to greet certain quite spectacular sacrifices as old familiar friends and, with luck, you may even find them appearing in your own games. Consider, for instance, the position shown in the following diagram:

White to Play

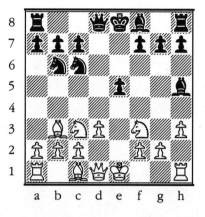

There are several obvious affinities between the previous two diagrams. In each position White's pieces are poised for a quick swoop on f7, and in each case there is an unprotected black bishop pinning a white knight on f3. No one who has seen Legall's mate before should be particularly astonished at what happens next, although this time the mate is not so simple and the whole combination is much more elaborately presented.

From the diagram play continued: 1.Nxe5!! Bxd1; 2.Bxf7+ Ke7; 3.Bg5+ Kd6; 4.Ne4+ Kxe5; 5.f4+ Kd4 (forced, for 5...Kf5 allows 6.Ng3 mate. We should not expect Black's monarch to be able to survive for long in White's half of the board, cut off from the rest of his army and from any hope of retreat) 6.Rxd1 Ke3 (White was threatening 7.Ke2 followed by 8.c3 mate; Black's move forestalls this but the reprieve is only temporary.) 7.0-0! (Now White's threat is 8.Rf3+ with mate to follow.) 7...Nd4; 8.Rde1 Ne2+; 9.Rxe2+ Kxe2; 10.Bh5+ Ke3; 11.Rf3+ Kd4; 12.Bf7. Black is helpless against the renewed threat of 13.c3 mate.

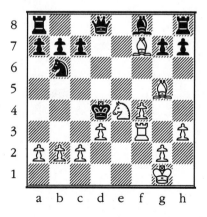

Puzzle 2:

The next diagram shows a common combinational idea involving an attack on f7. White has sacrificed two pawns for rapid development. How can he justify his previous play?

White to Play

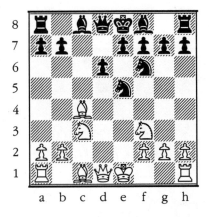

Puzzle 3:

Not all combinations in the opening are directed against the enemy king. Sometimes an unfortunate piece placement can form the basis of an early tactical skirmish. For example, in those openings where White has moved his e-pawn to e4 and has developed his king's bishop to c4, he should always be on his guard against a well-known black equalizing combination sometimes called the 'fork-trick'.

FORK TRICK

Black to Play

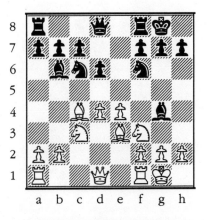

Our first impression is that White seems to have attained his opening objective of establishing a strong pawn center. Appearances, however, are deceptive, and Black has at his disposal a simple counter-stroke which assures him of equality at least. What is it?

GREEK GIFT

White to Play

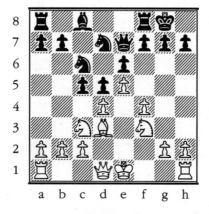

This diagram illustrates one of the most commonly encountered types of tactic to launch a mating attack: the classical Bxh7+ sacrifice (or, for Black, ...Bxh2+), which should have a place in every player's repertoire. This is a combinational idea of great antiquity. An identical sacrifice in a similar position is mentioned in Greco's handbook of 1619, and the basic theme has reappeared in countless numbers of games since then. The main variation runs 1.Bxh7+! Kxh7; 2.Ng5+ Kg8; 3.Qh5.

Black to Play

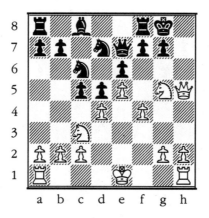

Black cannot avoid mate; 3...Rd8 (vacating f8 for the king) 4.Qh7+ Kf8; 5.Qh8 mate. An alternative defense is to bring the king forward instead:

Black to Play

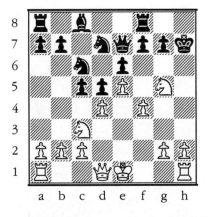

2...Kg6; 3.Qd3+ f5 (after 3...Kh5 White would play 4.Qh3+ Kg6; 5.Qh7 mate) 4.Qh3 and Black can only stop mate on h7 by giving up vast amounts of material. Declining the sacrifice is also of no avail: 1.Bxh7+ Kh8; 2.Ng5 g6 (necessary to stop 3.Qh5 followed by a lethal discovered check) 3.h4 followed by 4.h5 and 5.hxg6. Black's position will collapse once the h-file has been opened.

Puzzle 4:

Can the same thematic sacrifice be made to work in the position shown in this diagram?

White to Play

Puzzle 5:

Combinations in the late middlegame and ending frequently have as their objective the promotion of a pawn. There is little doubt about who is winning in the next diagram: White is already a pawn up, his rooks dominate the valuable open b-file, and Black's bishop is a totally passive piece. The winning process might still have been lengthy, but in fact White found an impressive sacrificial combination to batter down the last of Black's defenses. Can you discover it as well?

DEMOLITION TACTICS

White to Play

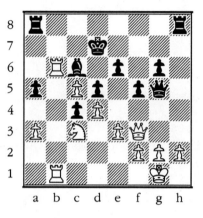

TACTICAL BREAKTHROUGH
Puzzle 6:

The next diagram, the finale of a famous game by the famous strategist Nimzowitsch, shows another position where Black's tactical objective is to force through a pawn. How did he manage it?

Black to Play

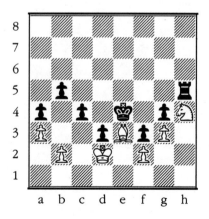

SOLUTIONS TO EXERCISES

Puzzle 1: Black played 1...c5! and then (after White's queen moved away) continued with 2...c4 trapping White's bishop on b3. One aspect of this elementary combination is the relative immobility of White's bishop - it could not retreat when attacked; another is the exposed position of White's queen which allowed Black to advance his pawn with gain of tempo.

Puzzle 2: 1.Nxe5 wins a piece. Black cannot recapture without suffering an even more horrible fate: 1...dxe5; 2.Bxf7+ Kxf7; 3.Qxd8 winning Black's queen for a bishop. This idea, decoying the king away with check to leave the queen unguarded, appears in several different opening variations.

Puzzle 3: 1...Nxe4!; 2.Nxe4 d5! forking White's bishop and knight. Whatever White now plays, Black will regain his piece on his next move and the net effect will be that White's pawn center has been demolished. Worse for White is 2.Bxf7+ Rxf7; 3.Nxe4, for Black's pressure against White's knight on f3 gives him the advantage.

Puzzle 4: Yes, the sacrifice is still successful, the play being 1.Bxh7+! Kxh7; 2.Ng5+ Kg8; 3.Qe4! (of course not 3.Qh5? Bf5! when White's attack has run out of steam) 3...f5; 4.Qh4 Rf7; 5.Qh8+!! Kxh8; 6.Nxf7+ Kg8; 7.Nxd8 and White should win on material. This time the sacrifice does not lead to mate, but merely to the gain of the exchange and a pawn. If Black decides to bring his king out into the open, however, he does get mated: 1.Bxh7+ Kxh7; 2.Ng5+ Kg6? (clearly bad is 2...Kh6?; 3.Nxf7+ winning Black's queen) 3.Qe4+ f5; 4.Qh4 f4; 5.Qh7+ Kxg5; 6.h4+ Kg4; 7.f3+ Kg3; 8.Qg6+ Kxh4; 9.Kf2! followed, whatever Black plays, by 10.Rh1 mate.

Puzzle 5: The game concluded: 1.Rxc6! Kxc6; 2.Nxd5! Rab8 (Black gets mated if he accepts the second sacrifice, e.g. 2...exd5; 3.Rb6+ Kc7; 4.Qxd5 and now 4...Qd8; 5.Qb7 mate or 4...Rab8; 5.Qd6+ Kc8; 6.Rxb8 mate or 4...Rhb8; 5.Rc6+ Kb7; 6.Qd7 mate or 4...Qe7; 5.Rb7+ etc.) 3.Nf4+ Kd7 (on 3...Kc7 White wins Black's queen while avoiding the back-rank mate: 4.Nxe6+ Kd7; 5.Qd5+! Ke7; 6.Qd6+ Kf6; 7.Nxg5+) 4.Rb7+! Rxb7; 5.Qxb7+ Ke8; 6.c6 and Black resigned since he has no defense to White's threats of 7.c7 and 7.Qd7+ with a knight fork to follow.

Puzzle 6: Black won by 1...b4!; 2.axb4 (Forced, since Black threatened 2...c3+; 3.bxc3 bxa3; 4.Kc1 Rb5! followed by 5...a2 and 6...a1Q) 2...Rxh4!; 3.gxh4 g3!; 4.fxg3 a3 and White resigned since after 5.bxa3 c3+; 6.Kxc3 Kxe3, Black will quickly obtain two new queens.

BACK RANK BOMBSHELLS

A frequently recurring danger is the possibility of a snap back rank checkmate. Watch out for them! Avoid them yourself, and try to inflict one on your opponent. The back rank checkmate is the ultimate expression of Emanuel Lasker's Theory of Immobility, stated at the front of this chapter. The immobile king is finally tracked down in its lair.

Sometimes the back rank checkmate is obvious, on other occasions, it is only set in motion by the most devious tactical preparation. Here are some progressively more sophisticated examples, so that you will be easily able to recognize the opportunities when they arise. We start with some examples by the early 20th century Grandmaster Duras, who seemed to be something of a back rank specialist.

DURAS VS. WOLF

White to Play

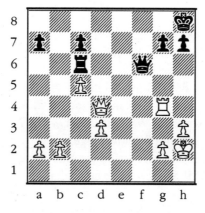

1.Rf4! Qe7 otherwise 1...Qxd4; 2.Rf8 mate **2.Qd7!!** The Black queen is deflected. Mate or loss of the queen is inevitable. Wolf resigned.

ZNOSKO-BOROVSKY VS. DURAS

Black to Play

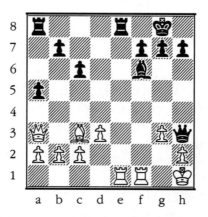

1...Re2!! White resigned. Qxh2 or Qg2 mate is threatened and if 2.Rxe2 then 2...Qxf1 with a back rank checkmate.

VON BALLA VS. DURAS

Black to Play

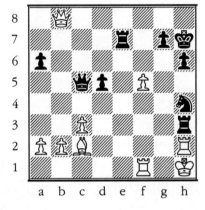

1...Qf2!! If 2.Rxf2 Re1+ or 2.f6+ Qxc2. Otherwise nothing can be done about ...Qg2 mate. White resigns.

Sometimes a back rank mate materializes on a board full of pieces.

ZSOFIA POLGAR VS. ADAMS
Barbican Center, London 1989

White to Play

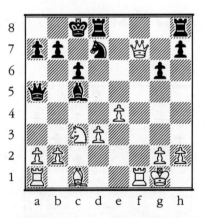

Although a pawn down, Black is threatening ...Rhf8 and is also giving check. Zsofia's next move is unfortunate, but forced, since her queen must be able to return to c4 and defend the rook on f1.

17.d4 Bxd4+; 18.Kh1 Rhf8; 19.Qc4 Bxc3.

White to Play

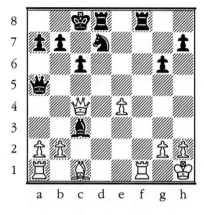

Now we can see the diabolical point of Black's play. If 20.bxc3 Qxc3!! (a superb deflection) 21.Qxc3 Rxf1 mate, exploiting the vulnerability of White's back rank.

20.Rxf8 Nxf8. White resigns. Suddenly the back rank mate threat looms on d1.

ACHILLES HEELS - THE ATTACK ON f7 AND h7

For Black, there are two major Achilles' Heels in his position as regards king safety. Before kingside castling, f7 is the main target, while after castling, h7 is also likely to come under attack. For White, danger lurks on the mirror image squares, f2 and h2.

This section shows a series of attacks on these key squares. First, a break-in at f7, even though Black had succeeded in castling!

KASPAROV VS. NUNN (BLITZ GAME)
London 1987

White to Play

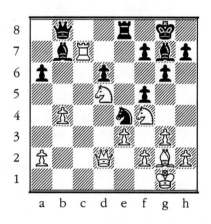

25.Qc2 Bxd5; 26.Nxd5 Qb5. Kasparov's coming move sets up a concealed battery against Black's most vulnerable point, the pawn on f7. **27.Qb3 Qe2; 28.Bxe4 fxe4.**

White to Play

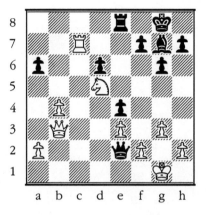

Kasparov has obtained decisive strategic pressure by securing absolute control of the open c-file. This will be utilized as the springboard to complete the invasion of Black's fortress. A White rook established on the seventh rank, or a Black rook on the second, is often a clear danger signal that tactical threats are building up!

As so often, Kasparov finishes off the game with a crisp display of tactics.

29.Nf6+. Black resigns. After 29...Bxf6; 30.Qxf7+ checkmate is forced.

WEAKNESS OF f7 - BEFORE CASTLING

NAJDORF VS. SAPIRO
Lodz 1929

White to Play

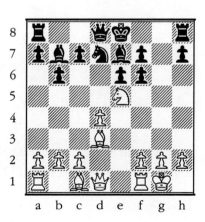

10.Nxf7!! A sacrifice based on the desire to persecute the black king. The pivotal point is f7. **10...Kxf7; 11.Qh5+ Kg8; 12.Re1 Nf8.** If 12...Bd5; 13.c4, forcing the bishop away from the defense of the black e-pawn.

White to Play

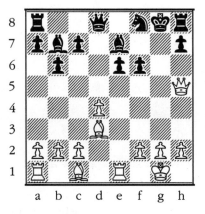

13.Rxe6. Already a piece down, White sacrifices a further rook to come to grips with the Black king. **13...Nxe6; 14.Bc4 Qd6; 15.Bh6 Bf8; 16.Re1 Bc8; 17.Qe8 Bd7.** Now White finishes with a flourish. **18.Rxe6 Rxe8; 19.Rxe8+.** The original f7 weakness has now translated itself into a generalized assault against Black's king across the entire light-square complex.

Black to Play

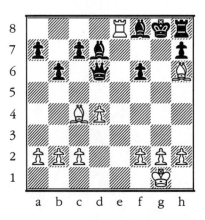

White's final combination giving up his queen is reminiscent of the great brilliancy won by Morphy at Paris, in 1858, against Count Isouard and the Duke of Brunswick. (We will see this game later.)
19...Be6; 20.Bxe6+ Qxe6; 21.Rxf8 mate.

WEAKNESS OF F2/UNCASTLED KING

FLEISSIG VS. SCHLECHTER
Vienna 1893
Orang-utan Opening

1.b4. An eccentric opening move, but in similar situations it has been adopted by Rèti, Smyslov and Larsen.

1...e6; 2.Bb2 Nf6; 3.a3 c5; 4.b5 d5; 5.d4. This is quite contrary to the spirit of the opening, in that White blocks the diagonal of his queen's bishop and simultaneously weakens the defense of his pawn on b5. White should have played 5.e3.

5...Qa5+. What is extraordinary about the remainder of this game is that Schlechter's superb artistry and accuracy mean that the entire continuation after White's error on move 5 is forced, right up to the checkmate.

6.Nc3. Necessary to prevent the loss of his pawn on b5, but from now on White is given no respite. **6...Ne4; 7.Qd3 cxd4; 8.Qxd4 Bc5; 9.Qxg7 Bxf2+; 10.Kd1 d4.** This attack on the traditional weak point forces White's king to wander around exposed in the center.

White to Play

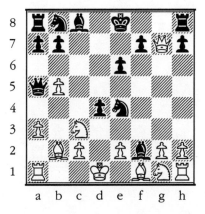

White cannot now play 11.Nxe4 on account of 11...Qe1 mate. Instead, White grabs at Black's rook sacrifice. Note the role of the black bishop on f2.

11.Qxh8+ Ke7; 12.Qxc8 dxc3; 13.Bc1 Nd7.

White to Play

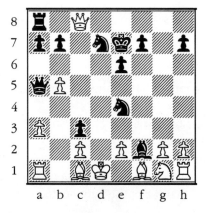

It is important to deflect the White queen, even at the cost of great material sacrifice. Now 14 Qxb7 Rd8 wins. **14.Qxa8 Qxb5; 15.Bf4 Qd5+; 16.Kc1 Be3+.**

White to Play

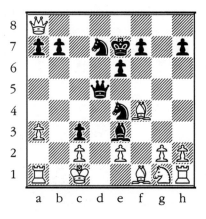

A brilliant clearance sacrifice.

17.Bxe3 Nf2. White resigns. On account of 18.Bxf2 Qd2+; 19.Kb1 Qd1+; 20.Ka2 Qxc2 mate. Incredibly, Black's 17th move is the final decisive exploitation of f2.

One of the revelations of my early chess studies was encountering the weird games of the Hungarian master Julius Breyer. Breyer, active in the early decades of the 20th century, had a short but glorious career. In particular, he had a curious knack of unleashing deadly attacks with pieces which appeared to be buried without trace, but which he could magically bring to life. The following game was characteristic of his attacking genius. Note the pivotal importance to White's attack of the h7-square.

BREYER VS. ESSER
Budapest 1917
Queen's Gambit Declined, Semi-Slav Defense

1.d4 d5; 2.c4 e6; 3.Nc3 c6; 4.e3 Nf6; 5.Bd3 Bd6; 6.f4 0-0; 7.Nf3 dxc4; 8.Bb1.

Black to Play

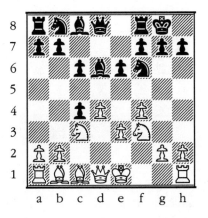

Most people would automatically capture on c4. Instead, Breyer gives up a pawn and buries his entire queenside army, simply to keep his king's bishop pointing at Black's king. **8...b5.** Symptomatic of the crass materialism which ultimately loses this game for Black. There was no immediate need to defend the pawn, hence the counterattack 8...c5 would have been more than adequate.

9.e4 Be7; 10.Ng5 h6; 11.h4 g6. Of course 11...hxg5; 12.hxg5 Nfd7; 13.Qh5 leads to immediate execution.

12.e5 hxg5. Hoping for 13.exf6 Bxf6; 14.hxg5 Bxd4, but Breyer disappoints him. **13.hxg5 Nd5.**

White to Play

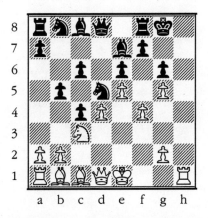

14.Kf1. An amazing move in the midst of a sacrificial attack. The point, and a very long range point it is, is to avoid a saving bishop check from Black on h4. If instead 14.Qg4 Kg7; 15.Rh7+ Kxh7; 16.Qh5+ Kg7; 17.Qh6+ Kg8; 18.Bxg6 fxg6; 19.Qxg6+ Kh8; 20.Qh6+ Kg8; 21.g6 then 21...Bh4+ followed by ... Qe7 refutes White's attack.

14...Nxc3; 15.bxc3 Bb7; 16.Qg4 Kg7; 17.Rh7+. Now this rook sacrifice works although there are still many piquant points to follow. **17...Kxh7.**

White to Play

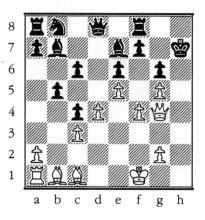

A rook and a knight down, White uses the situation of Black's king on h7 to bring up his reserves.

18.Qh5+ Kg7; 19.Qh6+ Kg8; 20.Bxg6 fxg6; 21.Qxg6+ Kh8; 22.Qh6+ Kg8; 23.g6 Rf7. Clearly forced since 23...Rf5 allows 24.Qh7+ Kf8; 25.Qh8 mate. If White had not played 14.Kf1 Black could once again have defended with ...Bh4+ and ...Qe7. This reveals the depth of Breyer's attacking conception and his extraordinary ability to build up dynamic energy in a position.

24.gxf7+ Kxf7; 25.Qh5+ Kg7.

White to Play

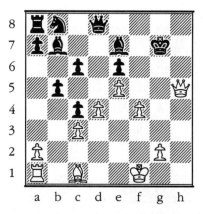

26.f5. At last White's bishop and rook enter the game. If now 26...Qh8 then 27.f6+ forces a quick win.

26...exf5; 27.Bh6+ Kh7; 28.Bf4+ Kg7; 29.Qh6+ Kg8; 30.Qg6+ Kh8; 31.Ke2 Bh4; 32.Rh1. Black resigns.

Black to Play

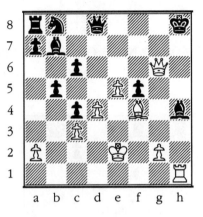

There is no defense to 33.Bg5. A tactical masterpiece, revealing many of the devices, both standard and non-standard, which can be used to destroy a castled king's palisade - based on a break-in at h7.

THE ROYAL HUNT

Themes we have so far observed in isolation can be combined to unleash the most devastating tactically based king hunts.

I am often asked what is the best way to improve, once the elementary stage has been passed in chess. If you are prepared to put some time in to study, one of the best methods is to pick a hero and study that player's games in some depth, or even write an article or book about that person. The Soviet expert Alexander Kotov freely admitted that his study of Alekhine, leading to a two-volume work on his hero's games, had been instrumental in transforming him from a first category player into a Grandmaster.

Similarly, Harry Golombek, Times Chess correspondent from 1945 to 1985, honed his skills by a deep study of both Capablanca and Reti. Again, in Golombek's case this ultimately led to the appearance of chess biographies of both players with deep comments on their outstanding masterpieces. In my own case, in 1973, I conducted an in-depth study of the games of the great chess strategist Aron Nimzowitsch and secured my first Grandmaster result the following year.

If you are an attacking player, choose Alekhine, Kasparov or Tal to emulate. If more strategically inclined, go for Botvinnik, Capablanca or Petrosian. Choosing a living player, such as Karpov (a noted strategist) brings the advantage that a constant stream of fresh games will be there to inspire you.

The American master, theoretician and author, Eric Schiller has recently started to follow the games of that great attacker Rudolf Spielmann and the effect on his style and strength has been extraordinary. Here is a sample, played under the Spielmann influence. Note the break-ins at f7 and f2!

SCHILLER VS. ARNE
Foster City 1995
Ruy Lopez

1.e4 e5; 2.Nf3 Nc6; 3.Bb5 a6; 4.Ba4 Nf6; 5.Qe2 b5; 6.Bb3 Bc5; 7.c3 0-0; 8.0-0 d6; 9.h3.

Black to Play

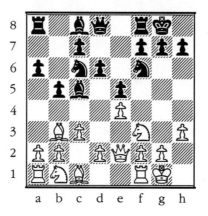

This is probably not necessary as Black's queen bishop is heading for b7, but White wanted to make sure that it was kept off g4, where the pin on the knight would weaken White's control of d4.

9...Bb7; 10.Rd1 Re8; 11.a4 b4; 12.a5 Qb8. In retrospect, this is an error. The simple 12...Qe7 would have given Black an equal game. **13.d4 exd4; 14.cxd4 Ba7.** 14...Rxe4 was playable, but White felt that he would then have sufficient compensation after 15.Be3 Ba7; 16.Qd3. However, after 14...Rxe4 White must avoid 15.Bxf7+ Kxf7; 16.Ng5+ Kf8; 17.Nxe4 Nxd4 when Black has the advantage.

15.e5 d5; 16.Qd3 Ne4; 17.Bxd5 Nxf2. An exciting battle is in prospect. First, Black tries to take White out by going for his Achilles Heel on f2.

White to Play

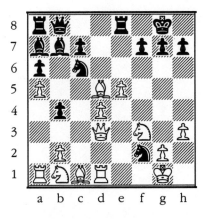

The idea is that if White captures the knight the pin on d4 allows captures at e5 with counterplay. For example 18.Kxf2 Nxe5; 19.Nxe5 Bxd5; 20.Be3 c5, when Black is a piece down but White's position is unstable. Instead, White launches a sacrificial attack, one virtually impervious to precise analysis, quite in the style of Spielmann himself.

18.Bxf7+ Kxf7; 19.Qf5+ Kg8; 20.Ng5 Nxd1. Having struck at f7, White now goes for h7 as well. **21.Qxh7+ Kf8; 22.Qh8+ Ke7; 23.Qxg7+ Kd8; 24.Nf7+ Kd7.**

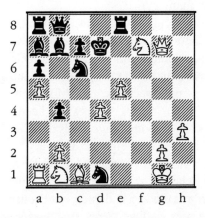

The position looks very good for White, but it is not so simple. Accurate tactical calculation is still required.

25.e6+ Kxe6; 26.Ng5+ Kd5; 27.Qd7+ Kc4; 28.Nd2+ Kd3; 29.Qf5+ Kxd4. White now closes the mating net with a problem-like move. **30.Ngf3+ Ke3; 31.Kf1. Black resigns.**

Black Resigns

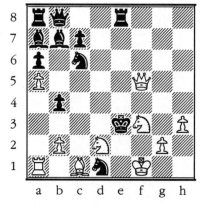

A quiet king move ends the spectacular combination. A discovered check, given by the bishop on c1, will be deadly.

BRONSTEIN AND THE DARK DOMINION

It is amazing, but true, that one sides' entire position in a chess game can utterly collapse if it becomes weak across a certain square-color complex. This is an advanced piece of information which will help you to win many games.

This scenario can become particularly pronounced for example, if Black, in the King's Indian Defense (or related fianchetto lines, where a bishop is developed on the flank) can retain the powerful fianchetto bishop, operating on g7, whilst somehow eliminating the opposing dark-square bishop by other means. In the next two games, that ingenious Russian Grandmaster David Bronstein is even prepared to sacrifice a rook for White's queen's bishop. After this, once the principal guardian of White's dark squares has been removed, a dark-square firestorm, orchestrated simultaneously on both wings, tears through the White positions and lays them waste, as if scorched and blasted by a gigantic dragon.

Whenever I see Bronstein's name, I am reminded of these two very brilliant games he played at the start of his career, when he was pioneering the King's Indian Defense. These are games which may be unfamiliar to a modern audience, but Bronstein's spectacular exploitation of a dynamic dark square strategy is well worth resurrecting for contemporary admiration.

ZITA VS. BRONSTEIN
Prague-Moscow 1946
King's Indian Defense

1.c4 e5; 2.Nc3 Nf6; 3.Nf3 d6; 4.d4 Nbd7; 5.g3 g6; 6.Bg2 Bg7; 7.0-0 0-0; 8.b3 c6; 9.Bb2. More active is 9 Ba3. **9...Re8; 10.e4 exd4; 11.Nxd4 Qb6.** The first intimation that Black intends to strike out at White's pieces which are based on the dark squares. **12.Qd2 Nc5; 13.Rfe1 a5; 14.Rab1 a4.** The energy displayed by Bronstein in this game is truly remarkable. The text inaugurates a plan of attack designed to harass White on both extremities of the board. **15.Ba1 axb3; 16.axb3 Ng4; 17.h3 Rxa1.** A thunderbolt with many elegant pirouettes and ramifications to follow. **18.Rxa1 Nxf2.**

White to Play

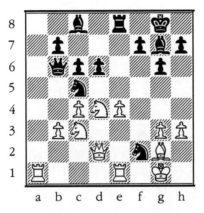

A shattering blow. The knight is immune. If 19.Qxf2 Nd3 or 19.Kxf2 Nxb3 with dark square carnage in both cases.

    19.Re3 Nxh3+; 20.Kh2 Nf2. An extraordinary return. If now 21.Qxf2 Bxd4. **21.Rf3 Ncxe4; 22.Qf4 Ng4+; 23.Kh1 f5; 24.Nxe4 Rxe4; 25.Qxd6 Rxd4; 26.Qb8 Rd8; 27.Ra8 Be5; 28.Qa7 Qb4; 29.Qg1 Qf8; 30.Bh3 Qh6. White resigns.**

   After 31.Qf1 Rd2; 32.Rxc8+ Kf7 Black's threat of ...Rh2+ is deadly.

PACHMAN VS. BRONSTEIN
Prague-Moscow 1946
King's Indian Defense

    1.d4 Nf6; 2.c4 d6; 3.Nc3 e5; 4.Nf3 Nbd7; 5.g3 g6; 6.Bg2 Bg7; 7.0-0 0-0; 8.b3 Re8; 9.e4 exd4; 10.Nxd4 Nc5; 11.Re1 a5.

    This was one of the earliest games to achieve prominence in which Bronstein adopted his new strategy in the King's Indian Defense. In earlier times, it had been thought that White's solid position and powerful central pawns on c4 and e4, gave him a grip which would ultimately lead to his advantage. In particular, White's ability to generate pressure in the d-file against Black's backward pawn on d6 was thought to be almost decisive.

    In this game, and others of the same period, Bronstein demonstrated, though, that Black can generate dynamic counterattacking chances across the entire board to compensate for the seeming strategic inadequacies of his set-up. It is striking to observe, in the further course of play, that these counterchances arise almost exclusively along the dark square complexes of the entire board.

12.Bb2 a4. The same counterattacking theme as we met in the previous game. Black will parry 13.b4 with 13...a3. **13.Rc1 c6; 14.Ba1 axb3; 15.axb3 Qb6; 16.h3 Nfd7; 17.Rb1 Nf8; 18.Kh2 h5.** Evidence of Bronstein's breadth of vision. Having first advanced on the queen's flank, he now begins to play on both sides of the board.

19.Re2. White would like to play 19.f4 but then 19...h4; 20.g4 Nfe6 begins to puncture White's camp along the infamous dark squares. **19...h4; 20.Rd2.**

Black to Play

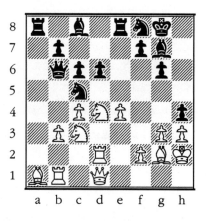

Pachman must have been feeling quite satisfied with his position, but now he is suddenly blown away by an amazing sequence of sacrifices which combine all of Black's previously disparate aggressive themes.

20...Rxa1. A sacrifice to annihilate the principal guardian of White's dark squares. **21.Rxa1 Bxd4; 22.Rxd4 Nxb3; 23.Rxd6.** It seems that all is in order, since 23...Nxa1 allows 24.Nd5 followed by 25.Nf6+ when White wins, but now Bronstein uncorks a further shattering surprise.

23...Qxf2.

White to Play

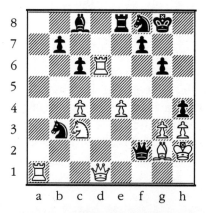

If now 24.Qxb3 hxg3+; 25.Kh1 Bxh3; 26.Rg1 Bxg2+; 27.Rxg2 Qf1+; 28.Rg1 Qh3 checkmate. **24.Ra2.** White plays cunningly to stay the exchange ahead but in the final analysis Black garners too many pawns and White's king becomes hopelessly exposed. However, if instead 24.Qxb3 hxg3+; 25.Kh1 Bxh3; 26.Rg1 Bxg2+; 27.Rxg2 Qf1+; 28.Rg1 Qh3 mate.

24...Qxg3+; 25.Kh1 Qxc3; 26.Ra3 Bxh3; 27.Rxb3 Bxg2+; 28.Kxg2 Qxc4; 29.Rd4 Qe6; 30.Rxb7 Ra8; 31.Qe2 h3+. White resigns. After 32.Kg1 Qe5; 33.Rd1 Ra3 followed by ...Nf8-e6-f4, White is entirely helpless. A grandiose example of play on both wings.

THE HOLLOW CROWN - ATTACK ON THE LONG DIAGONAL

"For within the Hollow Crown,
That rounds the mortal temples of a king
Keeps Death his count, and there the antic sits,
Scoffing his state and grinning at his pomp." – William Shakespeare, Richard II

Some of the most devastating tactics can arise if you can aim a fianchettoed bishop, operating from g2, b2, g7 or b7, directly at your opponent's king. Such tactics, as we might already guess from the two Bronstein examples, become especially powerful if we have already traded off the enemy bishop which opposes our own, or alternatively, if that enemy bishop cannot organize itself in defense along the critical diagonal of attack. These games illustrate this important tactical theme.

Breaking Open the Long Diagonal

In the following diagram, White's queen bishop is aiming ominously on the long diagonal towards Black's king. However, Black is well fortified in that sector. The question is, how does White commence the breakthrough, and undermine Black's resources on the diagonal?

KEENE VS. KOVACEVIC
Amsterdam 1973

White to Play

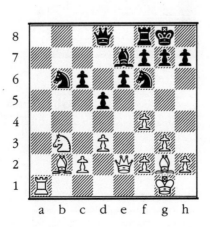

18.f5! Launching the decisive combination which rips away the defenses from around Black's king. **18...exf5; 19.Nd4 Qd7; 20.Bh3 g6; 21.Bxf5.** This sacrifice, combined with the one on the next move, gives White the requisite time to come directly to grips with the Black king. **21...gxf5; 22.Ra7.** A shocking move, the high point of the attack. White also hurls a rook on to the sacrificial pyre.

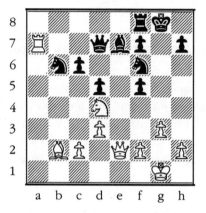

22...Qxa7; 23.Nxc6. This fork gives White the time he needs. **23...Qd7.** Alternatively, 23...Qa2; 24.Nxe7+ Kg7; 25.Nxf5+ Kg8 and now White can sacrifice his queen as well, to force checkmate with 26 Qg4+ Nxg4; 27.Ne7 checkmate. This variation, highlighting the power of White's bishop on the long diagonal, deserves an extra diagram.

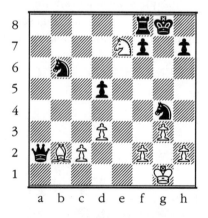

The game, in fact, continued... **24.Nxe7+ Kg7; 25.Qh5. Black resigns.** Black's position is hopeless, e.g. 25...Qxe7; 26.Qg5+ Kh8; 27.Bxf6+ or 25...h6; 26.Nxf5+ or 25...Ra8; 26.Qg5+ Kf8; 27.Bxf6 with Qg8 mate to follow.

Queen Sacrifice for Diagonal Control

Sacrificing the queen brings with it a special mystique. In the scale of values, the queen is worth almost twice as much as any other piece, so its loss is, of course, in normal circumstances, quite fatal. To be able to flout the orthodox rules and demonstrate the superiority of mind over matter by sacrificing the queen for a win is every chessplayer's dream. In world championship play it is so rare that when Garry Kasparov gave up his queen as the culmination of his brilliant final attack from game 20 of the 1990 world championship match, the moment of sacrifice was immortalized in a diagram on the front page of *The Times*. Here we see the queen sacrificed in the interests of a spectacular diagonal attack, with the black king as a target.

NORWOOD VS. MARSH
Walsall 1992

White to Play

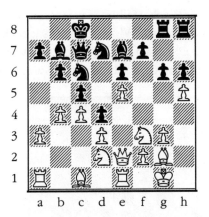

16.bxc5. It is essential now that Black recaptures with a piece on c5. The full opening of the b-file allows White to inaugurate a dangerous attack.

16...bxc5?;17.hxg6 Rxg6; 18.Rb1. An important move, aiming White's rook directly at Black's valuable defensive bishop. **18...h5; 19.Ne4 h4; 20.Bg5 Bf8.** Black also hopes to open lines for his rooks on the other wing against White's king. **21.Nxh4 Rgg8; 22.Nf3 Rh7; 23.Nd6+ Bxd6; 24.exd6 Qxd6; 25.Bf4 Qe7.**

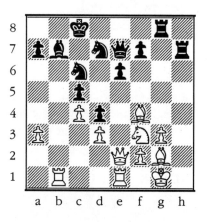

26.Rxb7. A just retribution for Black's failure to safeguard his interests on the light squares. As Black did in the Bronstein examples, White sacrifices a rook to knock out the opposite number of White's bishop on g2. 26...Kxb7; 27.Qe4 f5. Oblivious of the coming spectacular carnage, Black drives the white queen precisely where it wants to go.

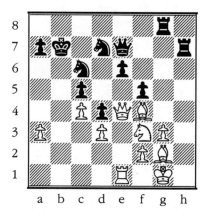

28.Qxc6+. Leading to a brilliant denouement with a forced checkmate. **28...Kxc6; 29.Nxd4+ Kb6; 30.Rb1+ Ka6; 31.Bb7+ Ka5; 32.Bd2+ Ka4; 33.Bc6+ Kxa3; 34.Bc1+ Ka2; 35.Rb2+ Ka1; 36.Nc2. Checkmate.**

Checkmate

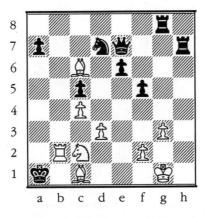

A most unusual position, worthy of a brilliancy prize itself. The distinction of checkmating the opposing king on one's own first rank has been accorded to very few Grandmasters.

The King's Indian Defense Scenario

The Diagonal Attack is often seen when White castles queenside against the King's Indian Defense, and Black can liberate the power of his king's bishop on g7.

TIMMAN VS. KASPAROV
Linares 1992

Black to Play

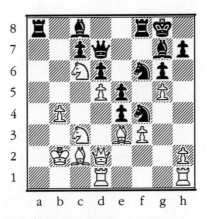

Were Black now obliged to play 21...N6h5 then 22.Bxe4 would in fact cement White's light-squared hegemony over the entire board. With the move Ra1 in the offing to secure the a-file, Timman would have been able to look forward to the future with confidence. Instead of falling in with this supine course, Kasparov sets the board alight with a sacrifice.

21...N6xd5!!; 22.Nxd5. Of course not now 22...Qxc6; 23.Ne7+ winning for White. **22...Nd3+.**

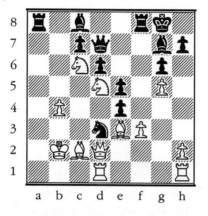

23.Bxd3. If 23.Kb3 Bb7 either wins back the material or leads to a mating attack, e.g. 24.b5 Bxc6; 25.bxc6 Rfb8+. Another possibility is the spectacular queen sacrifice 23.Kb3 Qxc6; 24.Ne7+ Kh8; 25.Nxc6 Be6+; 26.Kc3 Ra3+; 27.Bb3 Rxb3+; 28.Kc2 Rb2+; 29.Kc3 Rxd2 followed by ...Rxf3 when Black's central pawns should guarantee victory. However, by playing 23.Kb1 White could still have put Black's idea to the test.

23...exd3; 24.Nce7+ Kh8; 25.Nxc8 e4+.

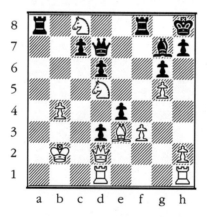

The concluding point of Black's tactics. Black's king's bishop enters the fray against White's king. It was so devastating that **White resigns.** After 25...e4+; 26.Kb3 Qa4+; 27.Kc4 Qc6+; 28.Kb3 Qxd5 is checkmate. Also; 25...e4+; 26.Nc3 Qa4; 27.Kc1 Qa1+; 28.Nb1 Ra2 and Black wins or 25...e4+; 26.Nf6 Rxf6; 27.Bd4 Rxf3; 28.Bxg7+ Qxg7+ and Black wins again.

SHORT'S PIN

The pin is one of the commonest tactical motifs to win material or hamstring an opponent's ability to maneuver. It is a further fine example of Lasker's dictum on mobility, quoted at the start of this chapter.

SHORT VS. TIMMAN
Hilversum 1989
KRO Match - Game 4

Black to Play

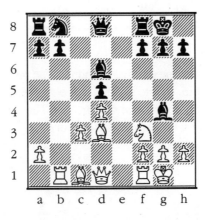

Black is being provoked into a slight, but ultimately significant weakening of his queenside pawns. It would appear natural to play 12...Qc7 which performs the triple function of defending b7, attacking c3 and threatening White's pawn on h2. However, this dream move fails tactically, e.g. 12...Qc7; 13.Bxh7+ Kxh7; 14.Ng5+ Kg8; 15.Qxg4 with advantage to White. We are already well familiar with this kind of strike.

12...b6; 13.Rb5 Bc7; 14.c4 dxc4. This position has occurred before in Short's games. Timman now produces a new idea which, at first sight, appears to lose material. In fact, Black's defense is based on complex tactics and comes close to succeeding.

15.Be4 Nc6. If now 16.Bxc6 Qd6 threatens both ...Qxc6 and ...Bxf3 followed by ...Qxh2 mate. Short prefers to prosecute his kingside offensive. **16.Rg5 Bxf3.** This move commits Black to the loss of rook for bishop, but he hopes to gain ample compensation in terms of central control. **17.Qxf3 Qd6; 18.Rg3 Nxd4; 19.Qg4.** This is the key move. White threatens mate on g7 as well as the black rook on a8.

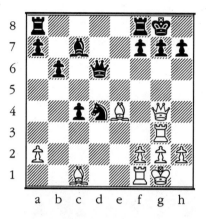

19...g6; 20.Bxa8 Rxa8. White's next move introduces the pin, nailing down Black's knight on d4. **21.Rd1 Rd8; 22.Kf1 Qd5.** White's 22nd move was excellent. Black suffers from a serious pin on the d-file which cannot sensibly be broken. The point of 22.Kf1 was to prevent Black lifting the pin by means of a knight check on e2 or f3.

23.Re3.

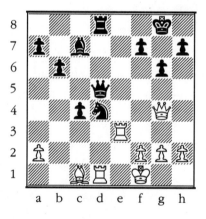

The crisis has been reached. White threatens 24.Rxd4 Qxd4; 25.Re8+ (deflection) 25...Kg7; 26.Qxd4+ Rxd4; 27.Bb2 introducing yet another murderous pin. In order to ward off this horror, as well as other variations based on the augmentation of the pin by Bb2, Timman must irrevocably weaken the fortifications surrounding his king.

23...f5; 24.Qh4 f4; 25.Re7 h5; 26.Qf6 Black resigns. White has exploited the various pinning motifs to close in decisively around the Black king.

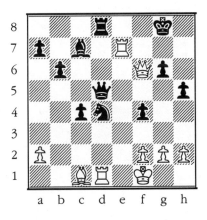

THE DEADLY ZWISCHENZUG

Zwischenzug is a German term, now adopted around the world in chess circles, meaning intermezzo or 'in-between' move. It is a key component in your tactical arsenal. Imagine the shock value: you play 'X' and your opponent responds 'Y', expecting you then to play 'Z'. It sometimes pays, however, to slip in 'A' before playing 'Z'.

Now play through this masterpiece by Kasparov. His 15th move 15 e6!! destroys Karpov's entire strategy.

KASPAROV VS. KARPOV
Tilburg 1991
Scotch Game

1.e4 e5; 2.Nf3 Nc6; 3.d4.
The Scotch Game, leading to open gambit style positions. It was a great favorite in the 19th century, but languished in relative neglect until Kasparov revived it.
3...exd4; 4.Nxd4 Nf6. A different way to counter the Scotch Game is 4...Bc5; 5.Be3 Qf6; 6.c3 Nge7. **5.Nxc6 bxc6; 6.e5 Qe7; 7.Qe2 Nd5; 8.c4.** Now 8...Nb6; 9.Nd2 Qe6; 10.b3 a5; 11.Bb2 was played in a previous game between Kasparov and Karpov. **8...Ba6; 9.b3 g6.** A relatively new idea. A risky continuation had been seen in another earlier Kasparov-Karpov game, 9...0-0-0; 10.g3 Re8; 11.Bb2 f6.
10.f4. 10.Bb2 is possible, but Kasparov perceives more lucrative perspectives for his queen's bishop on a3 rather than b2.

10...f6; 11.Ba3 Qf7; 12.Qd2 Nb6; 13.c5 Bxf1; 14.cxb6 axb6. A spirited piece sacrifice, intending to meet 15.Rxf1 with 15...Bxa3, or the more plausible 15.Bxf8 with 15...Rxf8; 16.Rxf1 fxe5, when Black has a solid position plus two good pawns for his sacrificed piece. Yet another possibility after 15.Bxf8 is 15...Bxg2; 16.Qxg2 Rxf8, followed by ...0-0-0. Nevertheless, better would have been 14...Ba6, since Kasparov now has a brilliant riposte which cuts across Black's plans.

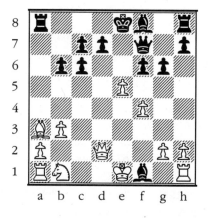

15.e6!! A perfect example of a zwischenzug. Now we experience in graphic form the shock of playing unexpected "A" before expected "Z"! The point of this intermezzo is that now 15...Qxe6+ would fail to 16.Kxf1 Bxa3; 17.Nxa3 Rxa3; 18.Re1 devilishly netting the black queen with a pin.

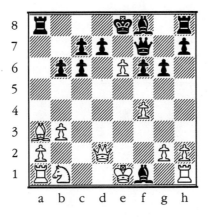

15...dxe6. This way White still wins the piece, but by virtue of his splendid fifteenth move he shreds Black's pawn structure and prevents Black castling.

16.Bxf8 Rd8; 17.Qb2.

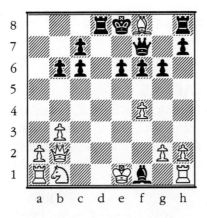

A highly original position, possibly unique in the annals of chess, in which both players simultaneously have a queen's bishop on the starting square of their opponent's king's bishop.

17...Bxg2; 18.Qxg2 Kxf8; 19.Qxc6 Rd6; 20.Qc3 Kg7; 21.Nd2 Rhd8; 22.0-0-0 Qe8.

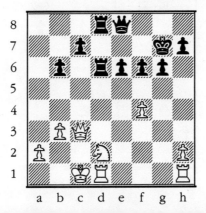

Up to now Karpov has maintained a measure of compensation for his lost piece, but if he wanted to continue resistance he had here to play 22...Qd7. The text is a miscalculation which overlooks the fact that White can safely snatch one more pawn.

    23.Qxc7+ R8d7; 24.Qc2 Qb8; 25.Nc4 Rd5; 26.Qf2 Qc7; 27.Qxb6.

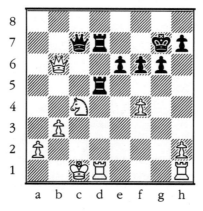

Black's case is now hopeless since Kasparov not only has an extra knight but a decisive armada of passed pawns on the queen's wing. White duly won the game on move 44. The zwischenzug on move 15 did not just win material, it shattered Karpov's morale.

KASPAROV'S LETHAL TACTICS

    We have already seen world champion Garry Kasparov in action. He ranks, along with Alexander Alekhine and David Bronstein, as one of the all-time great tactical geniuses.

    In this section we again see Kasparov at work, now combining various major tactical themes, which I have already demonstrated in isolation, to crushing effect.

SHORT VS. KASPAROV
Savoy Theatre, London 1993
Speed Game (2)

Black to Play

34...d5!! Interestingly, this both exposes the weakness of White's back rank, and exploits the pin, by Black's queen, of White's knight on c3 to the rook on e1. If now 35.Nxd5 Qxe1+ or 35.exd5 e4; 36.Nxe4 Qxe1+, therefore White must take with the bishop. **35.Bxd5 Nxd5; 36.exd5 e4.** If White now plays 37.Rxe4 then 37...Qxc3; 38.Rxc3 Rb1+; 39.Rc1 Rcxc1+; 40.Re1 Rxe1+; 41.Qf1 Rxf1 checkmate. A superb finish.

37.Qxe4 Rxc3; 38.Rd4 Qd6; 39.f6 Bxf6. White resigns

In game three of the same contest, White's advantage appears to be on the queen's flank, but Kasparov switched fronts to devastating effect using the Greek Gift sacrifice on h7.

KASPAROV VS. SHORT
Savoy Theatre, London 1993
Speed Game (3)

White to Play

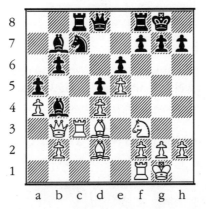

20.Bxh7+! Kxh7; 21.Ng5+ Kg8; 22.Rh3 Re8. If 22...Bxd2 then 23.Rh8+ Kxh8; 24.Qh3+ Kg8; 25.Qh7 checkmate. A beautiful tactical conception, with the rook sacrificing itself, to make way for the white queen. **23.Qf3 Qd7.** If Black plays 23...f6 then 24.Rh8+ Kxh8; 25.Qh3+ Kg8; 26.Qh7+ Kf8; 27.Qh8+ Ke7; 28.Qxg7 checkmate.

24.Qh5 Kf8; 25.Nh7+ Ke7; 26.Bg5+ f6; 27.Nxf6. Black resigns. After 27...gxf6; 28.Bxf6+ Kf8; 29.Qh8+ Kf7; 30.Qg7 is checkmate.

In game four Kasparov clearly had a great advantage in space, and now broke through with a cascade of sacrifices. Note the menacing position of the Black queen, hovering near the White king. Such proximity is frequently an extreme danger signal!

SHORT VS. KASPAROV
Savoy Theatre, London 1993
Speed Game (4)

Black to Play

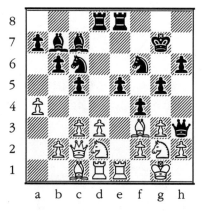

28...e4! Black threatens the terminal ...Ne5, bringing up deadly reinforcements, so White must take with the rook. **29.Rxe4 Nxe4; 30.Bxe4 Rxe4; 31.dxe4 Ne5; 32.Ne1 Ba6.** The point of Black's play is to try to give checkmate on f1. **33.c4 Rxd2.** A final sacrifice forces the penetration of White's defenses.

34.Rxd2 Bxc4; 35.Rd3 Bxd3; 36.Nxd3 Nf3+; 37.Kh1 Qf1. Checkmate.

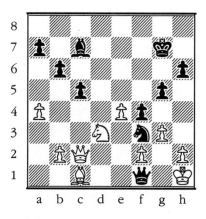

A TACTICAL MASTERPIECE

I conclude this chapter with a game that weaves together many of the threads we have been examining. A tactical masterpiece, queen sacrifice, back rank threats, king hunt, this game has it all.

Austrian Grandmaster Rudolf Spielmann was active around the first three decades of the

20th century. Spielmann was a noted giant-slayer, with wins against both Capablanca and Alekhine to his credit. His one literary masterpiece was his book, *The Art of Sacrifice*, in which he detailed his own aggressive concept of how chess should be played.

Indeed, Spielmann's best games provide a shining example to any aspiring player who wishes to master the art of the initiative. The following game is a superb jewel of the imagination. It will repay close investigation at every stage, from Spielmann's powerful counterattacking opening right up to the superlatively imaginative king hunt, based on a breakthrough into White's back rank, which crowns his plan of campaign.

RUBINSTEIN VS. SPIELMANN
San Sebastian 1912
Dutch Defense

1.d4 e6; 2.c4 f5. True to form, Spielmann immediately unbalances the central pawn constellation and indicates with this aggressive move that he plans, ultimately, to operate against White's kingside, where he perceives that White's king will take shelter. **3.Nc3.** This allows Black too easy a development. 3.Nf3 or 3.g3 would be superior.

3...Bb4. This pin helps to combat White's influence over the center. **4.Bd2 Nf6; 5.g3 0-0; 6.Bg2 d6; 7.a3 Bxc3; 8.Bxc3 Nbd7; 9.Qc2 c5; 10.dxc5 Nxc5.**

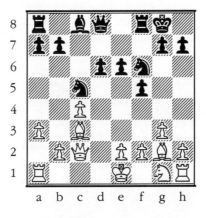

The opening has given White the advantage of the bishop pair and more mobile queenside pawns. In compensation Black's knights have a firm grip over e4, as a possible springboard to invasion of the white camp.

11.Nf3 Nce4; 12.0-0 Bd7; 13.Rfd1 Rc8; 14.Bxf6.

Black's development has, in fact, been so rapid and efficient that White now feels constrained to part with the bishop pair. All that remains of a possible White edge is Black's backward pawn on d6, but, over the coming moves, Spielmann expertly masks its weakness.

14...Qxf6; 15.Qb3 Rc7; 16.Ne1 Nc5; 17.Qb4 f4. Black's kingside attack now starts in earnest.

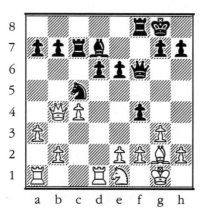

18.Nd3. If 18.Rxd6 fxg3 grants Black a terrible attack in the f-file. **18...fxg3; 19.fxg3 Nxd3; 20.Rxd3 Qf2+.** Already penetrating with his most powerful piece to f2, one of the typical Achilles Heels in White's camp. **21.Kh1 Bc6; 22.e4.** White could trade on c6 but Rubinstein clearly felt that his king needed the added protection provided by the bishop on g2.

22...Rcf7. Black's rooks mass on the f-file, generating tangible tactical energy. **23.Re1.** If 23 Rxd6 Qe2 threatening ... Rf1+ with mate to follow. **23...a5; 24.Qc3 Qc5; 25.b4.** With this move White must have felt, at long last that he had restored the balance and neutralized Black's initiative. The Black queen is apparently driven away from its commanding post and the further threat of b5 by White will also press Black's bishop into a defensive situation. However, White is in for a terrible shock.

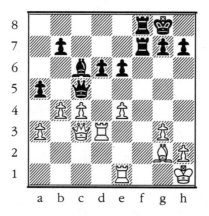

25...Bxe4!! A fantastic move. Spielmann offers up both his queen and bishop to generate tactical threats against White's king. If 26.bxc5 Rf1+; 27.Rxf1 Rxf1+ with a beautiful back rank checkmate. Alternately, if 26.Bxe4 Rf1+; 27.Rxf1 Rxf1+; 28.Kg2 Rg1+; 29.Kf3 Qh5+; 30.Ke3 Qxh2 with a murderous attack. Doubtless stunned by the sudden turn of events, though, Rubinstein misses the most tenacious, indeed, problem-like counter-tactical defense which consists of 26.Rf3!!. After this Black has nothing better than 26...Qc6; 27.b5 Rxf3; 28.Qxf3!!

Bxf3; 29.bxc6 Bxc6; 30.Bxc6 bxc6; 31.Rxe6 Rf6. In this case, Black is a pawn ahead in the endgame and should win, though White's resistance is by no means at an end. As played in the game, although a rook ahead, White is overwhelmed by a further sequence of tactics, exploiting the exposed nature of his king.

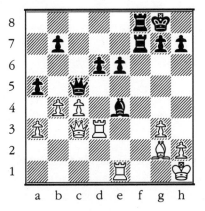

26.Rxe4 Rf1+. Blasting his way into White's back rank to chase out the king. **27.Bxf1 Rxf1+; 28.Kg2 Qf2+; 29.Kh3 Rh1; 30.Rf3 Qxh2+; 31.Kg4 Qh5+; 32.Kf4 Qh6+; 33.Kg4 g5.** The key move to Black's offensive. The threat of 34...Qh5 checkmate now obliges White to jettison material, after which White's wandering king spells his doom.

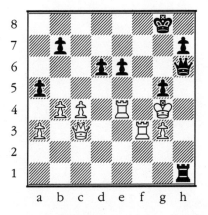

34.Rxe6 Qxe6+; 35.Rf5 h6; 36.Qd3 Kg7. A decisive reinforcement, threatening 37...Kg6 and introducing the possibility (should White defend with 37.Qd5) of 37...h5+; 38.Kxg5 Qh6.

37.Kf3 Rf1+. A fitting final sacrifice which transposes directly into a won king and pawn endgame.

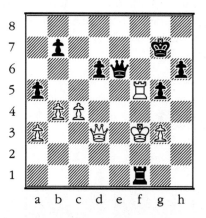

38.Qxf1 Qxf5+; 39.Kg2 Qxf1+; 40.Kxf1 axb4; 41.axb4 Kf6; 42.Kf2 h5. White resigns.

One of my all-time favorite games. The variations after Black's 25th move are truly astonishing. This brilliant tactical win spins together many of the themes in this chapter.

ELEMENTARY CHESS OPENINGS
Seize the Advantage and Win

MAJOR OPENING PRINCIPLES

Even if we consider the first three moves by each side, there are hundreds of millions of ways to start a game of chess! If we eliminate those which are obviously ridiculous, there are still several thousand possibilities which make sense to a greater or lesser extent and which have been tried in over-the-board play. To discuss, or even list, all of the opening variations which you are likely to meet in your career as a player would take far too long and, in any case, you would be unlikely to learn much from the exercise; I would merely be burdening your memory with a vast mass of indigestible detail.

There is a large amount of published material on the openings, ranging from 'encyclopaedias', which cover all openings, to detailed monographs on one particular opening system. As reference works, these books are of great value to the experienced player; to the beginner they are both daunting and stultifying, for it is tempting to substitute memorization for the more rewarding task of thinking about a position and developing your own ideas.

Chess is a game of infinite possibilities. Not all the computing power in the world could calculate all the possible moves in all possible games that could ever be played. Yet, for all the richness and variety, there are a number of well-trodden pathways and strategic schemes around which most players build their games. Even novice players quickly come to understand that some squares on the board are more important than others, and that success in a game will depend on quickly seizing control of them. In this chapter, I address the crucial question of the opening - the initial phase of the game in which the players must wrestle for territorial and tactical control. Some of the commonest openings, favored by Grandmasters and amateurs alike, are set out for you to learn, practise and improvise upon. And, just to make sure that you can finish what you have started, I describe some of the classic methods of using a powerful opening to arrive at a speedy and decisive and victorious conclusion.

The initial phase of any game of chess is known as the **opening**. It begins with the first pawn moves and ends at the point where the players have "developed" most of their pieces into strategic positions. After that the "middle game" begins.

The importance of the opening can hardly be overstated. It has been subject to more analysis than any other part of the game, and modern Grandmasters carry thousands of variations in their heads (plus hundreds of thousands more on computers). Many standard openings are named after the players who invented them (Alekhine, Gruenfeld, Ruy Lopez); others, more picturesquely, after the shapes they make on the board.

It is during the opening that players vie for mastery of the center, trying to provide maximum mobility for their own pieces, while denying space and initiative to their opponents. In the early 19th century the main objective during the opening was to attack the enemy king, but Wilhelm Steinitz, the first world champion, who captured the supreme title in 1886, advanced the art of defensive play to such a pitch that, among top players at least, premature attacks thereafter have been doomed to failure.

Fashion plays a large part in the selection of openings. Most games in the 19th century began:

1.e4 e5. By the 1930's White would more commonly open with: **1.d4.** Both of these remain popular today, though the flank openings **1.c4** or **1.Nf3** or **1.g3** also have their devotees.

It would take a lifetime's study to master all the, but there are a number of standard openings, good and extremely reliable for both sides, with which every player should be familiar.

The Importance of the Center and Fast Development

It is time now to consolidate the diverse elements I have introduced and to formulate an overall picture of the correct way to open a game - to expand our strategical insight.

There is danger in oversimplification. There are as many different methods of playing the chess openings as there are ways of fighting a battle, and there are chessboard analogies to nearly every form of combat, from trench warfare to Blitzkrieg. The way a particular game develops will be a function of the ideas which you and your opponent bring to bear on each position. Chess would be frightfully dull if there were a unique 'best' way to play (i.e. a winning strategy). Fortunately, this is not the case. Frequently, situations will be reached in which it is impossible to point to a single 'best' continuation, in which several different plans present themselves, each of them in keeping with the basic strategic and tactical necessities of the position, and each of them possessing some merit.

At such times a player's choice of move will be influenced, not only by exact calculation, but by intangible psychological considerations: do you like simple positions or complicated positions, open positions with possibilities of direct attack, or closed positions which require subtle maneuvering against enemy weaknesses, and (if this information is known) what sort of game does your opponent prefer to play, and how can you do your best to upset him or her?

A Question of Style

Very few chess players (perhaps none) feel equally at home in all positions; *style* is an important factor. In the roll of former world champions we find players with widely differing styles: Karpov and Kasparov, for instance. Karpov is ultra-solidity personified; he rarely takes risks and has the patience of a cat sitting in front of a mouse hole, ready to pounce on any inaccuracy on his opponent's part. In contrast, Kasparov revels in complications of which neither he, nor his opponent, can completely predict the outcome; he is the master of the speculative sacrifice.

As your playing strength increases, you too will develop an individual style. You should get to know it and to play in accordance with it. In the opening especially, style is important, for there the pattern is set which the rest of the game must follow. You should not expect to like equally each of the opening variations I discuss in this chapter. You should choose some which suit your style and learn to play them well.

Start Position

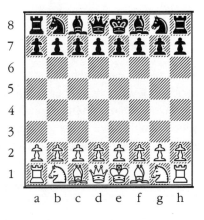

Development

In spite of the diversity indicated above, all chess games have at least one thing in common: they all start from the same position (diagram). If we look closely at this diagram, certain basic facts begin to emerge. The first thing we notice is that neither side has its pieces well-placed. The rooks, bishops, and queen are all out of play - none of them has any legal move. The knights can move, but it will be some time before they are able to cause concern to the enemy. Even for defense, our forces are badly disposed. In particular the squares f2 for White and f7 for Black are vulnerable, since each is protected only by the king.

Our first duty in the opening phase of the game is to change this state of affairs: to secure active and aggressive posts for all our pieces from which they can threaten the opposition and protect our own weak points. This mobilization process is called **development**. A move which contributes to it is called a **developing move**; a move which does not is called a **non-developing move**.

Pawn moves may also be developing moves, for of necessity we shall have to advance some pawns before our pieces can come to life. Thus, in the diagram, 1.Nf3 is a developing move (it develops a knight) and so is 1.e4 (it opens up diagonals for our queen and king's bishop) but 1.h3 is non-developing, since this move does not assist any of our pieces to reach a useful square. A very sound maxim is that non-developing moves should be avoided if possible in the opening.

The Center

In mobilizing our chessboard army, two factors should primarily engage our attention: where should we put our troops and how fast can we activate them? The reader should be able to guess the answer to the first question. In the opening phase of the game the struggle revolves mainly around the four central squares d4, d5, e4, and e5. The center dominates the board, in much the same way as a mountain dominates the surrounding landscape. Any side which gains control of the center obtains a considerable advantage.

Minor pieces, placed in the center, radiate strength and can attack both sides of the board with equal freedom. In addition, control of the center by one side usually gives the other side a communication problem: the position becomes cramped and it is difficult to transfer forces from one flank to the other.

This does not mean that we should charge out into the center with our knights and bishops at the earliest opportunity. In the first place, such a plan is too slow. Even with no pawns blocking the way, none of our minor pieces can reach a central square in one move, and if we move the same piece twice in the opening we may fall behind in development and find that our opponent has activated an entire army, while only half of our forces are ready for battle. Even if we could afford the time, our pieces would have no security of tenure, when they reached the center, and could easily be repulsed from their advanced posts by enemy pawns.

A more sensible and limited objective is to occupy the center with pawns, thus establishing a position in the center, denying its use to the enemy, and laying the groundwork for future occupation by our pieces. In keeping with this policy, we should develop our pieces onto squares where they can influence events in the center and help support our central pawns. For example, White's king's knight is usually better developed on f3 than on h3, for on f3 the knight helps control the vital central squares d4 and e5.

Time

The second factor we must consider when deciding on our opening plan is time. The unit of time corresponding to one move on the chessboard is called a **tempo** (plural: **tempi**). Thus, in the initial position, White is a tempo ahead because he has the first move. Again, consider the following two ways of starting the game:

A. 1.e4 e5.
B. 1.e3 e5; 2.e4.

In each case we reach the same position but once, with White to move, and once, with Black to move. By playing as in "B" White has lost a tempo - in effect he has given Black an extra move.

Exchanges frequently lead to gain or loss of tempi. Here is another way in which a game could commence: 1.e4 e5; 2.Nf3 Nf6; 3.Nxe5 d6; 4.Nf3 Nxe4; 5.d3 Nf6; 6.Qe2+ Qe7; 7.Bg5 Qxe2+; 8.Bxe2 Be7 reaching the diagram.

White to Play

If we put White's bishop on g5 back on c1 the position would be symmetrical, even as the starting position is symmetrical. Thus in the diagram, White has gained a move, namely Bg5. This gain of tempo happened because Black had played two queen moves (6...Qe7 and 7...Qxe2+) and White had played only one (6.Qe2+) before the exchange of queens took place.

How valuable, then, is this tempo? Unhappily, I cannot provide a simple answer - it all depends on the position. In blocked positions, where nothing much is happening, tempi are relatively insignificant. In positions where both sides are attacking furiously, a single tempo often spells the difference between defeat and victory. The position of the diagram (which is actually one of the main ideas in an opening called the Petroff Defense) is about midway between these two extremes. White's gain of tempo is meaningful, but hardly decisive, because, in order to win the tempo, he had to encourage Black to exchange queens, and this reduction of forces has lessened the chances of a successful direct attack, by either player, in the immediate future.

The Initiative

Closely bound up with the question of tempi is the concept of *the initiative*. This is easy to understand but hard to define. It is rather like getting in the first bid at bridge, or like getting the net position in a tennis game. In chess, the player who has the initiative has the ability to dictate (at least partially) the further course of play. The initiative should not be confused with the attack - these concepts are related, but not identical.

At the start of the game White has a slight initiative by virtue of his extra tempo. During the opening he will try to transform this initiative into some more tangible advantage: the better central position, more spatial control, a material advantage, or perhaps an attack. If he fails, his initiative will probably gradually peter out, for his extra tempo will become less valuable as the game continues. Consider this opening variation: 1.e4 e5; 2.Nf3 Nc6; 3.Bc4 Bc5; 4.d3 Nf6; 5.Nc3 d6.

The moves played by both sides have been perfectly reasonable and logical. Both players have developed their pieces rapidly and staked out a claim in the center with pawns. The position reached (diagram) is symmetrical and White has the move, so he still has the lead of one tempo, with which he started the game. But White's initial advantage is fast disappearing, because he has failed to exploit his initiative. None of White's moves so far has posed Black any serious problems or caused Black to do anything he would not have wished to do in any case.

White to Play

Black's control of space and central position are not inferior to White's and he is well on the road to full equality. A modern master would tend to dismiss White's choice of opening as being insufficiently aggressive.

So far, our discussion has been somewhat abstract, so let us see now how our ideas work in practice in the context of a complete game:

SHIROV VS. KARPOV
Seville 1995
Center Game

1.e4 e5; 2.d4 exd4; 3.Qxd4 Nc6; 4.Qe3.

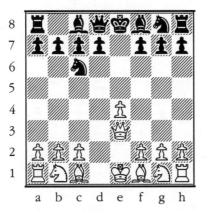

The Center Game is a shock weapon which is often successful against lesser fry. However, against the great masters it has been notably unsuccessful on those rare occasions on which it has been brought out of the closet. Blackburne tried it against Lasker once, Mieses risked it against both Capablanca and Alekhine, while Tartakower employed it against Reshevsky. In each case, White was blown away. In this game Shirov joins that list of unfortunate predecessors. The problem with White's position is that in seeking to maneuver White's queen into an early attacking location, White may simply lose time and find his most powerful piece being pushed from pillar to post.

4...Nf6; 5.Nc3 Bb4; 6.Bd2 0–0; 7.0–0–0 Re8; 8.Qg3.

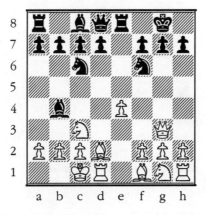

8...d6. It is possible to take the gambit pawn on e4. Mieses-Capablanca, Berlin 1913 continued 8...Nxe4; 9.Nxe4 Rxe4; 10.Bf4 when White enjoyed some initiative for his pawn. Typically, Karpov avoids complications in the opening, preferring to render things more complex in the middlegame. **9.f3 Ne5; 10.h4 Kh8.** This is Karpov's improvement on 10...c6 which led to a quick victory for White in Morozevich-Hebden, London Lloyds Bank 1994.

11.Nh3 Nh5; 12.Qh2 c6; 13.a3 Ba5; 14.Be2. White wants to play g4 but the immediate 14 g4 fails to 14...Nxf3, hence White's decision to protect the f3-pawn. Shirov has, though, overlooked a devastating counterplay. Better is 14.Ng5 threatening g4 (since f3 is now protected) as well as setting the trap 14...h6; 15.Qxe5 dxe5; 16.Nxf7+.

14...Bxh3; 15.Qxh3. Shirov must have been feeling quite pleased with himself but Karpov's next move dispels all illusions.

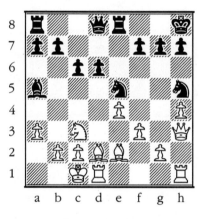

15...Bxc3!;16.bxc3. Horrible but forced. The sad truth has dawned on White that the move he wanted to play 16.Bxc3 loses at once to 16...Nf4 forking White's queen and bishop. **16...Nf6; 17.c4 Qb6; 18.f4 Ned7; 19.Bd3 Nc5; 20.e5 Na4.** With White's king's fortress shattered Karpov is now able to wrap things up quickly.

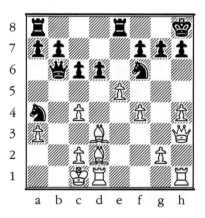

21.Bb4 dxe5; 22.c5 Qc7; 23.Bc4 a5. White resigns. White's position has dissolved spectacularly.

I strongly recommend that during your first few months playing chess you do not study 'book' variations too seriously. Rather, you should simply use your common sense, remembering the basic point: that every worthwhile opening system is an attempt to solve two problems - the problem of the control of the center and the problem of development. Nevertheless, I shall include over the next nine sections a brief sketch of the main systems of attack and defense, so that my readers will be aware of what to expect when they sit down to play.

THE KING'S GAMBIT

I start with this wonderfully exciting and energetic opening, a gambit to blast open the f-file and accelerate White's development and central control. It has been responsible for a multitude of brilliant games.

1.e4 e5; 2.f4.

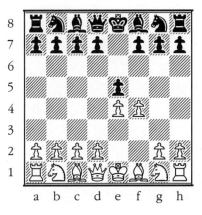

There are three reasonable courses of action:
a) 2...exf4; 3.Nf3 g5.

White to Play

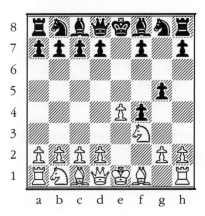

Black intends to hold on to the gambit pawn and weather White's coming attack. This is risky but suitable for the tactically-minded player.

b) 2...Bc5. Declining the pawn and developing normally: 3.Nf3 d6; 4.Nc3 Nf6; 5.Bc4 Nc6; 6.d3 0-0.

White to Play

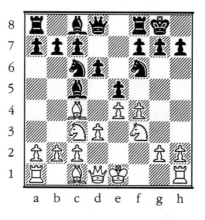

This plan should equalize.

c) 2...exf4; 3.Nf3 d5. Counterattack. Black returns the gambit pawn to open lines for his pieces. Play might continue: 4.exd5 Nf6; 5.Bb5+ c6; 6.dxc6 Nxc6; 7.d4 with a sharp struggle.

Black to Play

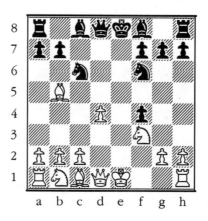

SPASSKY VS. FISCHER
Mar del Plata 1960
King's Gambit

1.e4 e5; 2.f4. The King's Gambit is an heroic opening, which both Fischer and Spassky have revived to great effect. **2...exf4; 3.Nf3 g5; 4.h4 g4; 5.Ne5.**

Black to Play

For a long time, the ancient Allgaier gambit 5.Ng5 was considered unsound here, but after 5...h6; 6.Nxf7 Kxf7; 7.Nc3 Nf6; 8.d4 d5; 9.Bxf4 no less an authority than Paul Keres has suggested that the exposed nature of Black's king still gives White good chances for an attack. See diagram below.

Black to Play

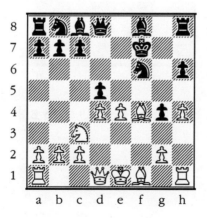

5...Nf6; 6.d4 d6; 7.Nd3 Nxe4; 8.Bxf4 Bg7; 9.Nc3. Fischer himself criticizes this move and suggests instead 9.c3 Qe7; 10.Qe2 but after 10...Bf5 Black appears to have a splendid position.

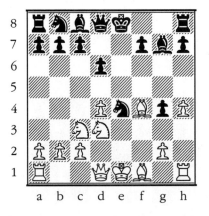

9...Nxc3; 10.bxc3 c5; 11.Be2 cxd4; 12.0-0 Nc6; 13.Bxg4 0-0; 14.Bxc8 Rxc8; 15.Qg4 f5. White had been threatening to win with Bh6! Fischer always liked to win material and then hang on for a grim defense. This move nets a second pawn but weakens his kingside. 15...Kh8 would be stronger. Nevertheless, the text still leaves Fischer with excellent prospects.

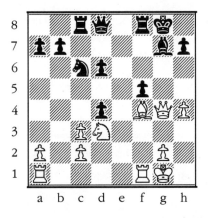

16.Qg3 dxc3; 17.Rae1 Kh8; 18.Kh1 Rg8; 19.Bxd6 Bf8. Striving to eliminate one of White's active attacking pieces.

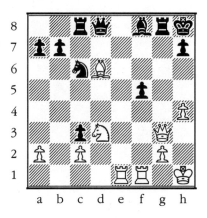

20.Be5+ Nxe5; 21.Qxe5+ Rg7; 22.Rxf5 Qxh4+; 23.Kg1 Qg4. Black threatens mate on g2. A pawn up, Fischer dreams of launching an attack of his own, but he has underestimated the power of White's centralized forces. Correct is 23...Qg3! trying to bring about an exchange of queens, which would evidently favor Black.

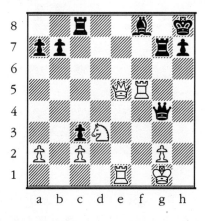

24.Rf2 Be7; 25.Re4 Qg5. Here Black should have played for a draw with 25...Qd1+.

26.Qd4 Rf8; 27.Re5. A dramatic moment. Black's queen is attacked and it has no good square. If 27...Qg6 then 28.Rxe7 wins or 27...Qh4; 28.Rxf8+ or 27...Bf6; 28.Qd6, when Black can resign.

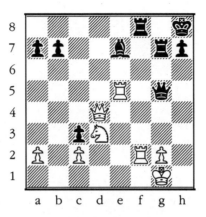

27...Rd8; 28.Qe4 Qh4. Fischer wrote of this position: "I knew I was losing a piece, but just couldn't believe it. I had to play one more move to see if it was really true!"

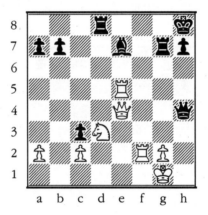

29.Rf4. Black resigns. After 29...Qg3; 30.Rxe7 is deadly. The verdict is that White was lucky to win. But if you play a gambit like this, you must be prepared to take risks!

THE FRENCH DEFENSE

The French Defense is one of Black's most solid options. Black intends to blunt White's initiative by constructing a solid wall of pawns in the center.

1.e4 e6; 2.d4 d5; 3.Nc3 Nf6; 4.Bg5 Be7; 5.e5 Nfd7; 6.Bxe7 Qxe7; 7.f4.

White has a spatial advantage, but Black's position is fairly solid. The chief problem is that Black's queen's bishop on c8 is restricted by its own pawn wall.

The main alternative to this for Black is the Winawer variation:
1.e4 e6; 2.d4 d5; 3.Nc3 Bb4; 4.e5 c5; 5.a3 Bxc3+; 6.bxc3 Ne7.

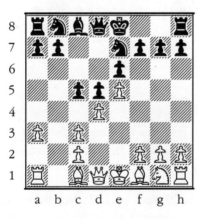

Now White can develop normally with **7.Nf3.** (best) or he can try to exploit the absence of Black's king's bishop by the sharp 7.Qg4 which leads to exciting play after 7...cxd4 (7...0-0? gives White a ready-made attack) 8.Qxg7 Rg8; 9.Qxh7 Qc7 when Black's attack is at least as strong as White's.

White to Play

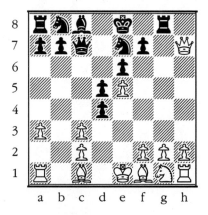

White too has an important alternative:
1.e4 e6; 2.d4 d5; 3.Nd2.

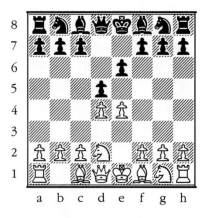

This is the Tarrasch variation. If Black plays 3...Nf6 White will close the center with 4.e5 and he will be able to support his center later with c3 when Black counterattacks. If Black counterattacks immediately with **3...c5.**

White will change his strategy and play **4.exd5 exd5; 5.Ngf3 Nc6; 6.Bb5 Bd6; 7.dxc5 Bxc5; 8.0-0 Nge7.**

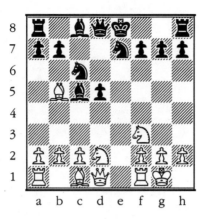

This gives Black an isolated queen pawn. Black must seek active piece play in compensation.

KARPOV VS. LJUBOJEVIC
Brussels 1986
French Defense - Tarrasch Variation

1.e4 e6; 2.d4 d5; 3.Nd2 Nf6.

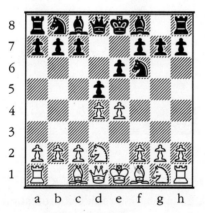

Karpov has a tremendous record against this line of the Tarrasch variation. The reason, of course, is that Black's third move invites White to seize vast tracts of central terrain. Black then hopes to puncture this extended structure, but Karpov is an adept at maintaining a space advantage and ducking the counterplay. Korchnoi has been highly successful at obtaining draws against Karpov with the more fluid 3...c5, but the patient defense, to which this inevitably leads, is not to everyone's taste.

4.e5 Nfd7; 5.c3 c5; 6.f4 Nc6; 7.Ndf3 Qb6; 8.g3 a5. Black hopes to strike back with ...a4. Karpov promptly squashes this possibility.

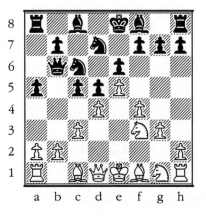

9.a4 cxd4; 10.cxd4 Bb4+; 11.Kf2. With Black's forces cramped White avoids exchanges even though he forfeits the right to castle. **11...g5.** A wild bid for counterplay which, however, may simply undermine the solidarity of his own structure.

12.h3 f6; 13.Be3 0-0; 14.Rc1 Rf7; 15.Rh2. Typical Karpov. The move looks insignificant, but is, in fact, very farsighted. Later on, this rook's coordination along the second rank will play a decisive role.

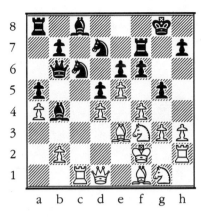

15...Bf8; 16.Qd2 Qb4; 17.Qxb4 axb4. Exchange of queens does not completely relieve Black's problems. **18.b3 Na5; 19.Rb1 gxf4; 20.gxf4 Bh6; 21.Bd3 b6; 22.Rg2+ Kh8; 23.Ne2 Ba6.** A logical attempt to seek further relief by exchanges and simultaneously rid himself of his restricted Queen's bishop. But Karpov has prepared a crushing and artistic refutation.

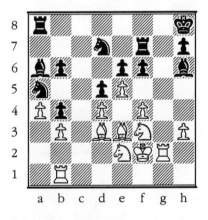

24.Bxa6 Rxa6; 25.f5! The decisive coup. White now gains material and launches a deadly attack against the Black king. **25...Bxe3+; 26.Kxe3 b5.** 26...exf5; 27.e6 Re7; 28.Nf4 with threats such as 29 Rbg1 or 29 Nh4, while 26...fxe5; 27.fxe6 exd4+; 28.Kf2 leaves Black without sufficient compensation for the lost material.

27.axb5 Rb6; 28.Rbg1. Threatening mate.

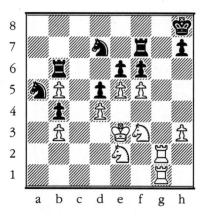

28...h5; 29.Nf4 fxe5; 30.Ng6+ Kh7; 31.Ng5+ Kg7; 32.Nxe5 Nxe5; 33.Nxf7+ Kxf7; 34.dxe5. Black resigns.

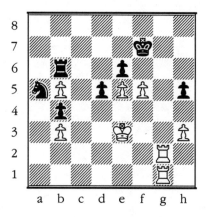

This game is typical of the problems Black can encounter in the French Defense. In spite of the possibility of a vicious attack against White's big pawn center, with moves like ...c5 and ...f6, and even ...g5, White has more space, and the Black queen bishop is difficult to develop.

THE SICILIAN DEFENSE

The Sicilian Defense is by far the most popular choice at master and Grandmaster level against 1.e4. By immediately attacking d4, Black thwarts White's ambition of setting up a big pawn center, as in the French Defense.

1.e4 c5; 2.Nf3 d6; 3.d4 cxd4; 4.Nxd4 Nf6; 5.Nc3 Nc6; 6.Bg5 Bd7; 7.Qd2 Rc8; 8.0-0-0.

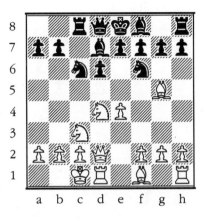

White castles queenside and plays for a quick attack. Black must defend actively, counter-attacking along the half-open c-file while completing his development as quickly as possible. There are many alternative deployments which Black can consider. For example:

1.e4 c5; 2.Nf3 d6; 3.d4 cxd4; 4.Nxd4 Nf6; 5.Nc3 g6; 6.Be3 Bg7.

White to Play

This introduces the Dragon variation. White can continue by advancing his f-pawn: **7.Be2 Nc6; 8.0-0 0-0; 9.Nb3 Be6; 10.f4.**

Black to Play

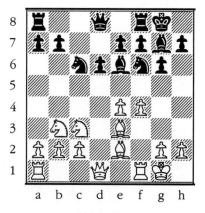

Or White can castle queenside and try to pry open the h-file: **7.f3 Nc6; 8.Qd2 0-0; 9.Bc4 Bd7; 10.h4 Qa5; 11.0-0-0.**

Black to Play

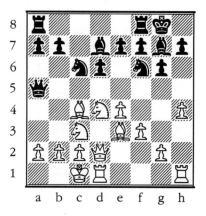

Both plans lead to a double-edged game with chances for both sides.

Other possibilities for Black include systems where Black plays 2...e6, hoping to be able to play ...d5 later.

OLL VS. HODGSON
Groningen 1993
Sicilian Defense

1.e4 c5; 2.Nf3. A common alternative for White now is 2.c3, still planning d4. Black can react with 2...d5, 2...e6 or 2...Nf6; 3.e5 Nd5, all of which are playable. **2...d6; 3.d4 cxd4;**

4.Nxd4 Nf6; 5.Nc3 Nc6; 6.Bg5 e6; 7.Qd2 Be7; 8.0-0-0 0-0. Castling on opposite wings is typical of many lines of the Sicilian.

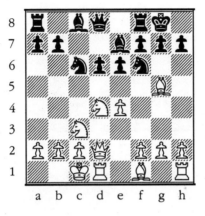

9.f4 Nxd4; 10.Qxd4 Qa5; 11.Bc4 Bd7; 12.e5.

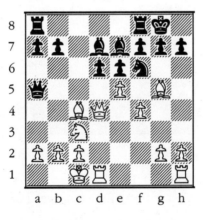

This line of the Sicilian Defense is one of the most fashionable in contemporary Grandmaster circles. Nevertheless, the forcing variation Oll now chooses, although it captures the bishop pair for White, cedes Black a solid position. For this reason, the alternative 12.Rd3 is gaining in credibility.

12...dxe5; 13.fxe5 Bc6. This is the saving grace, otherwise Black would lose material. If now 14.exf6, Black has the perfect riposte 14...Qxg5+. Alternatively, 14.Bxf6 gxf6; 15.exf6 Qg5+; 16.Kb1 Bxf6. Although Black's kingside is weakened, his bishops are so active that White would never contemplate this.

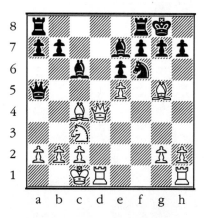

14.Bd2 Nd7; 15.Nd5. Uncovering an attack on Black's queen. The whole point of White's play, which gains the bishop pair.

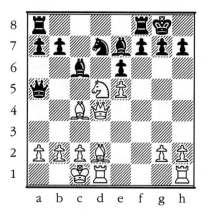

15...Qc5; 16.Nxe7+ Qxe7; 17.Rhe1 Rfd8; 18.Qg4 Nf8; 19.Bd3. White's bishops look dangerous, but Black's next move, sacrificing the exchange, grants him excellent counterplay.

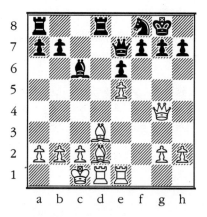

19...Rxd3; 20.cxd3 Qd7; 21.Kb1. This position is still theory. Other moves which have been tried in this position are 21.Bb4 and 21.Re3. The text tempts Black to take the White d-pawn with check in order to open up central files for White's rooks.

21...Qxd3+; 22.Ka1 h5. An important innovation, improving on 22...Qf5 of Ivanchuk-Anand, 7th match game, Linares, 1992. In that game, after 23.Qg3 Ng6; 24.Bc3 h6; 25.Rf1 White gradually took control and won on the 51st move. Hodgson's move deflects White's queen, thus allowing Black's bishop to enter the fray.

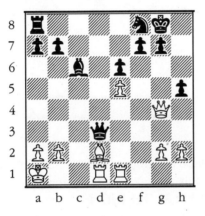

23.Qxh5 Ba4; 24.Bc3. It is impossible for White to retain his material advantage, for if 24.b3 Qd4+; 25.Kb1 Bb5 with a deadly bishop check coming on d3.

24...Bxd1; 25.Rxd1 Qe4; 26.Qg5 a5; 27.Qd2 Ng6; 28.g3 Ne7; 29.Qd7 Nd5. Setting the trap 30.Qxb7 Nxc3 when Black wins material. However, if White avoids this the position appears equal. Although Black's knight, entrenched in the center, appears superior to White's bishop, there is no evident way for Black to make use of his rook, which seems caged help-lessly on its own back rank. The way in which Hodgson solves this problem, and introduces his rook into the attack, is a stroke of genius.

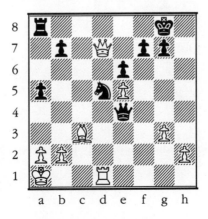

30.Bd4 Qe2; 31.Rc1 b5; 32.Bc5 Qd3; 33.Qc6 Rd8; 34.Bd6 Kh7. Black appears to be marking time, but there is a hidden purpose to the king move.
   35.Qc5.

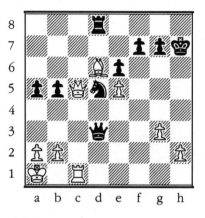

   35...Kg6! At last all becomes clear. Hodgson is marching his king into the battle in order to free the h-file as an avenue for his rook. Wonderfully imaginative play by the former British Champion. **36.h4 Rh8; 37.a3 Rh5; 38.Qg1 Kh7.** Now that the Black rook is in full action the king drops back into safety.
   39.Rd1 Qb3; 40.Rd2 Rf5; 41.g4 Rf4. Having been dormant for so much of the game, Black's rook has now become a tower of strength. Doubtless unnerved by this sudden turn of events, Oll panics and permits a brilliant finale.

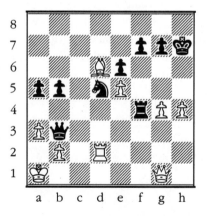

   42.Qb1+ Kg8; 43.g5 b4. Proceeding vigorously to dismantle the fortress around White's king. **44.Rd3.**

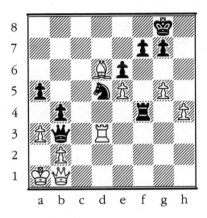

44...Nc3! The first brilliant coup. If now 45.bxc3 Qxa3+; 46.Qa2 Rf1+ wins.

45.Bxb4. The Estonian Grandmaster meets fire with fire. He threatens 46.Rd8 checkmate, while 45...Nxb1 is adequately countered by 46.Rxb3 Rf1; 47.Ka2 axb4; 48.Rxb4 when White has dangerous passed pawns to make up for his missing knight. But Hodgson is ready with a thunderbolt. **45...Qa2+!!**

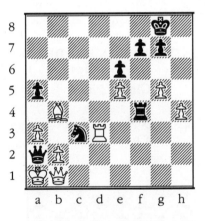

Black's move is the kind of move which knocks you off your chair. After **46.Qxa2 Rf1+.** White can only strew pieces helplessly in the path of Black's rook before the inevitable checkmate, thus **47.Rd1 Rxd1+; 48.Qb1 Rxb1** checkmate.

This is a superb example of Black strategy in the Sicilian Defense.

THE GIUOCO PIANO

1.e4 e5. Usually there follows 2.Nf3 Nc6 (this is the most active way to defend the e-pawn) and now 3.Bc4. White builds up pressure against f7. Black's safest course is to develop normally: 3...Bc5 (3...Nf6 inviting White to attack f7 by 4.Ng5 is also sound, but very complicated) 4.c3 Nf6; 5.d4 exd4; 6.cxd4 Bb4+; 7.Bd2 Bxd2+; 8.Nbxd2 d5! countering White's pawn center.

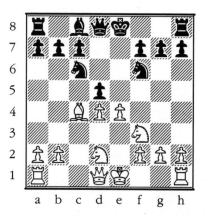

The Giuoco Piano (Italian - literally 'Quiet Game') is probably the opening which is most popular at elementary level. White develops quickly and simultaneously sets up a pawn center.

Wilhelm Steinitz claimed the world title in 1886, the first man to do so, after his match win against Zukertort, and he is universally regarded as the founding father of the line of world champions, which stretches from those days until the present time. The following win by Steinitz is a classic Giuoco Piano, not only a worthy representative of the play of the first world champion, but also a brilliant achievement with which every student of chess should be familiar.

STEINITZ VS. VON BARDELEBEN
Hastings 1895
Giuoco Piano

1.e4 e5; 2.Nf3 Nc6; 3.Bc4 Bc5; 4.c3 Nf6; 5.d4 exd4; 6.cxd4 Bb4+; 7.Nc3. The modern continuation, as we have seen, is 7.Bd2 Bxd2+; 8.Nbxd2 though after 8...d5 the position is considered level.

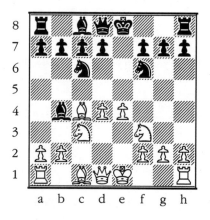

7...d5. Here too this thrust is perfectly playable. The sharpest alternative is, however, 7...Nxe4; 8.0-0 Bxc3; 9.d5, the Moller Attack. Although very complicated modern analysis indicates that this too probably burns out to no more than equality. In round 2 of Hastings Steinitz met 7...Nxe4; 8.0-0 Bxc3 with 9 bxc3 d5; 10.Ba3 Be6; 11.Bb5 with chances for both sides, as in the game Steinitz-Schlechter. Nevertheless, a later game from the 1896 World Championship match (with Steinitz White and Lasker Black) demonstrated that the whole concept is completely unsound. Black met 10.Ba3 with 10...dxc4; 11.Re1 Be6; 12.Rxe4 Qd5; 13.Qe2 0-0-0 with an extra pawn and a better position.

8.exd5 Nxd5; 9.0-0 Be6; 10.Bg5 Be7; 11.Bxd5 Bxd5; 12.Nxd5 Qxd5; 13.Bxe7 Nxe7; 14.Re1 f6; 15.Qe2 Qd7; 16.Rac1.

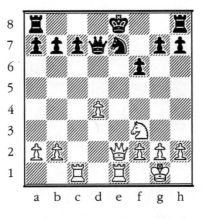

Black's position is perfectly solid, with the exception of the slight difficulty posed by the fact that White's pressure in the e-file prevents him from castling. Believing that he has all the time in the world to consolidate, Black now commits a serious inaccuracy. He should have played the cold-blooded 16...Kf7, breaking the pin, when the position is equal. Various sacrificial ideas have then been suggested for White, namely 17.Qxe7+ Qxe7; 18.Rxe7+ Kxe7; 19.Rxc7+ Kd6 or 17.Ne5+ fxe5; 18.dxe5 Qe6; 19.Qf3+ Qf5; 20.Qxb7, but neither is very convincing. White's best is probably 17.Rc5 c6; 18.Re5 Rhe8; 19.Qc2 with a little pressure but not enough to win.

16...c6; 17.d5. A powerful sacrifice which leaves Black tied in knots.

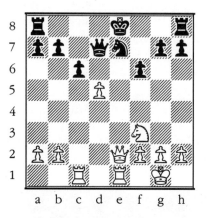

17...cxd5; 18.Nd4 Kf7; 19.Ne6 Rhc8; 20.Qg4 g6; 21.Ng5+ Ke8.

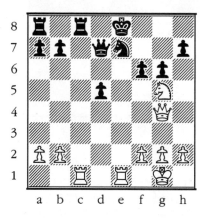

22.Rxe7+. This looks decisive, since if 22...Qxe7; 23.Rxc8+ or 22...Kxe7; 23.Re1+ Kd6; 24.Qb4+ Kc7; 25.Ne6+ Kb8; 26.Qf4+ Rc7; 27.Nxc7 Qxc7; 28.Re8 mate. However, Black has an amazing defensive resource.

22...Kf8. An extraordinary position. White is a piece ahead, but all of his pieces are under attack and he is threatened with a back rank mate. It takes the vision of a genius to demonstrate the win **23.Rf7+ Kg8; 24.Rg7+.** Amazing. The rook is immune. If 24...Qxg7; 25.Rxc8+ or 24...Kxg7; 25.Qxd7+.

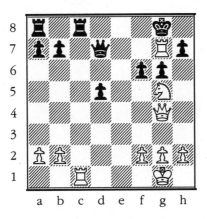

24...Kh8; 25.Rxh7+. Here Black conceded the game, simply by walking out of the room. After 25...Kg8; 26.Rg7+ Kh8; 27.Qh4+ Kxg7; 28.Qh7+ Kf8; 29.Qh8+ Ke7; 30.Qg7+ Ke8; 31.Qg8+ Ke7; 32.Qf7+ Kd8; 33.Qf8+ Qe8; 34.Nf7+ Kd7; 35.Qd6 is checkmate.

THE RUY LOPEZ

1.e4 e5; 2.Nf3 Nc6; 3.Bb5.

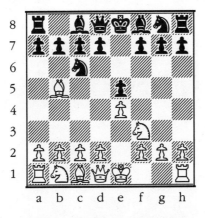

This is White's logical continuation of the attack on Black's e5-pawn, inaugurating a positional struggle. It has been a favorite of Bobby Fischer and Garry Kasparov. In the main line White develops his kingside and then plays c3 and d4, while Black counters this with a strong point on e5: 3...a6 (preparing in advance to break the coming pin on the knight) 4.Ba4 (Note that White cannot win a pawn: 4.Bxc6 dxc6; 5.Nxe5? Qd4!) 4...Nf6; 5 0-0 Be7 (After 5...Nxe4 Black's extra material cannot be held for long and White gets good play in the center) 6.Re1 b5; 7.Bb3 d6; 8.c3 0-0; 9.h3 Na5; 10.Bc2 c5; 11.d4 - a position which has arisen many times in master play and which offers scope for both sides.

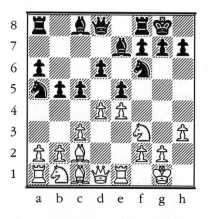

ANAND VS. KAMSKY
PCA Candidates, Las Palmas 1995
Ruy Lopez

1.e4 e5; 2.Nf3 Nc6; 3.Bb5 a6; 4.Ba4 Nf6; 5.0-0 Be7; 6.Re1 b5; 7.Bb3 d6; 8.c3 0-0; 9.h3 Bb7. This is the Zaitsev Defense in the Ruy Lopez, Karpov's favorite, a variation from the popular 9...Na5 and one which has led to a number of fascinating clashes in championship games between Kasparov and Karpov.

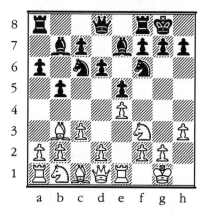

10.d4 Re8; 11.Nbd2 Bf8; 12.a4 h6; 13.Bc2 exd4; 14.cxd4 Nb4; 15.Bb1 Qd7. This is highly unusual. Karpov has tended to inject life into the situation here by means of 15...c5; 16.d5 Nd7 followed by the risky ...f5 to explode White's pawn center. Given White's preponderance of mobile pawns in the middle of the board, Kamsky's treatment now seems much too slow.

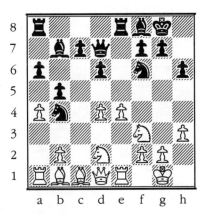

16.b3 g6; 17.Bb2 Bg7; 18.Qc1. At first sight a strange move, but it is the initial link in a plan to embarrass both Black knights. The long range intention is to proceed with Bc3 followed by Qb2, with veiled threats against the Black knights on b4 and f6.

18...Rac8; 19.Bc3 c5; 20.d5 Qe7; 21.Nf1 Nh7. Already an admission of strategic defeat. Once the dark squared bishops are exchanged, definite holes appear in the fortifications around the Black king. **22.Bxg7 Kxg7; 23.Ne3.**

Black to Play

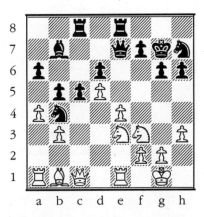

Black's bishop on b7 is locked out of play and meanwhile White threatens unpleasant tactics against the Black king commencing with Ng4. This provokes further weaknesses in the Black king's field.

23...h5; 24.Qd2 Kg8; 25.axb5 axb5; 26.Nd1 Na6; 27.Nc3 b4; 28.Nb5 Nc7; 29.Bd3 Nxb5; 30.Bxb5 Red8; 31.Bc4 Nf6; 32.Qh6 Qf8; 33.Qg5. Anand's feints against the Black king have caused Kamsky's queenside defenses to be depleted. White now takes advantage of this to force a decisive invasion via the a-file. Nevertheless, if Black decides to contest the invasion on the queen's flank by means of 33...Nh7; 34.Qf4 Ra8 then 35 Rxa8 Rxa8; 36.e5 dxe5; 37.Nxe5 grants White a huge attack with moves like d6 to follow, unmasking a devastating battery against Black's pawn on f7.

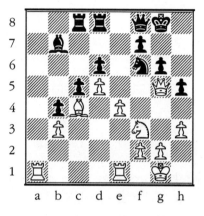

33...Qg7; 34.Ra7 Rc7; 35.Ba6 Rb8; 36.e5 Ne8. Abject retreat but if 36...dxe5; 37.d6 Rd7; 38.Nxe5 wins on the spot. **37.Rxb7 Rcxb7; 38.Bxb7 Rxb7; 39.Qd8 Qf8; 40.Ra1 Nc7; 41.Qd7 Qb8.** Black's defenses have now collapsed for if 41...dxe5; 42.d6 wins at once

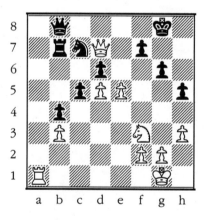

42.Qxd6 c4. Black stakes everything on a last desperate attempt to create a passed b-pawn but Anand has events well under control. **43.bxc4 b3; 44.Rb1 b2; 45.Qc5 Rb3; 46.Qd4 Qb4; 47.Ng5 Rc3; 48.Qf4 f5; 49.exf6 Nxd5; 50.f7+. Black resigns.** After 50...Kf8; 51.Ne6+ is decisive.

QUEEN'S GAMBIT

In the 1.d4 openings, White aims initially for pawns on d4 and c4 as his pawn center. He will only play e4 after suitable preparation has paved the way - his e-pawn may rest on e3 first for a while. White's central formation has considerable latent power, but his development is slower than after 1.e4, and this gives Black great scope in choosing a defense.

If Black occupies the center immediately **1.d4 d5**, then **2.c4** leads to the Queen's Gambit. This is not a real gambit, since Black cannot actually win a pawn. After 1.d4 d5; 2.c4 dxc4 White can even, should he so desire, regain the pawn at once with 3.Qa4+, forking e8 and c4. The strength of 2.c4 is that if Black exchanges on c4, White will be left with a pawn majority in the center and this may give him the better prospects in the middle game. A typical main line of the Queen's Gambit Declined (QGD) is: **2...e6; 3.Nc3 Nf6; 4.Bg5 Be7; 5.Nf3 0-0; 6.e3 Nbd7; 7.Rc1 c6; 8.Bd3 dxc4** (surrendering the center in order to initiate a series of exchanges to free his position) **9.Bxc4 Nd5; 10.Bxe7 Qxe7; 11.0-0 Nxc3; 12.Rxc3 e5** (when White still has a slight initiative after **13.Qc2**).

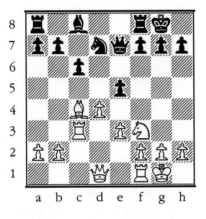

It is important in top level clashes to avoid inferior positions when playing Black, as I well know from my experiences as second to Korchnoi against Karpov in the World Championship of 1978. If a player can equalize easily with Black, then half the battle is won.

KARPOV VS. YUSUPOV
Candidates Semi-Final, London 8th match game 1989
Queen's Gambit Declined

1.d4 Nf6; 2.c4 e6; 3.Nf3 d5; 4.Nc3 Be7; 5.Bg5 0-0; 6.e3 h6; 7.Bh4 Ne4. This is another method of freeing Black's position by exchanges, attributed to Emanuel Lasker, world champion from 1894-1921.

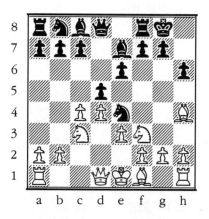

8.Bxe7 Qxe7; 9.Rc1 c6; 10.Bd3 Nxc3; 11.Rxc3 dxc4.

White to Play

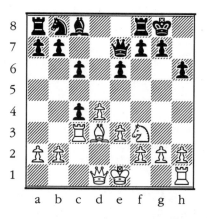

White can now try 12.Rxc4 but Karpov was clearly aiming for a position he had studied thoroughly. **12.Bxc4 Nd7; 13.0-0 e5.** Safer here would be 13...b6 For example, 14.Bd3 c5; 15.Bb5 Rd8; 16.Bc6 Rb8; 17.Qc2 cxd4; 18.Nxd4 e5! (Smyslov-Kasparov, Candidates Final, Vilnius 1984) as given in BCO 2. **14.Bb3 exd4.**

This is very similar to the main line I gave in the introductory comments to this section. The main difference is that Black has the extra move ...h6, which is more of a liability than a strength.

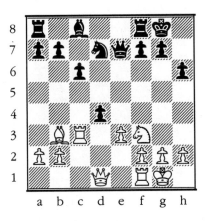

At this stage Black should prefer 14...e4 to seal up the center. Black's play merely serves to accentuate White's lead in development.

15.exd4. White could recapture on d4 with his knight or queen, but taking back with the pawn, although it leaves White with an isolated queen's pawn, opens more lines for White's attack. **15...Nf6; 16.Re1 Qd6; 17.Ne5 Nd5.**

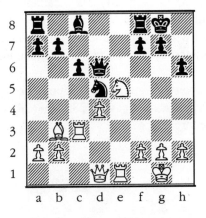

18.Rg3. Karpov's attack is already running on oiled wheels. **18...Bf5.** Yusupov is in grave danger, all due to the opening. Black's problem is that the extra ...h6 move means he can never expel White's knight with ...f6, because of Ng6. In trying to defend the g6 square he cedes Karpov further targets for attack. **19.Qh5.** An energetic continuation of the offensive. White's control of the center permits him to swing his pieces into a direct attack on the Black king. **19...Bh7; 20.Qg4 g5.**

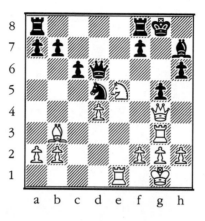

White's fierce concentration of forces obliges Black to breach the pawn shield around his king. Obviously, after this extreme loosening move, Black's prospects of survival become remarkably thin. By advancing the pawns in front of his king Yusupov offers a ready made object for twin White battering ram thrusts, h4 and f4.

21.h4 f6. Not so much to threaten the knight on e5 as to bolster up the protection of the vulnerable pawn on g5. **22.hxg5 hxg5.** Naturally Black cannot play 22...fxe5 which is refuted by 23 gxh6+. Now Karpov could consider 23.Nf3 with the idea of sacrificing the knight on g5. there is, however, nothing at all wrong with the logical move he chooses. This continues the plan of stripping away, at no material cost, the pawn wall tenuously separating Black's king from disaster.

23.f4 Rae8. Yusupov had a very long think at this point and then resigned himself to the game continuation, which costs him several pawns. 23...Kh8; 24.fxg5 fxe5; 25.g6 is also hopeless, since White has added the threat of g7+.

24.fxg5 fxe5; 25.g6 Bxg6.

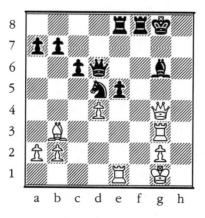

26.dxe5! A brilliant in-between, or 'zwischenzug', move which ensures a winning position. It is much more convincing than the immediate 26.Qxg6+. **26...Qe6.** Black could well have resigned instead, but since losing this game spelled defeat in the match Yusupov fights on till his resources are utterly exhausted. Of course, Black cannot capture on e5, while 26...Qc5+; 27.Kh2 leaves him helpless against the imminent Qxg6+.

27.Bxd5 cxd5; 28.Qxg6+ Qxg6; 29.Rxg6+ Kh7; 30.Rd6 Rc8. The opening has been a triumph for White.

NIMZO-INDIAN DEFENSE

Another way for Black to play against **1.d4** is to attempt to control the key central squares with pieces rather than pawns. One popular method for black is the **Nimzo-Indian Defense: 1...Nf6** (preventing e4) **2.c4 e6; 3.Nc3 Bb4** (again preventing e4). In this opening Black tries to avoid the slightly cramped formations which result from the d5-e6 pawn chain in the Queen's Gambit Declined while still preventing White from enlarging his center. Black must be prepared, however, to surrender the bishop pair, but the doubled pawns White suffers in return will be valuable compensation. One continuation is **4.e3 c5; 5.Bd3 Nc6; 6.Nf3 Bxc3+; 7.bxc3 d6; 8.e4.** White looks to have the superior game, but Black can block the position with 8...e5! and does not stand worse.

Black to Play

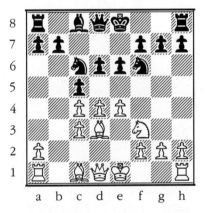

When I first started to take an interest, as a junior, in playing over the games of masters and Grandmasters, I remember being puzzled by the designation of one particular defense, the Nimzo-Indian.

For those who are similarly confused, Nimzo-Indian is an abbreviation of the Nimzowitsch Indian Defense. The so-called Indian defenses became popular in the 1920s, and were based on the perception that Black could hold back his pawns in the opening and concentrate instead on observation of the center by piece play. The connection with Indian chess was tenuous, referring mainly to the fact that in the older, slower Indian version of the game the pawns could move only one square at a time.

Aron Nimzowitsch, the inventor of the Nimzo-Indian, was also active in the twenties, during which period he scored some excellent tournament successes. He was the leader of the hypermodern school of chess, a great strategist and a champion of the somewhat misnamed "Indian" ideas. His most famous book, in which he expounded his theories, was *My System*, which is still in print after many editions. The strategic goal of the Nimzo-Indian Defense is for Black to blockade the White central pawns. Black is successful in this in the game I show, an all-time doubled-pawn formation classic.

JOHNER VS. NIMZOWITSCH
Dresden 1926
Nimzo-Indian Defense

1.d4 Nf6; 2.c4 e6; 3.Nc3 Bb4; 4.e3 0-0; 5.Bd3 c5; 6.Nf3 Nc6; 7.0-0 Bxc3. An important component of Nimzowitsch's Defense. Black hopes, by doubling White's pawns on the c-file, to restrict the mobility of White's central pawn mass.

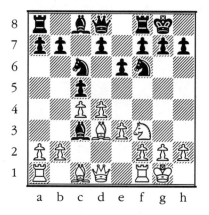

8.bxc3 d6; 9.Nd2 b6; 10.Nb3 e5. The commencement of Black's central blockading maneuvers, further intended to hinder White's possibilities for expansion.

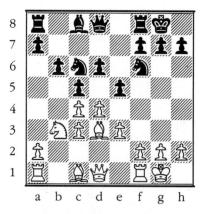

11.f4 e4; 12.Be2 Qd7. It is important to prevent White gaining space by means of g4 **13.h3 Ne7; 14.Qe1.** If White now plays 14.g4 then 14...h5; 15.f5 hxg4; 16.hxg4 Nh7 would leave White's kingside full of holes.

14...h5; 15.Bd2 Qf5; 16.Kh2 Qh7. The completion of a remarkable concentration of Black's forces on the king's flank, which more or less paralyzes White's chances for freedom of action. In particular, it should be noted what a miserable role is now played by the White bishop pair.

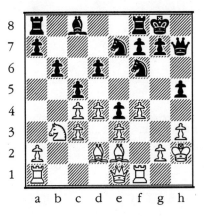

17.a4 Nf5; 18.g3 a5; 19.Rg1 Nh6; 20.Bf1 Bd7; 21.Bc1 Rac8; 22.d5 Kh8; 23.Nd2 Rg8; 24.Bg2 g5. With White tied up in knots, the time has come for Black to start his own assault in earnest.

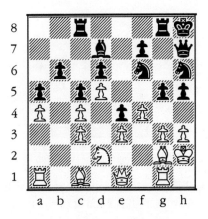

25.Nf1 Rg7; 26.Ra2 Nf5; 27.Bh1 Rcg8; 28.Qd1 gxf4; 29.exf4 Bc8; 30.Qb3 Ba6; 31.Re2 Nh4.

As so often happens when one side has been strategically out-played, wonderful combinations begin to arise naturally from the position. Thus, had White chosen to defend himself with 32.Nd2, then Black could sacrifice his queen most aesthetically with 32...Bc8; 33.Nxe4 Qf5; 34.Nf2 Qxh3+; 35.Nxh3 Ng4 mate.

32.Re3 Bc8; 33.Qc2 Bxh3; 34.Bxe4. If instead 34.Kxh3 Qf5+; 35.Kh2 Ng4+ with mate to follow.

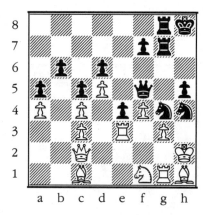

Analysis Diagram

34...Bf5; 35.Bxf5 Nxf5; 36.Re2 h4. Although material is still level, White's position has been crushed. Black's blockading strategy has been supremely successful.

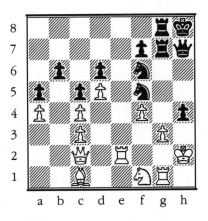

37.Rgg2 hxg3+; 38.Kg1 Qh3; 39.Ne3 Nh4; 40.Kf1 Re8. White resigns.

KING'S INDIAN DEFENSE AND ATTACK

A third and very modern way for Black to treat the opening after 1.d4 is to allow, indeed encourage, White to build up an extended center, in the hopes that it will prove vulnerable to a counter attack. Black deliberately holds back his central pawns until his pieces are well placed to support them. Typical of these aggressive counter attacking openings is the **King's Indian Defense** (Classical variation):

1.d4 Nf6; 2.c4 g6; 3.Nc3 Bg7; 4.e4. (accepting the challenge) **4...d6; 5.Be2 0-0; 6.Nf3 e5; 7.0-0.** 7.dxe5 dxe5; 8.Qxd8 Rxd8; 9.Nxe5 Nxe4! is good for Black. **7...Nbd7; 8.d5 Nc5** when White's advantage is minimal.

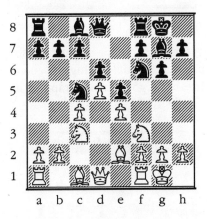

A major plan for Black in this type of position is to move the f6-knight and then attack with ...f5.

The King's Indian Defense is a great favorite with Kasparov.

KRAMNIK VS. KASPAROV
Intel Grand Prix, Paris 1995
King's Indian Defense

1.d4 Nf6; 2.c4 g6; 3.Nc3 Bg7; 4.e4 d6; 5.Nf3 0-0. Kasparov can almost always be relied upon to wheel out the King's Indian. **6.Be2 e5; 7.d5.** The patent variation of Tigran Petrosian, who was world champion from 1963 to 1969. White's plan is to continue with Bg5, and clamp down on Black's counterplay. Kramnik has beaten Kasparov with this in the past, but in this game Kasparov avoids his former experimentation and heads straight down the main line approved by theory.

7...a5; 8.Bg5 h6; 9.Bh4 Na6; 10.0-0 Qe8. The point of this move is to break the pin against his king's knight, without losing the cohesion of his kingside pawns. The alternative 10...g5 would achieve a similar goal, but Black would, in that case, forfeit the fluidity of his kingside pawn mass.

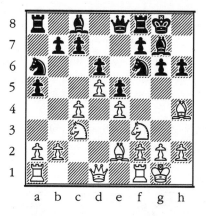

11.Nd2 Nh7; 12.a3 h5. Creating a square for his king's bishop on h6. Operating from this point the bishop often plays a useful role, both in kingside and queenside operations.

13.f3. He has to meet the threat of ...g5 and ...h4, trapping his bishop. **13...Bd7; 14.b3 f5; 15.Rb1 Nc5; 16.Nb5 Bxb5; 17.cxb5 Bh6.**

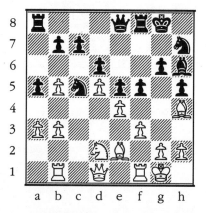

The situation has crystallized. White has promising pressure on the queen's flank, but Black is active on the opposite wing, his pawns are mobile and his remaining bishop is able to conjure up all kinds of tactical perspectives.

18.exf5 gxf5; 19.b6 cxb6; 20.Nc4 Qg6. There is no satisfactory way to defend both the pawn on b6 and d6. **21.Be7.** Not content with the simple 21.Nxb6, Kramnik seeks to annihilate Black's central pawn constellation. The corresponding danger is that Black is given time to accelerate his counterplay against the White king. **21...Rf7; 22.Bxd6 Rg7; 23.Rf2 e4; 24.Bxc5 bxc5; 25.fxe4.** White would like to play 25.f4, to blockade the Black attack, but this fails tactically to 25...Bxf4; 26.Bxh5 (not 26.Rxf4 Qxg2 mate) 26...Qh6, when Black's pieces enjoy multiple avenues of attack against the white king.

25...fxe4; 26.d6. White's passed d-pawn now becomes a danger to Black. If now 26...e3 then the response 27.Qd5+ defends g2.

26...Nf6; 27.Qf1 Nd7; 28.Rd1?

Obsessed with Black's threats on the kingside, Kramnik overlooks that Black may also strike on the other wing. The correct move here is 28.a4, restraining Black's queenside pawns and thus maintaining the knight in its strong position on c4. In that case White's passed d-pawn is counter-balanced by Black's passed e-pawn. The situation then would still be in a state of dynamic equilibrium.

28...b5. Disaster has struck. White dare not move his knight on account of ...Be3. **29.Rd5 bxc4; 30.Bxh5 Qe6; 31.bxc4 Be3.** Having overlooked Black's 28...b5, White has collapsed. Black's last move wins further material as well as introducing the deadly threat of ...Rf8. Kramnik, therefore, resigned.

KING'S INDIAN ATTACK

Club players and home enthusiasts often ask me to suggest an opening system for White which is safe, yet aggressive, and does not require a superb memory and months of intense learning. In such cases I invariably recommend the King's Indian Attack. In this system White's first four or five moves are fixed (1.Nf3, 2.g3, 3.Bg2, 4.0-0, 5.d3) and White can develop in isolation, without devoting any attention at all to how Black is proceeding. In the middle game

White has plenty of opportunity to unleash an attack based on either c4 or e4, advancing in the center.

One of the first games I saw with this opening (and the game which forms the topic of this analysis) was a deeply impressive struggle between Vassily Smyslov and Mikhail Botvinnik, the two Soviet champions, played during the period when they were at the height of their battle for the world chess title, a struggle which dominated the fifties. I was particularly attracted by the way in which Smyslov whipped up an attack against the Black king, commencing with a pawn sacrifice on the other extremity of the board.

SMYSLOV VS. BOTVINNIK
USSR Championship 1955
King's Indian Attack

1.Nf3 Nf6; 2.g3 g6; 3.Bg2 Bg7; 4.0-0 0-0; 5.d3 c5; 6.e4 Nc6; 7.Nbd2 d6; 8.a4 Ne8. Botvinnik prepares a vigorous counterattack in the f-file, but the safest and best treatment is ...Rb8 followed by ...a6, shifting the weight of the struggle to the queen's side.

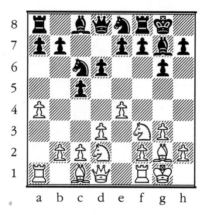

9.Nc4 e5; 10.c3 f5. Rather too enterprising. Sounder is 10...h6 followed by 11.Be6. **11.b4!** A well founded sacrifice: the b-file is opened and White diminishes Black's influence in the center by attacking the pawn on c5.

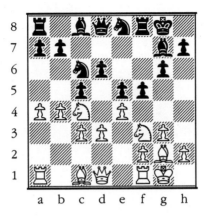

11...cxb4; 12.cxb4 fxe4. If 12...Nxb4; 13.Qb3! with fierce diagonal pressure towards the Black king. The text plans to accept White's offer at a later stage, but 12...h6 would still have been a safer alternative.

13.dxe4 Be6; 14.Ne3 Nxb4; 15.Rb1 a5; 16.Ba3 Nc7; 17.Bxb4 axb4; 18.Rxb4 Bh6. Botvinnik relies on active defense. He hopes to meet 19.Rxb7 with 19...Bxe3; 20.fxe3 Na6 followed by ...Nc5.

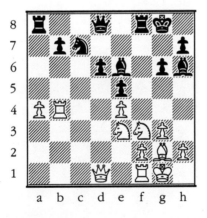

19.Rb6! Establishing pressure against Black's d-pawn is more important than capturing the pawn on b7. **19...Bxe3; 20.fxe3 Bc4; 21.Rxd6 Qe8; 22.Re1.**

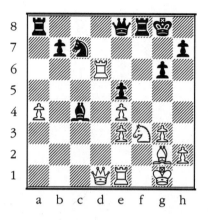

White's material advantage is of little importance, as Black can easily regain his pawn. The chief defect of Black's position is the slightly exposed situation of his king and the lack of coordination between his other pieces.

22...Rf7. If 22...Rxa4 then 23.Nxe5! Qxe5; 24.Qxa4 Qxd6; 25.Qxc4+ and Black is clearly losing. The best chance, in fact, would have been 22...Qxa4; 23.Qxa4 Rxa4; 24.Nxe5, and although Black is a pawn down he has chances of survival since White's pawns are doubled. **23.Ng5 Re7; 24.Bf1! Bxf1; 25.Rxf1.** Threatening Qb3+ followed by Rdf6. **25...Qxa4.** If 25...h6 then 26.Rff6! hxg5; 27.Rxg6+ with a winning attack. **26.Rd8+ Re8; 27.Qf3!**

Suddenly, after such a sophisticated and ultra-modern opening, Smyslov has generated a brutal attack in the f-file which might just as well have arisen from a good old King's Gambit.

27...Qc4; 28.Rd7. Black resigns. After **28...Rf8.** White wins beautifully with **29.Rxc7 Qxc7.**

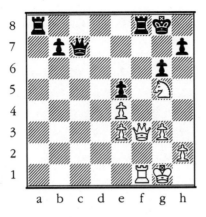

And now a superb forking device. **30.Qxf8+ Rxf8; 31.Rxf8+ Kxf8; 32.Ne6+** leaving White a knight ahead in the endgame.

I well remember that I used precisely this game as inspiration to prepare for my first truly important face-off in a junior championship. I hope it will prove equally useful to you, the readers.

OPENING TRAPS

It so often happens that a Grandmaster is deluded into following a hazardous or downright inferior line, simply because it has become a popular highway of chess openings theory. When everyone is doing it there is a temptation to challenge one's own instincts and follow the trend, which can lead to unpleasant surprises.

Something of a sensation was created when Leonard Barden published an astounding miniature in his columns in both The Guardian and the Financial Times. It was a Grandmaster game from Biel 1988 which was over in a mere six moves, and I repeat the moves here.

ZAPATA VS. ANAND
Biel 1988
Petroff Defense

1.e4 e5; 2.Nf3 Nf6; 3.Nxe5 d6; 4.Nf3 Nxe4; 5.Nc3 Bf5?? Repeating a blunder from an earlier Grandmaster game, between Christiansen and Miles, when 5...Bf5 had been played, but not punished.

6.Qe2. Black resigns!

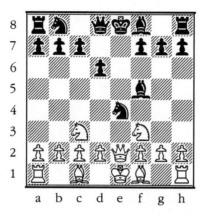

This is the shortest game ever lost by a Grandmaster. For if 6...Qe7; 7.Nd5 wins or 6...d5; 7.d3 wins.

THREE OPENING MISTAKES

Another common error is to neglect development, leave the king stuck in the center, and move the same piece twice. This usually leads to summary execution!

NUNN VS. SOKOLOV
Dubai Olympiad 1986
Sicilian Defense

1.e4 c5; 2.Nf3 e6; 3.d4 cxd4; 4.Nxd4 Nc6; 5.Nc3 a6; 6.Be2 d6; 7.Be3 Qc7; 8.f4 Na5.

Moving the knight again before developing other pieces is most unwise. This was, indeed, condemned 50 years ago, but Sokolov does not appear to be a student of chess history.

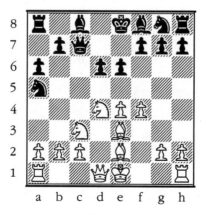

9.0-0 Nc4; 10.Bxc4 Qxc4; 11.f5 Be7. Artificial, but if 11...Nf6; 12.fxe6 fxe6; 13.Rxf6! gxf6; 14.Qh5+ Kd8; 15.Qf7 Lasker-Pirc, Moscow 1935. White has a winning attack. **12.Qg4 h5; 13.Qf3 Bf6; 14.fxe6 fxe6**. Or 14...Bxd4; 15.Qxf7+ Kd8; 16.e7+.
15.e5! dxe5.

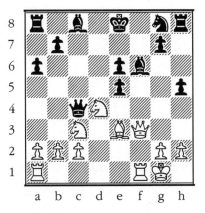

16.Ne4. Threatening Nd6+. **16...Qc7; 17.Qg3 Ne7; 18.Rad1 h4; 19.Nxf6+ gxf6; 20.Qg7 Rf8.** If 20...Rg8; 21.Qxf6 exd4; 22.Qf7+ Kd8; 23.Rxd4+ Bd7; 24.Qf8+. **21.Rxf6 Rxf6; 22.Qxf6 Qd6; 23.Bg5 exd4; 24.Rxd4 Nd5; 25.Rxd5. Black resigns.** There is no good recapture. A dashing win by John Nunn.

The last game in this chapter shows how to deal with an irregular and anti-positional opening. Rule Number 1: Don't panic, just follow the principles of central control and development, as explained in this chapter, and you will be fine!

BASMAN VS. KEENE
Manchester, 1981
Grob's Opening

1.g4. This has only surprise, or rather, shock, value. Strategically and tactically it is the worst opening move on the board. It both neglects development and weakens White's pawn structure. Black responds by seizing the center.
1...d5; 2.h3 e5; 3.Bg2 c6; 4.d4 e4; 5.c4 Bd6; 6.Nc3 Ne7; 7.g5. If 7 Qb3 0-0; 8.Bg5 f6; 9.cxd5 cxd5!; 10.Nxd5 Be6; 11.Nxe7+ Qxe7; 12.d5 Bf7; 13.Be3 Nd7 gives Black a superb position for his sacrificed pawn. Black's advanced pawn on e4 prevents White from developing his pieces.
7...Be6; 8.h4 Nf5; 9.Bh3 0-0; 10.cxd5 cxd5.

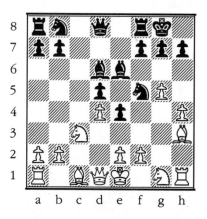

Black has followed all the rules against White's eccentric opening, and has achieved a dominating position. Realizing how serious his situation is, White now tries a desperate gamble to win a pawn.

11.Nxd5. Or 11.Bxf5 Bxf5; 12.Nxd5 Qa5+; 13.Nc3 Nc6 with a massive Black lead in development. **11...Ng3!!**

White to Play

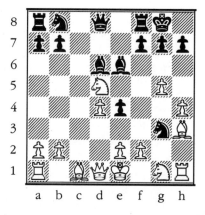

It is hardly surprising that Black has this devastating tactical shot, since his strategy has been impeccable, while White's has been unsound. If now 12.fxg3 Bxg3+ and ...Bxd5 or 12.Bxe6 Nxh1; 13.Bh3 Bh2! winning material.

12.Nf6+ gxf6; 13.fxg3 Bxg3+; 14.Kf1 Nc6; 15.Be3 Nb4; 16.Kg2 Nd5.

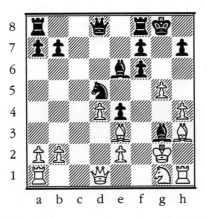

Now White's position dissolves. Note how White's entire structure was weakened by his erroneous first move 1.g4. **17.Kxg3 Nxe3; 18.Qd2 Qd6+; 19.Kf2 Qf4+; 20.Nf3 exf3. White resigns**. 21.Qxe3 Qxh4+ is too much.

MASTER THE MIDDLEGAME
The Art of Winning Attacks in Chess

KING IN THE CENTER
Attacking the Uncastled Enemy King

I start this chapter with one of the most common errors, which can be a real joy to exploit. If one side leaves the king uncastled in the center for too long, the attack against it can be devastating. It is an incredible disadvantage to have to conduct a standard middlegame with your king stuck in the firing line. In the following game, White hits hard with his pawns, and then follows up with a vicious piece attack, swiftly gunning down the black king.

KEENE VS. TIMMAN
Hastings 1973-74
Sicilian Maroczy (by transposition)

1.Nf3 g6; 2.c4 Bg7; 3.d4 c5. Black issues an invitation to the Benoni Defense but White declines, preferring to remain in the paths of the Maroczy Bind Sicilian. **4.e4.** Transposing into a line of the Sicilian Defense. Now after 4...cxd4; 5.Nxd4 Nc6; 6.Be3 Nf6; 7.Nc3 Ng4; 8.Qxg4 Nxd4; 9.Qd1 e5; 10.Nb5 0-0; 11.Qd2 Qe7!? 12 Be2! White maintains some advantage since Black's d-pawn is very weak. Timman opts for a move favored by Fischer and Tal.

4...Nc6; 5.dxc5. Here it is less effective to play 5.d5 Nd4; 6.Nxd4 cxd4 since White's queen's knight cannot enter play at any good square. After the move played, Black has to waste time with his queen in order to recapture the pawn. **5...Qa5+; 6.Nfd2!** An idea of Petrosian's. The idea is to chase Black's queen with the king's knight and then develop the queen's knight on the excellent square c3.

6...Qxc5; 7.Nb3 Qb6; 8.Be2. Later I discovered the more accurate move order 8 Be3! Qc7; 9.Qd2 Nf6; 10.Nc3 d6; 11.Be2 0-0; 12.0-0 Ne5; 13.Nd5, Keene-Sanz, Orense 1976.

8...d6; 9.0-0 Qc7! A tremendous move which improves on the game Petrosian-Fischer, Zagreb 1970. Fischer played 9...Nf6 but after 10.Nc3 White clearly has an excellent game since his queen's knight is ready to jump into the key square d5 (c.f. Keene-Sanz). Timman delays ...Nf6 so that he can answer 10.Nc3 with 10...Bxc3; 11.bxc3 Nf6 and White's doubled c-pawns are severely exposed. In his turn White now has to find a good waiting move.

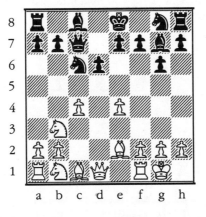

10.Kh1! Waiting, but useful too. It's a valuable precaution to tuck the king in the corner away from disturbing checks along the g1-a7 diagonal. **10...Be6; 11.f4 a5?**

Much too optimistic. Black had to obstruct the further advance of White's f-pawn with 11...f5! **12.Na3.** It's okay to develop the knight on this inferior square since Black has seriously weakened b5. **12...a4.** Continuing with his plan, but now all hell breaks loose. **13.Nb5 Qb6.** See my note to White's tenth move!

14.c5! Black confessed after the game that he had overlooked this move. White obtains an irresistible attack by means of this pawn sacrifice.

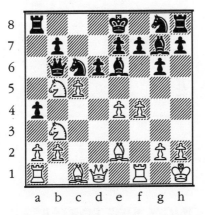

14...Qd8. The line of least resistance. Probably Black's best chance was to test the accuracy of White's idea: e.g. 14...dxc5; 15.Nxc5! Qxc5 (15...Rd8; 16.Nxa4 wins a pawn) 16.Nc7+ Kf8; 17.Nxa8. Thus White wins the exchange but the knight in the corner is trapped. However, if Black goes after the knight White's attack crashes through: 17...Qa5; 18.f5 gxf5; 19.exf5 Bc8; 20.Bf3 Nf6 (20...Qxa8; 21.Bxc6 bxc6; 22.Qd8 mate) 21.Bxc6 bxc6; 22.Bf4 Qxa8; 23.Qd8+ Ne8; 24.f6 Bxf6; 25.Bh6+ Bg7; 26.Bxg7+ Kxg7; 27.Qxe7 and at the trifling cost of rook for two minor pieces Black's position has been laid waste. **15.cxd6!** This sacrifice still holds.

White's attack virtually conducts itself. **15...axb3; 16.Nc7+ Kf8; 17.Nxa8 Qxa8; 18.f5.** Going forwards all the time. White's pieces occupy logical and strong squares and Black can resign.

18...gxf5; 19.exf5 Bd7; 20.dxe7+ Ke8; 21.Bc4. Threatening 22.Bxf7+ and 23.Qxd7; **21...Ne5; 22.Bxb3 Qa6; 23.Bf4 Nh6; 24.Qd5!** Black is quite powerless against White's dominating centralization.

24...Nhg4; 25.Bxe5 Nxe5; 26.Rfe1. Black resigns. There is no defense to 27.Rxe5 and 28.Qxf7 mate.

DEMOLITION OF THE KING'S SIDE FORTRESS

There are a number of standard ways of breaking down the defenses of a castled king. This section demonstrates four of them:
1. A breakthrough at h7
2. A breakthrough at f7
3. Exchange of a fianchettoed bishop on g7 which had been an important defender of the king.
4. A sacrifice against Black's pawn on h6

Paul Keres, the Estonian grandmaster, established the extraordinary record of coming second in four World Championship Candidates tournaments, those of 1953, 1956, 1959 and 1962. Additionally, at the AVRO tournament of 1938, he shared first prize with the American grandmaster Reuben Fine ahead of no less than four past reigning or future world champions. Twenty-five years later, Keres was still able to demonstrate super class, when he again shared top honors with the reigning world champion of the day, Tigran Petrosian, in a tournament composed only of the elite.

This game is a superb example of Keres's tactical skills, culminating, as it does, in a sacrificial breakthrough on h7, with f7 one of the main Achilles Heels of the fortifications of a castled Black king.

KERES VS. FINE
Ostend 1937
Queen's Gambit Declined

1.Nf3 d5; 2.d4 Nf6; 3.c4 e6; 4.Nc3 c5; 5.cxd5 Nxd5; 6.e4 Nxc3; 7.bxc3 cxd4; 8.cxd4 Bb4+; 9.Bd2 Bxd2+; 10.Qxd2 0-0; 11.Bc4.

The opening has been standard. White has a strong pawn center, with a potential passed pawn in the d-file, good development and some makings of an attack against the Black king. On the other hand, though, Black has no obvious weaknesses, and has also succeeded in effecting simplification which could complicate White's task of whipping up an attack.

11...Nd7; 12.0-0 b6; 13.Rad1 Bb7; 14.Rfe1 Rc8; 15.Bb3 Nf6; 16.Qf4 Qc7; 17.Qh4.

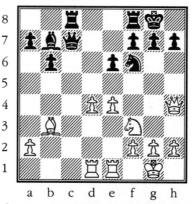

Evidently an exchange of queens would be entirely in Black's favor. After such a trade, White's attacking chances would evaporate and Black's majority of pawns on the queen's flank would assume at least equal significance with White's center pawns. Instead of this su-pine course, Keres transfers his queen into direct alignment with the black king.

17...Rfd8; 18.Re3. In his notes Keres prefers the immediate 18.e5, though after 18...Nd5; 19.Ng5 h6; 20.Ne4 Nc3; 21.Nf6+ Kh8 things are not clear. **18...b5; 19.Rde1 a5; 20.a4 b4; 21.d5.** Having massed his forces, White must strike. Further delay would allow Black gradu-ally to profit from his own powerful passed pawn on b4. With the text White prepares to hurl all his forces at the Black king.

21...exd5; 22.e5 Nd7; 23.Ng5 Nf8. Black should have preferred 23...h6 when great com-plications arise after 24.e6 hxg5; 25.exf7+ Kxf7; 26.Re7+.

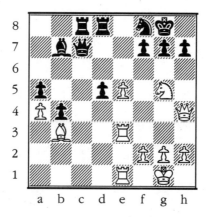

24.Nxh7. A brilliant breakthrough on one of Black's most sensitive squares, even though it appears to be heavily guarded. Fine had clearly overlooked that this breakthrough was pos-sible. **24...Nxh7; 25.Rh3 Qc1.** An ingenious riposte, speculating on the weakness of White's back rank. The attacked knight on h7 cannot, of course, move in view of Qh8 mate. Neverthe-less, in spite of Black's resourcefulness, Keres can now power through with a brutal frontal assault.

26.Qxh7+ Kf8; 27.Rhe3 d4; 28.Qh8+ Ke7; 29.Qxg7 Rf8; 30.Qf6+ Ke8; 31.e6. Black resigns. After the forced line 31...dxe3; 32.exf7+ Rxf7; 33.Bxf7+ Kd7; 34.Qe6+ Black either loses his queen or is mated. In the middle of this 32...Kd7; 33.Qe6+ Kc7; 34.Rxc1+ is also fatal for Black.

Keres' style was fluent and tactical, much easier to grasp, for example, than the recondite maneuvers of a Smyslov, Karpov or Petrosian. His games often resulted in slashing attacks, even against the world's best. In the following game, against his co-winner from AVRO 1938, Keres pulls off an amazing sacrificial combination, based on the traditional weakness of one of the Achilles Heels of the Black camp, the pawn on f7. Even though, in this case, it appeared to be heavily guarded, Keres found a way to effect a surprise breakthrough.

KERES VS. FINE
USSR-USA Match, Moscow 1946
English Opening

1.c4 c5; 2.Nf3 Nf6; 3.Nc3 d5; 4.cxd5 Nxd5; 5.e3. In this position the great Nimzowitsch favored the paradoxical 5.e4 Nb4; 6.Bc4, inviting weaknesses in the d-file, in exchange for advantages elsewhere. Keres, though, preferred to keep his pawn structure sound and prepares, instead, to build up a solid pawn center. **5...Nxc3; 6.bxc3 g6; 7.Qa4+.**

Later Keres was to recommend 7.h4 h5; 8.Bc4 Bg7; 9.Ng5 0-0; 10.Qc2. **7...Nd7.**

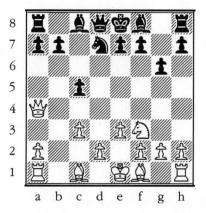

8.Ba3. Keres was always on the lookout for sharp tactical solutions. Here, for example, he had originally intended to bowl Fine over right in the opening with 8.Bc4 Bg7; 9.Bxf7+ Kxf7; 10.Ng5+ but noticed just in time that after 10...Ke8; 11.Ne6 Qb6; 12.Nxg7+ Kf7 White's knight would be trapped. Note, though, that this motif of sacrificing on f7 does, indeed, recur with great force later in the game. **8...Qc7; 9.Be2 Bg7; 10.0-0 0-0; 11.d4 a6; 12.c4 e5; 13.Rad1 exd4; 14.exd4 b6; 15.d5 Bb7; 16.Qb3 Rab8; 17.Bc1**

Keres is still playing for tactics, but here the strategic exchange 17.Bb2 would have been most embarrassing for Black, e.g. 17...Bxb2; 18.Qxb2 b5; 19.cxb5 axb5; 20.Bxb5 Ba6; 21.a4 Bxb5; 22.axb5 Qb7 when White's passed pawn in the d-file, combined with the weakened dark squares around the Black king, conspire to give White a significant advantage.

17...b5. Black fights back well, trying to rid himself of his weaknesses. **18.cxb5 axb5; 19.Bxb5 Ba6; 20.a4 Bxb5; 21.axb5 Qb7; 22.Ng5.** Black has solved his problems on the queenside, so White hastens to stir up trouble on the other wing.

22...Qxb5; 23.Qh3 Nf6; 24.Bf4 Rbc8. Fine utterly overlooks a neat tactical point. By playing 24...Rb7 he might have been able to ward off White's pressure. It must, though, be conceded that White's passed pawn and concentration of force against the Black king would continue to make Black's life difficult.

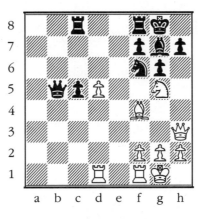

25.Nxf7. A terrible shock for Black, the more so since f7 seems perfectly well defended. Sadly this is not the case. If 25...Kxf7; 26.Qe6 is mate while 25...Rxf7; 26.Qxc8+ leads to an overwhelming win of material. **25...Qd7; 26.Qxd7 Nxd7; 27.Nd6 Rcd8; 28.Be3.**

White has not just won a pawn, he also retains the superior position. The result is no longer in doubt. **28...Nb6; 29.Bxc5 Na4; 30.Ba3 Nc3; 31.Nb7 Nxd1; 32.Nxd8. Black resigns.**

KASPAROV VS. KRAMNIK
Immopar, Paris 1992
Sicilian Defense

1.e4 c5; 2.Nf3 Nc6; 3.Bb5. This slight deviation from the normal 3.d4 is becoming increasingly popular after the rematch between Bobby Fischer and Boris Spassky. One example from that match was game 11, which continued 3...g6; 4.Bxc6 bxc6; 5.0-0 Bg7; 6.Re1 e5 where Fischer introduced the surprisingly powerful pawn sacrifice 7.b4 and went on to a crushing victory. Later investigation revealed Black could play 6...f6 with a fully playable position.

3...e6. This procedure seems somewhat less effective than a defense based on ...g6 and ...f6, as intimated in the previous note. **4.0-0 Nge7; 5.c3 d5; 6.exd5 Qxd5; 7.Re1 g6.** At this point the fianchetto of Black's king's bishop is too much of a time-consuming luxury. The simple 7...a6 would have been preferable.

8.b4! A vigorous pawn sacrifice, similar in nature to the one introduced by Fischer against Spassky. Kasparov's idea is to exploit Black's lack of development after 8...cxb4; 9.c4 Qd8; 10.Bb2 Rg8; 11.d4 when, at the cost of a mere pawn, White would have succeeded in thoroughly disorganizing the Black camp. Kramnik prefers to decline the gambit but still lands in hot water. **8...Bg7; 9.Bb2.**

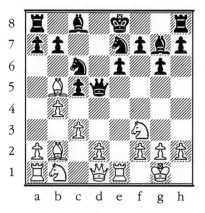

Setting a further cunning trap, for if Black plays the seemingly innocent capture 9...cxb4 then 10.c4, unmasking the full power of White's bishop on b2, would lead to decisive gain of material. **9...0-0; 10.c4 Qh5; 11.Bxg7 Kxg7; 12.bxc5 Qxc5; 13.d4.**

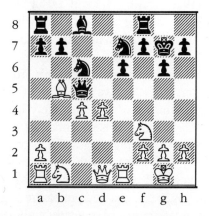

Kasparov's opening strategy has triumphed. Not only does he dominate the center but he has also succeeded in eliminating Black's valuable defensive dark-squared bishop. Consequently, Black's king will soon be drawn into the firing line.

13...Qb6; 14.Nc3 Rd8; 15.Bxc6 Qxc6; 16.Qe2 a6; 17.Rac1 Qc7; 18.d5. The commencement of the final attack. Black's reply is somewhat desperate but he is faced with horrible threats such as Ne4 followed by Qb2+. **18...f6; 19.dxe6 Rd6; 20.Nd5 Qd8; 21.Nxf6.** Completing the demolition. 21...Kxf6 is of course ruled out on account of 22.Qe5 checkmate.

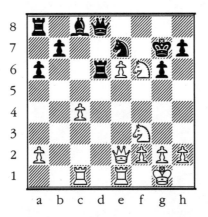

21...Rxe6; 22.Ne4 Nc6; 23.Qb2+ Kg8; 24.Nfg5 Re5; 25.f4 Rf5; 26.Rcd1. Black resigns. Not a moment too soon, for if 26...Qc7; 27.Nf6+ or 26...Qe7; 27.Nd6.

TOPALOV VS. TIMMAN
Amsterdam 1996
Caro-Kann Defense

1.e4 c6; 2.d4 d5; 3.e5. The Advance Variation against the Caro-Kann was popularized briefly by Nimzowitsch in the 1920s and by Mikhail Tal in his 1961 World Championship match against Botvinnik. Neither practitioner had much luck with this variation, and it was not until Nigel Short found new ways for White to handle the position that 3.e5 was finally honed into a dangerous weapon.

3...Bf5. Black takes the opportunity granted by White's 3rd move to develop his bishop onto a seemingly favorable diagonal. **4.Nf3.** It was Nigel Short's insight that the development of Black's queen's bishop did not have to be immediately challenged by means of Bd3. Nimzowitsch tried this against Capablanca at New York in 1927, but it turned out that the exchange of bishops did more to drain the White position of its potential than to impede Black's prospects. Tal, on the other hand, went berserk with moves such as h4 and c4, prematurely committing White to a strategy of out and out aggression. In this game Topalov profits from the Nigel Short approach, both avoiding exchanges and premature aggression and building up for a later onslaught when White's forces are more efficiently mobilized.

4...e6; 5.Be2 Nd7; 6.0-0 h6. On the surface a waste of time but Black wants to be able to develop his king's knight to e7 without allowing White to play Nh4 and trade off the black queen's bishop. 6...h6 grants Black a haven on h7 for that piece. **7.b3.** At first sight White has the modest plan in view of developing his own queen's bishop in fianchetto, or flank mobilization, on b2. As we shall soon see, however, the point behind this wing pawn move is considerably more profound and is, in fact, aimed at future domination of the center.

7...Ne7; 8.c4 Ng6. The fact that White has prepared c4 by means of b3 means that Black can hardly exchange in the center. At any stage ... dxc4 met by bxc4 would cede White a powerful central majority of pawns. Meanwhile, Black's bishop on f5, although well placed, finds no direct targets.

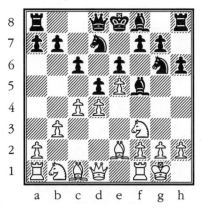

9.Na3 Nf4. A surprising move but one based on the tactical observation that White's knight on a3 is prone to attack. **10.Bxf4 Bxa3.** With the threat of ... Bb2 winning material.

11.Bd3 Bg4. This cedes White a dangerous attacking diagonal for his bishop. Black would have been better advised to play 11...Bxd3; 12.Qxd3 Be7, to avoid having his bishop on a3 cut off. Black's position would remain passive but solid. The game now enters a phase of more rapid warfare.

12.Rb1 Be7; 13.h3 Bh5; 14.Qe2 0-0; 15.Qe3 a5. Black remains naively oblivious to White's coming sacrificial intentions. True 15...Bxf3; 16.Qxf3 (not 16.gxf3 Bg5! blocking White's attack) leaves White with all the play but the preemptive 15...Bg6; 16.Bxg6 fxg6, although it weakens Black's pawn structure, would take much of the immediate steam out of White's attack. **16.cxd5 cxd5.**

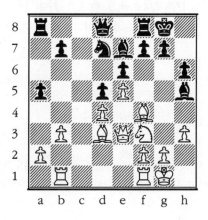

Now Topalov is quick to strike. **17.Bxh6 Bxf3.** Timman had clearly been relying on this move, but it turns out to be inadequate. If instead 17...gxh6; 18.Qxh6 Bg6; 19.Bxg6 fxg6; 20.Qxg6+ Kh8; 21.Qh6+ Kg8; 22.Qxe6+ followed by Qxd5 with five pawns and an attack for the piece. **18.gxf3 Bh4; 19.Kh1.** Preparing to mass more reserves on the g-file.

19...f5; 20.Rg1 Rf7.

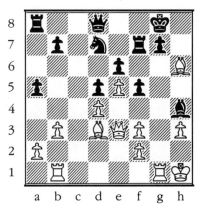

21.Bxg7. Without this further sacrifice Black might still survive since White's extra pawn is doubled and isolated and Black was threatening to drive White back by means of ... Kh7. **21...Rxg7; 22.Qh6 Bg5; 23.Qxe6+ Kh8; 24.Qxf5 Qe7; 25.Qg4 Nxe5.** Hoping to confuse matters before White carries out his threat of Qh5+ followed by doubling rooks on the g-file. **26.dxe5 Qxe5; 27.Rbe1 Qf4; 28.Qh5+ Kg8; 29.Rxg5.** This final sacrifice batters Black into submission. If now 29...Qxg5; 30.Re8+ Rxe8; 31.Qxe8 mate.

29...Rxg5; 30.Qh7+ Kf8; 31.Qh6+ Kf7. 31...Kg8; 32.Bh7+.

32.Bg6+. Black resigns. 32...Kf6; 33.Bh5+ Kf5; 34.Qe6 mate or 32...Kg8; 33.Qh7+ Kf8; 34.Qh8 mate.

THE ISOLATED QUEEN'S PAWN AS A LAUNCH-PAD FOR ATTACK

The isolated queen's pawn can be a liability but it can also provide its owner with a huge grip on the center, especially offering a powerful knight outpost on e5. The next game shows White's resultant attack in ideal form.

KEENE VS. MILES
Hastings 1975-76
Queen's Gambit, Semi-Tarrasch Defense (by transposition)

1.Nf3 Nf6; 2.c4 c5; 3.Nc3 Nc6; 4.e3 e6; 5.d4 d5; 6.cxd5 Nxd5; 7.Bd3 cxd4. Perhaps 7...Be7 is more accurate, maintaining central tension. **8.exd4 Be7; 9.0-0 0-0.**

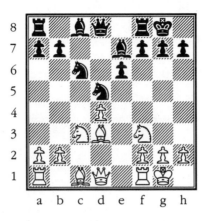

One of the classical isolated queen's pawn positions, in which White's extra space and attacking chances compensate for the structural weakness. **10.Re1 Nf6.** A solid alternative is 10...Bf6; 11.Be4 etc. **11.Bg5!?** Fashionable is 11.a3, but the text is not bad.

11...Nb4. The immediate 11...b6 deserves attention. Black's plan to dominate the blockade square d5 instantly is possibly too straightforward. **12.Bb1 b6.** 12...Bd7 is a more cautious treatment, planning a later ...Bc6.

13.Ne5 Bb7; 14.Re3!! A difficult and bold move. When I played it I already had to be sure that my kingside attacking chances would be sufficient compensation for my lack of queenside development and the clumsy position of my rook on the third rank. Strangely, a similar rook maneuver occurred in a game Filip-Pogats, played 14 years previously, but neither Miles nor I had any notion of this until I discovered the theoretical background after our game. Incidentally, the Filip game ended in a draw.

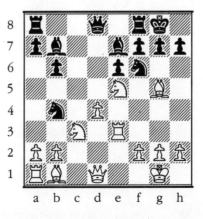

14...g6. To prevent 15.Bxf6 Bxf6; 16.Bxh7+ Kxh7; 17.Qh5+ and 18.Rh3. **15.Rg3!** It looks odd to aim the rook against a granite wall (g6) but the granite has faulty foundations. In contrast the more natural 15.Rh3 achieves nothing.

15...Rc8?! At the time the course I feared most was 15...Nc6!; 16.Bh6 Qxd4! when Black breaks White's attack by sacrificing the exchange. In view of the lack of weaknesses in Black's position it would then be a distinctly uphill struggle for White to win. After the move played the solution became susceptible to precise tactical analysis.

16.Bh6 Re8; 17.a3 Nc6. 17...Nbd5 does not alter things significantly. **18.Nxg6! hxg6; 19.Bxg6.**

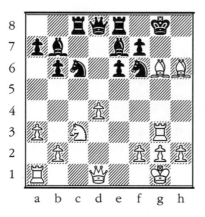

Apart from capturing the bishop Black has two other defenses:

a) 19...Bf8; 20.Bc2+ Kh8; 21.Bxf8 Rxf8; 22.Qd2 Ng8; 23.Rh3+ Kg7; 24.Rh7+ Kf6; 25.d5+.

b) 19...Bd6; 20.Bxf7+ Kxf7; 21.Rg7+ Kf8; 22.Qf3+-. In this position Black is quite helpless, in spite of his extra material.

19...fxg6.

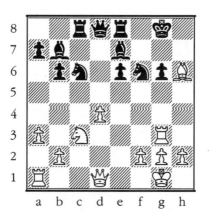

20.Qb1! An original square for the queen in a mating combination, but neither 20.Qd3 Ne5 nor 20.Qc2 Ne5!; 21.dxe5 Ne4 (exploiting the pin on the c-file) would be good enough for White. **20...Ne5; 21.dxe5 Ne4.** Without the c-file pin this is sheer desperation.

22.Nxe4 Kh7; 23.Nf6+ Bxf6; 24.Qxg6+ Kh8; 25.Bg7+ Bxg7; 26.Qxg7 mate.

THE GREAT RACE - OPPOSITE CASTLING

Many of the most important opening systems, for example the Sicilian Defense and the King's Indian Defense, often witness both sides' kings castling on opposite sides of the board. You must know what to do in such situations.

This section is designed to help you master the techniques of attacking your opponent's king, when castled on the other side to your own. The usual method will be by a pawn storm, to open lines for your pieces.

MESTEL VS. GUFELD
1986 Hastings Foreign and Colonial
King's Indian Defense

1.c4 g6; 2.e4 Bg7; 3.d4 d6; 4.Nc3 Nf6; 5.f3 0-0. A standard variation of the King's Indian Defense. **6.Bg5 Nc6; 7.Nge2 a6; 8.Qd2 Rb8; 9.h4 h5.** White advances and Black blocks White's h-pawn.

10.0-0-0 b5. The die is cast. Both sides have committed their kings to opposite wings.

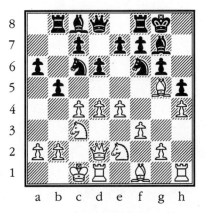

11.Bh6 e5; 12.Bxg7 Kxg7; 13.dxe5 dxe5; 14.Qg5 Qe7; 15.Nd5 Nxd5; 16.exd5 f6; 17.Qd2 Rd8; 18.g4 bxc4.

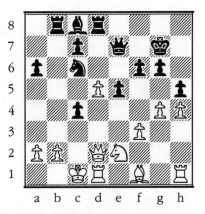

19.Nc3. After 19.gxh5, Gufeld proposes the following remarkable variation: 19...Nb4; 20.Nc3 Bf5; 21.Bxc4 (not 21.hxg6? Rxd5! intending ...Nxa2) 21...Qc5; 22.Qe2 Bd3!! 23 Bxd3 Nxa2+; 24.Kc2 Rxb2+; 25.Kxb2 Qxc3+; 26.Kxa2 Rb8; 27.Qd2 Qb3+; 28.Ka1 Qa3+; 29.Qa2 Qc3+ and Black wins.

19...hxg4; 20.Bxc4. Now Black whips up a decisive attack by gaining time with his rook against the exposed White bishop. However, on 20.h5 Gufeld gives 20...g5; 21.Qc2 Nd4; 22.Qg6+ Kf8; 23.d6 cxd6; 24.h6 Bf5; 25.h7 Bxg6; 26.h8Q+ Kf7; 27.Bxc4+ d5; 28.Bxd5+ Rxd5; 29.Qxb8 Ne2+; 30.Nxe2 Qc5+; 31.Nc3 Qe3+ with mate.

20...Nd4; 21.fxg4 Bxg4; 22.Rdf1 Rb4; 23.h5. A clear admission of defeat. But otherwise ...Rdb8 massing in the b-file must win easily.

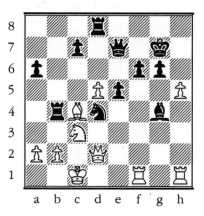

23...Rxc4; 24.hxg6 Rxc3+; 25.Qxc3 Ne2+; 26.Kc2 Nxc3; 27.Rh7+ Kxg6. White resigns.

XIE JUN VS. LALIC
Erevan Olympiad 1996
Caro-Kann Defense

1.e4 c6; 2.d4 d5; 3.e5 c5. A bold gambit continuation, frowned on by theory. 3...Bf5 is the standard move, but it does not allow Black to escape from a complicated middlegame.

4.dxc5. The theoretical recommendation, regarded as strong for White ever since the Tal-Botvinnik world championship match of 1961. **4...Nc6; 5.Bb5 e6; 6.Be3 Nge7; 7.c3 Bd7; 8.Nf3.** Was this move a blunder, overlooking Black's neat tactical response which regains the pawn, or did White hope to gain time for an attack by returning the material? In any case 8.Bxc6 Nxc6; 9.Nf3 Qc7; 10.Bd4 cements the extra pawn and gives Black more problems.

8...Nxe5; 9.Nxe5. If 9.Bxd7+ Nxd7. **9...Bxb5; 10.Na3 Bd7; 11.Qb3 Nc6; 12.Nxd7 Qxd7; 13.0-0-0 Be7; 14.h4.**

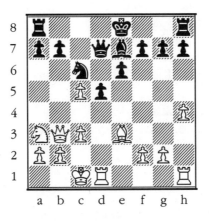

By returning the pawn, White has gained active play for her pieces, and the Chinese former champion now launches a dangerous strike against the future destination of the Black king. However, Black retains the residual plus of a sturdy central pawn majority. This factor could well prove important in future hand to hand fighting.

14...0-0; 15.h5 b6. A bold counter, offering a pawn to open up lines against the White king. **16.h6 g6; 17.cxb6 axb6; 18.Nc2.** If 18.Bxb6 Bxa3; 19.bxa3 Rfb8 leaves White badly pinned. **18...Bc5; 19.c4 d4.** So, Black has avoided losing a pawn, while her central pawn majority has now furnished a passed pawn and is generally on the march.

20.Kb1 e5; 21.Bc1 Qe6; 22.Rhe1 Rfe8. Also possible is the immediate 22...Na5, but Black prefers to maintain this possibility as a threat. **23.f3 Na5; 24.Qd3 Nxc4; 25.b3 b5!**

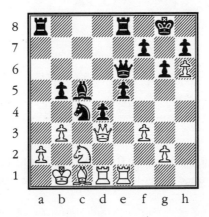

A wonderful concept. If White accepts the sacrifice with 26.bxc4 then 26...bxc4 followed by ...Reb8+ and ...c3 would give Black an overwhelming attack.

26.Re2 Qa6; 27.Ne1 Na3+; 28.Bxa3 Bxa3; 29.f4 Bf8. Not only clearing the a-file for Black's attack, but also targetting White's weakness on h6. **30.fxe5 Rxe5.** An unpleasant shock for White. If now 31.Rxe5 Qxa2+; 32.Kc1 Ba3 mate.

31.Rdd2 Rxe2; 32.Qxe2 Bxh6; 33.Rxd4 Qc6; 34.Qc2 Qf6; 35.Nf3 Bg7; 36.Qc5 Qa6; 37.Rd2 b4; 38.Qd5 Rc8; 39.Qd7 Bh6. Material down, and with her king exposed, White's resistance is futile. **40.Rd1 Ra8; 41.Qa4 Qxa4; 42.bxa4 Rxa4; 43.Rd7 Ra5; 44.Kb2 Bg7+; 45.Kb3 Bc3; 46.a4 bxa3. White resigns.**

An elegant final point. After 47.Kxc3 a2 Black wins further material.

THE CENTRAL PAWN ROLLER

A fearsome weapon at your disposal in certain situations is the pawn avalanche in the center. If you can work towards gaining a central pawn majority, and then set it in motion, it can become devastating. The player who controls the center tends to dominate the board as a whole.

KEENE VS. KUIJPERS
Rotterdam 1982
Nimzo-Indian Defense

1.d4 Nf6; 2.c4 e6; 3.Nc3 Bb4; 4.e3 0-0; 5.Bd3 d5; 6.a3 Bxc3+; 7.bxc3 c5. Black should preface this thrust with 7...dxc4. As played, White is given the chance to establish a mobile pawn center, a dream situation for White in this opening.

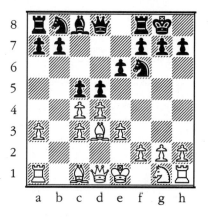

8.cxd5 exd5; 9.Ne2 b6; 10.0-0 Ba6; 11.Bxa6 Nxa6; 12.Qd3 Qc8; 13.f3. A key preparation for achieving the vital advance e4 which will crown White's opening strategy.

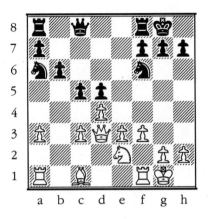

13...Qb7; 14.Ng3 Rad8; 15.Bb2 Rfe8; 16.Rae1 Re6; 17.Re2 g6.

Understandably Black wishes to deny the f5 square to the hostile knight, but this innocent looking move weakens the support for Black's knight on f6, thus permitting White to play e4.

18.e4.

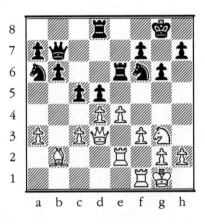

18...h5. Black must recognize that his entire defense has misfired. If now 18...cxd4; 19.cxd4 dxe4; 20.fxe4 Nc5, relying on the d-file pin to dismantle White's center, then White wins with 21.Qf3 Ncxe4; 22.Nxe4 Rxe4; 23.Qxf6 Rxe2; 24.Qxd8+. Alternatively, 22...Nxe4; 23.d5! and suddenly Black is losing, e.g. 23...Ng5; 24.Qc3 or 23...Rxd5; 24.Rxe4 or 23...Qxd5; 24.Qxf7 mate. Deprived of this defensive resource, Black can only watch helplessly as White's majority of pawns in the center and on the king's wing metamorphoses into a lethal bludgeon.

19.e5 Ne8; 20.f4 c4; 21.Qc2 h4; 22.f5 Rc6; 23.Nh1 Qe7; 24.f6 Qd7; 25.Rf4 h3; 26.Re3 hxg2; 27.Qxg2 Nac7; 28.Rh3. Black resigns.

STAUNTON VS. HORWITZ
London 1846
Philidor's Defense

1.e4 e5; 2.Nf3 d6; 3.d4 exd4; 4.Nxd4 Nf6; 5.Nc3 Be7; 6.Be2 0-0; 7.f4 c5; 8.Nf3 Nc6; 9.0-0 Bg4; 10.Be3 a6.

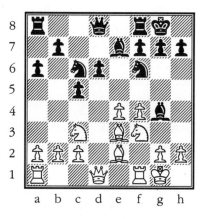

Black's opening, although seemingly passive, might generate some counterplay against White's center. Black seems to be steering for the advance ... b5 but, unaccountably, fails to carry this out.

11.a3 Bxf3; 12.Bxf3 Rc8; 13.Ne2 Qc7; 14.Ng3 Rfe8; 15.c3 Rcd8; 16.Qc2 Bf8; 17.Rad1 b6; 18.b4 Na7; 19.c4 cxb4; 20.axb4 d5. Desperate for counterplay, Black overlooks a neat switch of fronts by the White queen.

21.Qf2 Nc8. The only move to avoid loss of material though Black might have been better advised to throw caution to the winds with 21...dxe4. After the text, White establishes a mighty pawn center.

22.cxd5 Bxb4; 23.e5 Nd7; 24.d6 Qb8; 25.Bc6. If now 25...Nxd6, White can win with 26.exd6 Rxe3; 27.Qxe3 Bc5; 28.Rd4 Nf6; 29.Rfd1 Rxd6; 30.Nf5 Bxd4; 31.Rxd4.

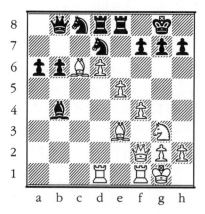

25...g6; 26.Ne4 Re6; 27.Qh4 Na7; 28.Bxd7 Rxd7; 29.Ng5 h5; 30.Nxe6 fxe6; 31.f5. This move contains a nasty sideways swipe from the white queen against Black's exposed bishop and, therefore, guarantees even further material gains. **31...a5; 32.fxe6 Rg7; 33.e7. Black resigns.**

OPPOSITE BISHOPS IN ATTACK

Opposite-colored bishops often indicate a draw, but when players have castled on opposite wings the fact that the live bishops are, so to speak, playing past each other can often lead to virulent attacks. This is especially so if one side's pawn defenses have been slightly weakened. This can swiftly prove deadly.

MARTIN VS. HODGSON
British Championship 1991
Queen's Pawn Game

1.Nf3 d6; 2.c4 Bg4; 3.Qb3 Qc8; 4.d4 g6; 5.h3 Bxf3; 6.Qxf3 Bg7; 7.e3 Nd7; 8.b3 e5; 9.Bb2 Ne7; 10.Na3 0-0; 11.0-0-0 a5; 12.g4 Nc6; 13.Nc2 a4; 14.b4 a3. This advanced pawn exerts a baleful influence around the White king.

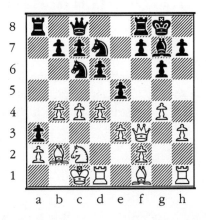

15.Bc3. If White wanted to decline the pawn, the immediate 15.Ba1 would have been a more accurate way of doing so. **15...Nb6; 16.h4 Na4; 17.Ba1 Nb2.** Stifling any aspirations White might have had in the long dark square diagonal.

18.Rd2 Ra4; 19.b5 Nb4; 20.Nxb4 Rxb4; 21.Bxb2 axb2+; 22.Rxb2 Rxb2; 23.Kxb2 exd4; 24.exd4 Bxd4+; 25.Kb1. Conventional wisdom dictates that opposite colored bishops increase the prospects of a drawn outcome. Here we have an instructive exception to the rule. When the players have castled on opposite wings and are each trying to attack the opponent's king, the side with the more active bishop will nearly always win. In this case, White has no defense at all on the dark squares and Black's king's bishop almost acts as an extra piece.

25...Re8; 26.Be2 Qe6; 27.Rc1 Bg7.

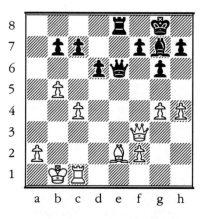

A further instructive moment. When conducting an attack with queen and bishop in the long diagonal against an opposing king, it always better to place the queen in front of the bishop. Accordingly, Black's king's bishop now retires, while Black's queen will aspire to reach one of the squares f6, e5 or d4, at which point the pressure against White's king will become overwhelming.

28.Qe3 Qd7; 29.Qf3 Qe7; 30.Qe3 Qd8; 31.Qf4 c6; 32.g5 Qa5; 33.Qxd6 Rxe2. White resigns.

ATTACK IN THE h-FILE

When a player has castled and also developed a bishop in fianchetto on g2 or g7, it is important to know the technique for launching an attack against this apparently superbly defended fortress. The basic method is to thrust forward your h-pawn, as in the following game.

SERPER VS. KORCHNOI
New York 1996
English Opening

1 c4 Nf6; 2.Nc3 e5; 3.Nf3 Nc6; 4.g3 Bb4; 5.Bg2 0-0; 6.0-0 Re8; 7.Nd5 Bc5; 8.d3. With this move White allows his center pawns to become doubled but hopes, in compensation, to gain counterplay on the light squares.

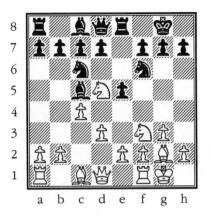

8...Nxd5; 9.cxd5 Nd4; 10.Nd2 d6; 11.e3 Nf5; 12.Nc4 a5; 13.Bd2 a4; 14.b4 Bb6; 15.Na5. I find this move hard to understand. Surely it would be more productive to shatter Black's pawns with 15.Nxb6 cxb6 and then take control of the c-file with 16.a3 to be followed by Rc1. After numerous gyrations with his knight, once White does get the idea of trading on b6, it turns out to be too late.

15...Qd7; 16.Qc2 h5. While White loses time on the other flank, Korchnoi organizes a direct strike against White's king.

17.Rac1 h4; 18.Qc4 Qe7; 19.Qc2 hxg3; 20.hxg3 g6. The simple retreat 20...Qd7 would reveal the full bankruptcy of White's strategy. The text, though, is even stronger. Black offers an unimportant wing pawn in order to gain sufficient momentum for his own onslaught against the white king.

21.Qxa4 Kg7; 22.Qc2 Rh8; 23.Nc4 Qg5; 24.Nxb6. If White had now expected Korchnoi to supinely recapture on b6 he is in for a rude shock. Korchnoi now conducts the final attack with superb elan.

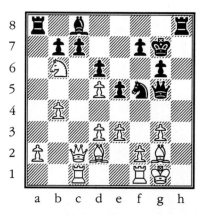

24...Qh5. Threatening mate on h2. **25.Rfe1 Qh2+; 26.Kf1 Nxg3+; 27.fxg3 Bh3; 28.Bxh3 Qxh3+; 29.Kf2 Qf5+ White resigns.** For the past few moves White has been a mere bystander as events have developed beyond his control. Now 30.Kg1 fails to 30...Qf3 while if 30.Kg2 Rh2+; 31.Kxh2 Qf2+; 32.Kh3 Rh8+; 33.Kg4 Qf5 mate.

SPACE CONTROL - PLAY ON BOTH WINGS

Control of more space, carried out by advancing center pawns, helps you:

1. to be more mobile than your opponent, and

2. to be able to play on both sides of the board at once. This can be most disconcerting for your opponent.

KARPOV VS. ROMANISHIN
Biel 1996
Queen's Indian Defense

1.d4 Nf6; 2.c4 e6; 3.Nf3 b6; 4.a3 Bb7; 5.Nc3 g6. A combative decision, aiming for a complicated middlegame. The solid 5...d5 is more usual.

6.Qd3. Striving to achieve e4 at all costs. If instead 6.Qc2 then 6...Bxf3; 7.gxf3 Nc6 quickly unbalances the situation. **6...Bg7; 7.e4 d6; 8.Be2 0-0; 9.0-0 Nbd7; 10.Qc2 c5; 11.d5 e5.**

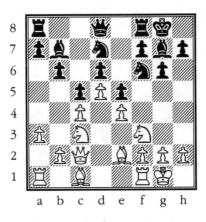

This type of position is well known. Broadly speaking, in such positions, White attacks on the queenside with b4, while Black counters on the other wing.

12.g3 Nh5; 13.Ne1 Ndf6; 14.Ng2 Bc8; 15.b4 Qd7; 16.bxc5 bxc5; 17.Rb1 Qh3; 18.Nb5 Qd7; 19.Bd2 a6; 20.Nc3. White's initial invasion of the Black queen's flank has tempted a weakness at b6 which can now be occupied by White's rook.

20...Qh3; 21.Na4 Ng4; 22.Bxg4 Bxg4; 23.f3.

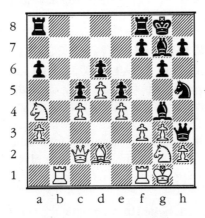

From now on Black is plagued by the lack of a good square for his queen's bishop. His next move is an initial attempt to solve this problem by tactical means.

23...Nf6; 24.Bg5. And not 24.fxg4 Nxg4 with a victorious incursion at h2 to follow. **24...Bd7; 25.Rb6 Rab8; 26.Rfb1.** Again Karpov avoids premature annexation of material by 26.Rxb6 Bxa4; 27.Qxa4 Rb2 when White is in difficulties. **26...Rxb6; 27.Nxb6 Rb8; 28.Rb3.** A move of tremendous subtlety, which has implications on both sides of the board. **28...Ne8; 29.Ne1 Rb7; 30.Nd3.**

Quite unexpectedly, Black's queen is in danger of being trapped. The immediate threat is Nf2. It is fascinating to observe how the knight on b6, seemingly engaged in far flung maneuvers on the left flank, in fact cuts off the line of retreat for the black queen.

30...Qh5; 31.Nxd7 Rxd7. More resilient is 31...Rxb3; 32.Qxb3 Qxg5 though after 33.Qb8, forcing 33...Qe7, Black is still badly tied up. It is obvious, though, from the text that Romanishin had not yet spotted Karpov's evil plan.

32.h4. With the terrible threat of g4, trapping Black's queen and if 32...f5; 33.Nf2 decisively renewing the threat. **32...Qxf3; 33.Nf2.**

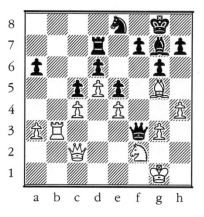

Black resigns. The horrible truth has dawned. Black's queen is trapped, for if 33...Qh5 once again 34.g4.

THE MINORITY ATTACK AND PAWN TARGETS

A very common type of unbalanced position is the kind where the two contestants have pawn majorities on opposite wings. If both sides have castled kingside, the player with the queenside majority often has an advantage. This happens for two reasons. In the middlegame, the queenside pawns are normally free to advance, while kingside pawns can only be advanced with great caution, because of the possibility that their forward march will create weaknesses in front of the castled king. Also, in the ending, when both players are trying to create passed pawns, it can be an asset to have a passed pawn on the queenside which cannot be blockaded by the opposing monarch.

An important strategical plan designed to counteract the latent superiority of the queenside pawn majority is the "minority attack". A minority attack consists of the advance of a pawn minority against an opposing pawn majority on the same wing. The minority attacker hopes that, after the smoke of battle has cleared, the "extra" pawn in his opponent's majority will become weak and exposed. As an example of the strategy involved I will give a game which was an extreme case of a successful minority attack.

KEENE VS. PATTERSON
Match, London 1963
Gruenfeld Defense

1.d4 Nf6; 2.c4 g6; 3.Nc3 d5; 4.Nf3 Bg7; 5.Bg5! Ne4; 6.cxd5 Nxg5; 7.Nxg5 e6; 8.Qd2 h6; 9.Nh3 exd5; 10.Nf4 c6; 11.e3 Bf5; 12.Bd3 Qf6; 13.0-0 0-0.

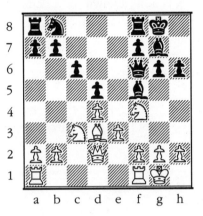

The stage is now set for a minority attack: White will advance his a and b-pawns. After these have been exchanged, Black's remaining queenside pawns will become weak.
14.b4 Nd7; 15.b5 Bxd3; 16.Qxd3 Nb6; 17.a4 Rac8; 18.a5 Nc4; 19.a6.

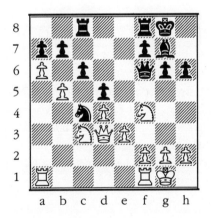

19...Qe7; 20.axb7 Qxb7; 21.bxc6 Rxc6. White's strategy has triumphed and the d-pawn cannot be defended. **22.Rfb1 Qd7; 23.Nfxd5** and with a healthy extra pawn, White soon won.

PILLSBURY VS. STEINITZ
Hastings 1895
Queen's Gambit Declined

1.d4 d5; 2.c4 e6; 3.Nc3 Nf6; 4.Bg5 c5; 5.cxd5 exd5. Black's opening is playable, but only as a gambit. Here both 5...Qb6 and 5...cxd4 have been tried, with varying degrees of success.

6.Bxf6 gxf6. If 6...Qxf6; 7.Nxd5 wins a pawn for nothing. Now, however, Black suffers from multiple fracturing of his pawns. One should, though, not be too hard on Steinitz. He was facing a relatively new opening and even now, a similar variation has been proved by Nigel Short to be playable for Black, namely 1.d4 d5; 2.c4 e6; 3.Nc3 Nf6; 4.cxd5 exd5; 5.Bg5 c6; 6.e3 Bf5; 7.Qf3 Bg6; 8.Bxf6 Qxf6; 9.Qxf6 gxf6 when Black's position is impervious, in spite of the shattered pawns.

7.e3 Be6; 8.Nge2 Nc6; 9.g3. An intelligent development of his bishop to put more pressure on Black's center. Pillsbury does not fear the apparent weakening of his light squares on the right flank.

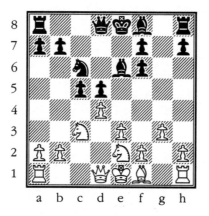

9...cxd4; 10.exd4 Bb4; 11.Bg2 Qb6; 12.0-0 0-0-0; 13.Na4 Qa6; 14.a3 Bd6; 15.b4. Pillsbury enjoys the unbelievable luxury of being able to advance his pawns to undermine Black's queenside, but with Black's king present there is an additional target.

15...Bg4; 16.Nac3. Obviously preferable to playing 16.f3. Black's problem is that queens are still on the board, so his broken pawns have an implication as far as king safety is concerned.

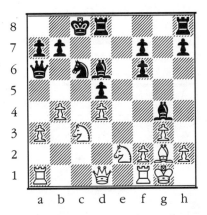

16...Ne7; 17.b5 Qa5; 18.Qb3 Kb8; 19.h3 Be6; 20.f4 f5; 21.Rfd1 Rd7; 22.Na4 Rc8; 23.b6 a6; 24.Nec3 Rc6; 25.Bf1 Rd8; 26.Na2 Bd7; 27.Nb4 Rcc8; 28.Nc3 Rg8.

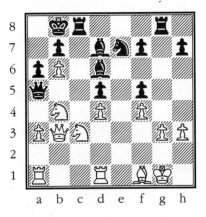

If 28...Qxb6; 29.Nxa6+. **29.Kf2 h5; 30.h4 Bxb4; 31.axb4 Qxb6; 32.Be2 Rg6; 33.Nxd5 Qe6; 34.Bf3 Bc6; 35.Re1 Bxd5; 36.Rxe6 Bxb3; 37.Rxe7 Rc2+; 38.Re2 Rc3; 39.Rae1.**

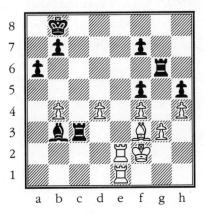

Steinitz's defense has been extraordinary, but he is still suffering because he has so many pawns fixed on light squares.

39...Rb6; 40.Rd2 Rxb4; 41.d5 Rc2; 42.Rxc2 Bxc2; 43.Bxh5 Be4; 44.Bxf7 Rd4; 45.Be6 Rd2+; 46.Re2 Rd3; 47.Re3 Rd2+; 48.Ke1 Rd4; 49.h5.

After a period of maneuvering White finally gains the time to exploit his trump, the passed h-pawn. **49...Bxd5; 50.Bxf5 Bf7; 51.h6 Rd8; 52.g4 a5; 53.g5. Black resigns.**

RESTRAINING THE CENTER PAWNS - "HYPERMODERN" STRATEGY

"First restrain, then blockade, finally destroy" – Aron Nimzowitsch, author of *My System* and chief apostle of hypermodernism.

In the final section of this chapter I want to introduce you to a most sophisticated attacking idea. This is the thought, first examined by British masters in the 1840's and 1850's, and brought to fruition by "hypermodern" grandmasters such as Nimżowitsch, Rèti and Gruenfeld in the 1920's, that it is possible to hold back your central pawns, and only unleash them once your opponent is committed to a set formation!

BUCKLE VS. LOWENTHAL
London 1851
Double Fianchetto

1.f4 f5; 2.b3 Nf6; 3.g3 e6; 4.Bb2 Be7; 5.Bg2. White's double fianchetto development of his bishops would not have seemed out of place amongst the hypermodern grandmasters of the 1920s. **5...c6.**

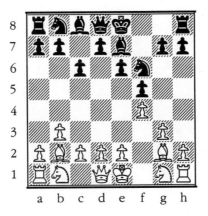

I doubt if such players as Nimzowitsch and Rèti were aware of Buckle's games, but had they been there was much to learn from them.

6.Nc3 Na6; 7.Nh3 d6; 8.0-0 0-0; 9.e3 Bd7; 10.Qe2 h6; 11.Rfe1 Qc7; 12.Nf2 e5; 13.fxe5 dxe5; 14.Nd3 Bd6; 15.e4.

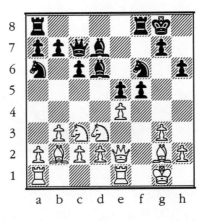

A device which became typical of the hypermoderns. White has so far restrained his central pawns but now, when the central advance is finally made, Black finds himself so seriously embarrassed that he makes a sacrifice that cannot be considered sound. Unfortunately for him, though, the main alternative 15...fxe4; 16.Nxe4 is also extremely unpleasant.

15...f4; 16.gxf4 Bg4; 17.Qf2 Qd7; 18.Qh4 Nh5; 19.f5 Nf6; 20.Ne2 Bxe2; 21.Rxe2. Preparing a decisive attack by doubling rooks on the open g-file.

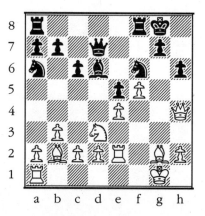

21...Rae8; 22.Kh1 b5; 23.Bf3 Qf7; 24.Rg1 Kh7; 25.Rg6 Rg8; 26.Reg2 Nb8; 27.Nf2 Nbd7; 28.d3 Kh8; 29.Bc1 Be7; 30.Bh5 Qf8; 31.Qh3 Nxh5; 32.Qxh5 Nf6; 33.Qh3 Ba3.

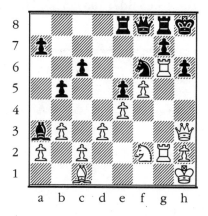

34.Bxh6. This sacrifice destroys Black's resistance and is, perhaps, even more decisive than the alternative 34.Bxa3 Qxa3; 35.Rxg7 Qc1+ (not 35...Rxg7; 36.Qxh6+) 36.Rg1 Qf4. **34...Nh7.** It would be utterly hopeless to accept, namely 34...gxh6; 35.Rxh6+ Qxh6; 36.Qxh6+ with a simple win. **35.Bxg7+ Rxg7; 36.Rxg7 Qxg7; 37.Rxg7 Kxg7; 38.Ng4 Bc1; 39.Qh5 Re7; 40.Qg6+ Kf8; 41.f6. Black resigns.**

CHESS STRATEGY
How to Win by Thinking Ahead

"Then shall I see, with vision clear, How secret elements cohere!"
– Johann Wolfgang von Goethe. FAUST PART ONE

INTRODUCTION

Grandmasters often amaze chess enthusiasts with brilliant cascades of sacrifices, resulting in remarkable and unexpected checkmates. It is easy to believe that the top players possess some kind of inner magic, a natural born talent, which it is hopeless to try to emulate. This is not true. What the best players have at their fingertips is an entire arsenal of strategic ideas, ideal positions and well remembered and rehearsed objectives, which they are constantly trying to achieve.

VICTORY BY OBJECTIVES

They know, for example, that a knight, sitting, seemingly harmlessly, in its stable on the back rank, can follow a tried and tested route to reach a vital attacking square. The key, therefore, to successful chess strategy is to master the arsenal of attacking ideas and objectives in certain important positions. Once you do this, you will find that setting up winning attacks becomes second nature to you.

Imagine that you are a military commander, in charge of a great and victorious army, that you are Hannibal, Julius Caesar, Boadicea, putting the Roman legions to flight, Napoleon or even stormin' Norman Schwartzkopf in Desert Storm. What strategic devices will you employ? I would suggest that they boil down to the following:

1. Blockading your opponent's possibilities while remaining highly mobile yourself.
2. Maneuvering your forces into effective advanced positions.
3. Staying flexible - adapting to your opponent's counterplay.
4. Aiming to deploy a mass attack at the critical weak point in your opponent's defenses.
5. Exploit surprise at the decisive moment; never do what your opponent expects.

VISUALISING KEY POSITIONS

KASPAROV VS. MEPHISTO COMPUTER
Hamburg, 1985

White to Play

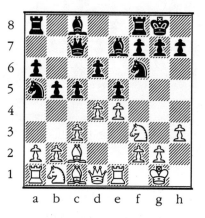

Now let us take a look at a game by Garry Kasparov, widely regarded as the greatest attacking player of all time.

The first position looks level. Both sides have mobilized their forces with equal efficiency, they control comparable amounts of space, and there appear to be no particular weaknesses in the Black camp. Now compare the situation just a few moves later.

Checkmate

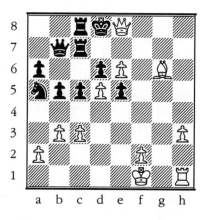

Here, Black has been entirely blown away. White, Kasparov, has had to make some substantial material sacrifices, but Black has been checkmated. How did Kasparov turn the first diagram into the second? The answer is logic, not magic! Kasparov's attacking process followed these stages:

1. Blocking the center to deprive Black of counterplay.

2. Maneuvering his queen's knight from b1 via d2, f1 and g3 to the attacking square f5. Kasparov knew from experience that this was the right route to position his knight for its greatest attacking potential. Having seen this game you now share that valuable information.

3. Flexibility. Once the knight reaches its best square, Black is forced to trade it off. White then obtains a gigantic mass of pawns in front of the black king. Kasparov is prepared to exchange the advantage of the dominating position of his knight in return for a flexible pawn mass.

4. Mass attack. The next stage involves hurling these pawns forwards to crush the defenses of the Black king.

5. Surprise. What looked like magic, the final sacrificial attack is now seen as the logical culmination of the earlier stages.

Play now continues from the first diagram:

12.d5. White blocks the center, so as not to be disturbed by Black pawn captures. **12...Bd7; 13.b3 Qb6; 14.Nbd2 Rfc8; 15.Nf1.** The queen's knight maneuvers away from the queenside, striving to reach its best square f5.

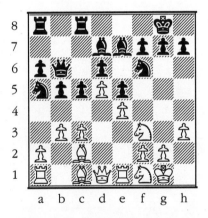

15...h6; 16.Be3 Qd8; 17.Qd2 Nh7; 18.Ng3 Rab8; 19.Nf5. Now the knight reaches the outpost square. White's strategy, envisioned with his 12th move, is running like clockwork.

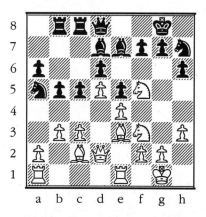

19...Bxf5; 20.exf5 Nf6; 21.g4 Nh7; 22.Kg2 Rb7; 23.Rh1 Nf6.

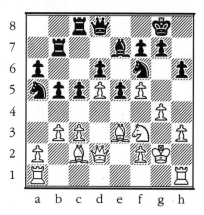

Black cannot find a plan and fails to work out an effective antidote to White's gradual build-up of forces against its king.

24.Rag1 Qb6; 25.Kf1 Rd7; 26.g5 hxg5; 27.Nxg5 Qb7.

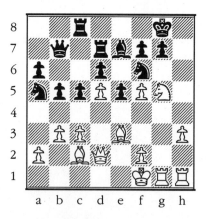

What follows is a demonstration of the devastating effects produced when the entire army of one player is hurled at the other's king.

28.Ne6 fxe6; 29.fxe6 Rdc7; 30.Rxg7+ Kxg7; 31.Bh6+ Kh8; 32.Bg7+!! This decisive third sacrifice tears open a route for White's queen to join in the carnage.

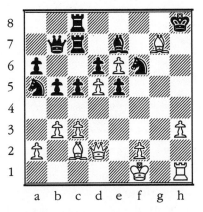

32...Kxg7. Or 32...Kg8; 33.Qh6; 33.**Qg5+ Kf8; 34.Qh6+ Ke8; 35.Bg6+ Kd8; 36.Qh8+ Black resigns.** Since 36...Bf8; 37.Qxf8+ Ne8; 38.Qxe8 is mate.

CHESS STRATEGY

To expand our discussion I must now make precise what we mean by the terms 'equality' and 'advantage'. There are two types of equality to be found on the chessboard; the contrast between them is illustrated in the following diagrams:

A drawish position

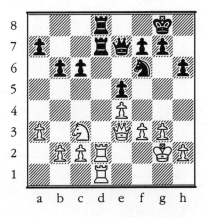

A position with equal chances

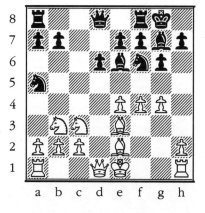

In the first diagram, all the features of the position indicate that a draw is the most likely outcome, and there is very little which either side can do to generate any winning chances. The heavy pieces will all be exchanged off sooner or later on the d-file and the balanced pawn structure will make the resulting ending very drawish. Neither side has any real weaknesses for the enemy to exploit.

In contrast, the position in the second diagram is also held to be equal, but something completely different is meant by this word in its new context. Now both sides have considerable winning chances and the final result is impossible to predict. White's future will be to castle queenside, and launch a vigorous kingside attack under cover of his advanced phalanx of pawns. Black's best plan is to react with an equally vigorous counterattack on the queenside, using as a basis the half-open c-file, on which he should post his major pieces. When we speak of this position as being 'level', we mean that the chances for both sides are roughly balanced, and a sort of dynamic equilibrium obtains. The victory will go to whichever side plays more precisely in the resulting complications.

An advantage in a game of chess can take many forms, of which the most common are:
a) Material advantage
b) Spatial advantage
c) A lead in development
d) Superior pawn structure
e) More active or better placed pieces

In shorthand, I express these as follows, and they will form the topics of the next five sections of this chapter:

Material
Space
Time
Structure
Mobility

The type of advantage which a player holds will usually determine his or her subsequent strategy, and the countermeasures taken by the side defending. For instance, experience has shown that a material advantage is most easily exploited in the ending, when the reduction of forces makes any disparity all the more acute. Thus a player with, say, an extra pawn, will strive to bring about an ending by judicious exchanges, while the inferior side will, in general, try to avoid any simplifications, provided that it can be done, without incurring any further disadvantage of a positional character.

MATERIAL - BALANCE AND IMBALANCE

First, a game by World Chess Federation champion Anatoly Karpov, in which he makes an advantage in material tell. A material advantage is, in fact, the easiest type of advantage to understand, since it is tangible, visible and usually quantifiable according to the point count discussed earlier and here reviewed:

> Queen = 9
> Rook = 5
> Bishop = 3
> Knight = 3
> Pawn = 1

The king is priceless, since checkmate ends the game. As a fighting unit in the endgame, though, a king is worth about the same as a bishop or knight.

KARPOV VS. KAMSKY
FIDE World Championship, Elista (Game 9), June 1996

Black to Play

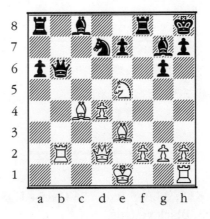

21...Nxe5. This queen sacrifice is too optimistic. Doubtless rendered nervous by his unfavorable score in the match, Kamsky felt that he had to strive for a win at all costs but in this

case the simple 21...Qf6 is preferable, though White retains his grip with 22.f4!
22.Rxb6 Nxc4; 23.Qb4 Nxb6; 24.Qxb6 a5; 25.0-0 a4; 26.Ra1 Bf5; 27.h4.

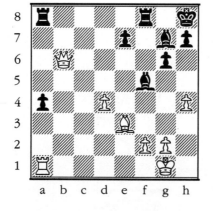

To be fair, Black's queen sacrifice for rook and bishop (9 points lost, 8 gained) looks quite promising, particularly since Black's passed a-pawn could become dangerous. Still, objectively speaking, Black can hope for little more than equality at best and, even to secure this modest benefit he must find some way of supporting his passed a-pawn with his queen's bishop. To this end, 27...Rfc8 now recommends itself, with the further idea of playing ...Bc2 and ...Bb3.

27...e6. In contrast, this move seriously weakens his dark squares. **28.Bf4 Be4; 29.Bd6 Rfc8; 30.Qb5 Bc6; 31.Qb4 Kg8; 32.Ra3.** Now White has established a perfect blockade of Black's pawn and can inexorably turn his attention towards Black's fragile kingside.

32...Ra6? And this move is a blunder which allows White to fork the Black rook and a valuable pawn. More Black material now goes down the tubes.

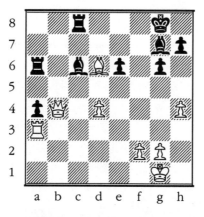

33.Qc4 Rca8; 34.Qxe6+ Kh8; 35.Be5 Bxe5; 36.Qxe5+ Kg8; 37.h5 Be8; 38.h6 R6a7; 39.d5 Rb7; 40.d6 Rd8; 41.Rf3. Black resigns.

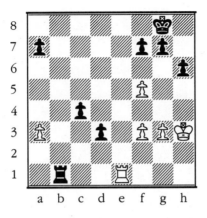

White resigns. After 41.Rxb1 c3 Black will automatically queen a pawn. A beautiful victory by Karpov.

SPACE - CONTROL THE CENTER

In a way, this game neatly symbolized the passing of the baton from one generation to another. As was common in his games, Steinitz dug himself in for a protracted trench-based war of attrition. Nevertheless, in the crisis, it was Lasker's reliance on central control, domination of space, as well as the speed and maneuverability of his forces which ultimately carried the day.

This is a game between the newly crowned world champion, the great Lasker, who was to stay champion until 1921, and his defeated rival, the mighty Steinitz, the father of modern strategic chess.

LASKER VS. STEINITZ
Hastings 1895
Ruy Lopez

1.e4 e5; 2.Nf3 Nc6; 3.Bb5 a6; 4.Ba4 d6; 5.0-0 Nge7; 6.c3 Bd7; 7.d4 Ng6. White already has a well-supported, ideal pawn center.

8.Re1 Be7; 9.Nbd2 0-0; 10.Nf1 Qe8.

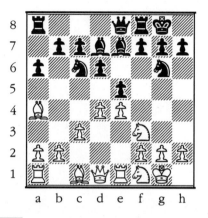

Commencing a somewhat artificial maneuver, the point of which, ultimately, is to provoke White into blocking the center by pushing his d-pawn to d5. Steinitz plans later counterplay based on the thrust ...f7-f5. This strategy is now well known from such defenses as the King's Indian, but in 1895 its subtlety was nothing short of revolutionary. Sadly for Steinitz, his splendid strategic conception is marred by some unnecessary to and froing with his pieces. He could have achieved an identical goal by playing the immediate 10...Bg4.

11.Bc2 Kh8; 12.Ng3 Bg4; 13.d5 Nb8; 14.h3 Bc8; 15.Nf5 Bd8; 16.g4 Ne7; 17.Ng3 Ng8. Steinitz's strategy has been spectacularly retrograde, as can be seen from the fact that he has retreated all of his pieces to the back rank. His plan, though, is a sound one. Ultimately he intends to play ...g6 followed by ...f5 to break out on the kingside and exploit White's weaknesses there.

18.Kg2 Nd7.

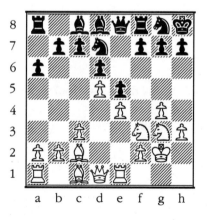

Steinitz mistakenly believes that he has all the time in the world to effect his desired flank advance ...f5, but this is not the case. If the mass retreats carried out by Steinitz's minor pieces from moves 13 to 17 were justified, his coming knight maneuver must, in contrast, be condemned as a pure waste of time. The American Grandmaster Reuben Fine, pointed out in his collection of Lasker's games that 18...g6 at once followed by ...Bf6-g7 and ...Ne7 and the prompt ...f5 would have granted Black a playable position. Now Lasker takes control.

19.Be3 Nb6; 20.b3 Bd7; 21.c4 Nc8; 22.Qd2 Nce7. Preferable here is 22...g6 followed by ...Bf6 and then ...Bg7. Once the bishop is securely placed as a defender to Black's king then the intended ...f5 will come with greater force.

23.c5 g6; 24.Qc3 f5.

Having waited for so long Black could have deferred this for just one more move and played 24...h6, to give his king a little more space. As played, Lasker, who controls more space and dominates the center, was able to sacrifice a piece and drag Black's king into the firing line.

25.Nxe5 dxe5; 26.Qxe5+ Nf6; 27.Bd4. This accurate move wins the game. Lasker had only to avoid the trick 27.g5? which would have been parried by 27...Nxd5. Now Black is quite without a satisfactory defense.

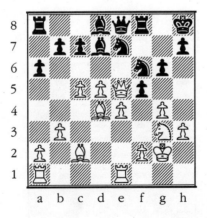

27...fxg4; 28.hxg4. Black's next move is a tragic blunder which loses material under unfavorable conditions. The right way to continue would have been 28...Kg8; 29.g5 Nexd5; 30.exd5

Qxe5; 31.Rxe5 Ng4; 32.Ree1 Bxg5; 33.Ne4 when White's superior centralization gives him the edge but Black can, of course, still fight on.

28...Bxg4; 29.Qg5 Qd7; 30.Bxf6+ Kg8; 31.Bd1 Bh3+; 32.Kg1 Nxd5. A desperate attempt to gain counterplay. **33.Bxd8 Nf4; 34.Bf6 Qd2.**

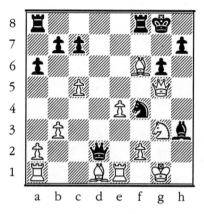

35.Re2. Rather than cling to an extra piece Lasker gives back material to break the back of Black's counterattack and seize the initiative himself. **35...Nxe2+; 36.Bxe2 Qd7; 37.Rd1 Qf7; 38.Bc4 Be6; 39.e5 Bxc4; 40.Nf5. Black resigns.** A whirlwind finale by Lasker.

As Harry Golombek once said of opening play similar to that of Steinitz in this game: 'Black played with the cumbrous slowness of another era. The contrast between the two players' styles presents the aspect of some antediluvian monster being annihilated by a modern weapon of destruction.'

In the next game the world champion uses his central grip to throttle Black's kingside. Note the dominating role played by White's knight at d5.

KASPAROV VS. ANAND
Moscow Speed Tournament, 1996

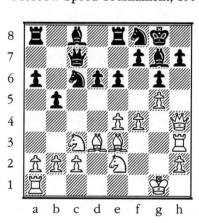

18.f5. White's advance commences in earnest. A variation to avoid now for Black is 18...exf5; 19.Nd5 Qd8; 20.Nf6+ Kh8; 21.Qxh7+ Nxh7; 22.Rxh7 checkmate. Even the superior alternative 20...Bxf6; 21.gxf6 still leaves Black facing the major threat of Bg5 followed by Qh6 exploiting the imprisonment of Black's king. **18...Ne5; 19.f6 Bh8.**

By playing f6 White abandoned any immediate ambition of checkmating the Black king, but with Black's bishop now marooned on h8, White can simply play a standard middlegame virtually a piece ahead. **20.a3 Rb8; 21.b4.**

Such a move by White in the Sicilian Defense is normally a sign of weakness, since it cedes Black vital squares in the c-file. Here, in contrast, White is virtually playing with an extra piece so moving the b-pawn is quite justifiable. **21...Bb7; 22.Rf1 Rbc8; 23.Bd4.** A false start which White soon repairs.

23...Nc6; 24.Be3 Ne5; 25.Rf4 Qd7; 26.Qh6 Nxd3; 27.cxd3.

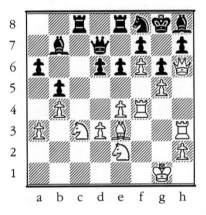

27...e5. Once Black plays this move, a 'hole' appears on d5, which a White knight hastens to occupy. Black's pawn on d6 now becomes 'backward'. **28.Rf1.** It is tempting to play 28.Rfh4 Qe6; 29.Qxh7+ Nxh7; 30.Rxh7 but then Black could defend with the counter-sacrifice 30...Bxf6 eliminating White's mating net. Kasparov's course is more prudent and maintains his grip.

28...Rc7; 29.Bb6 Rc6? A fatal error which allows the game to come to a sudden conclusion. Black had to play 29...Rcc8 in order to meet 30.Nd5 with 30...Bxd5.

30.Nd5 Bc8; 31.Re3 Qb7?

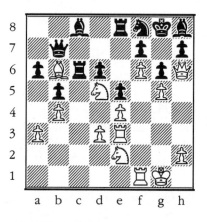

A further error which overlooks White's spectacular riposte.

32.Bd8! A horrible shock for Black. This move is more like a drop in Shogi, or Japanese chess, where the opponent's captured pieces can be reintroduced into the game at will. The sudden emergence of White's bishop on d8 ends matters at once for if 32...Nxd8; 33.Ne7+ wins Black's queen. **32...Ne6; 33.Ne7+ Rxe7; 34.fxe7 Qd7; 35.Rh3. Black resigns.**

The threat of Qxh7 mate can scarcely be parried. White's central grip, especially his knight on d5, was decisive.

TIME - MOMENTUM MATTERS

The game in this section proves that, even if you are White, wasting a couple of moves in the opening can be instantly fatal! It is vitally important to develop your pieces, mobilizing them all, swiftly and efficiently.

TOPALOV VS. LEKO
Bank of Austria, Vienna 1996
Caro-Kann Defense

1.e4 c6. As a result of Karpov's espousal of the Caro-Kann, it has become one of the most popular defenses in international practice. **2.d4 d5; 3.exd5 cxd5; 4.c4 Nf6; 5.Nc3 Nc6; 6.Bg5.** More normal is 6.Nf3 but Kasparov had used the bishop development to defeat Anand in the Amsterdam tournament earlier that year.

6...Be6. At first sight a beginner's move, blocking the black e-pawn. However, it has some deep points, one of which is to reinforce the black pawn on d5, another to develop Black's king's bishop on g7. **7.a3.** This looks like a waste of time, but Kasparov has played it and White's intention is to play c5 and b4 with a massive queenside advance.

7...Qd7. An improvement on 7...Bg4; 8.f3 Be6; 9.c5 Kasparov-Dreev, Moscow 1996. **8.Bxf6 gxf6; 9.g3.** Too slow. The consistent 9.c5 is better.

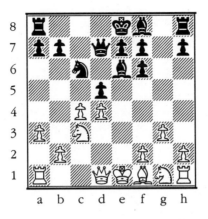

9...0-0-0; 10.Bg2 Bg4; 11.f3 Be6; 12.c5 Bf5; 13.b4 e5. Black's central counterattack is now the major force on the board.

14.Nge2 Qe6; 15.dxe5. White is being swept away by the tide of events and now Black's passed d-pawn smashes through his position. If instead White tries to man the barricades with 15.Kf2 Bh6; 16.Re1 then 16...Be3+; 17.Kxe3 exd4+; 18.Kf2 Qe3+; 19.Kf1 dxc3 is decisive.

15...d4; 16.Ne4 d3; 17.Nf4 d2+.

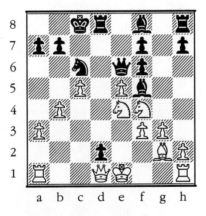

White's position is desperate, the black d-pawn is mowing him down. If 18.Nxd2 Qxe5+; 19.Ne2 Rxd2; 20.Kxd2 Bh6+; 21.Ke1 Rd8 with a slaughter.

18.Kf2 Qc4; 19.Bh3 Bxh3; 20.Nxh3 Qd4+; 21.Kg2 Nxe5; 22.Qb3 Nc4; 23.Rhd1 f5; 24.Neg5 Rd7; 25.f4 Bg7; 26.Nf2 Qd5+; 27.Nf3 Bxa1. Black's advantage in time translates into one of material. **28.Rxa1 Re8. White resigns**.

STRUCTURE - STRENGTHS AND WEAKNESSES OF THE PAWN CHAIN

I subdivide this section up into the following, each typifying a vitally important element in understanding pawns, the backbone of any strategic plan.

1. The Isolated Queen's Pawn
Can be a strength (central bastion) or weakness (cannot be defended by another pawn - cedes opponent useful blockading outpost directly in front of it).

2. Backward Pawn
Normally a weakness - hard to defend and, again, there is always a hole directly in front of it, which enemy pieces can invade.

3. Doubled Pawns
Often a static weakness - can be a target for hostile attack.

4. The Passed Pawn
A potential queen, unobstructed in any way by enemy pawns - usually very strong, especially if it can advance, heavily supported, far into the opponent's camp.

1. The Isolated Queen's Pawn
This was an historic game from the very first official world championship match. It was also the first important game between champions where the topic of the isolated queen pawn was seriously debated. Every student of strategy should know this game.

ZUKERTORT VS. STEINITZ
World Championship, St Louis 1886
Queen's Gambit Declined

1.d4 d5; 2.c4 e6; 3.Nc3 Nf6; 4.e3. The modern choice here would most likely be 4.cxd5 exd5; 5.Bg5. **4...c5; 5.Nf3 Nc6; 6.a3 dxc4; 7.Bxc4 cxd4; 8.exd4 Be7.** Now White has an isolated queen's pawn on d4.
9.0-0 0-0; 10.Be3. 10.Bg5 is more to the point.

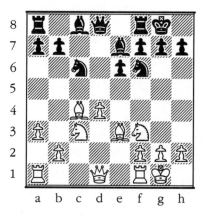

10...Bd7; 11.Qd3 Rc8; 12.Rac1 Qa5; 13.Ba2 Rfd8; 14.Rfe1. And here 14.Rfd1 looks stronger. **14...Be8; 15.Bb1 g6; 16.Qe2 Bf8; 17.Red1 Bg7; 18.Ba2 Ne7; 19.Qd2 Qa6.**

White has been vacillating with no clear strategy in view. Meanwhile, Steinitz has been piling up pressure against White's isolated queen pawn. **20.Bg5 Nf5.**

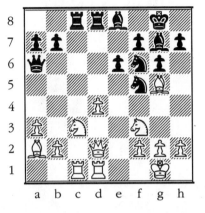

21.g4? A desperate move which should have been rejected in favor of 21.Qf4. **21...Nxd4.** A combination which throws a harsh searchlight on the weaknesses in White's camp. **22.Nxd4 e5.** The pin ensures that Black regains his material. **23.Nd5 Rxc1; 24.Qxc1 exd4; 25.Rxd4 Nxd5; 26.Rxd5 Rxd5; 27.Bxd5 Qe2; 28.h3 h6.**

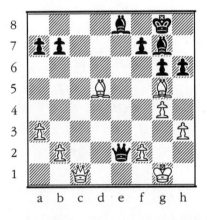

29.Bc4. Not 29.Bxh6 Bxh6; 30.Qxh6 Qd1+. **29...Qf3; 30.Qe3 Qd1+; 31.Kh2 Bc6; 32.Be7 Be5+.** A neat concluding combination to exploit the shattered nature of the White king's wing. **33.f4.** Or 33 Qxe5 Qh1+; 34.Kg3 Qg2+; 35.Kh4 Qxf2+; 36.Qg3 g5+ much as in the game. **33...Bxf4+; 34.Qxf4 Qh1+; 35.Kg3 Qg1+. White resigns.**

The finish would be 36.Kh4 Qe1+; 37.Qg3 g5+ etc. Having once contracted the isolated queen's pawn, subsequent pawn weaknesses spring up all over White's position, like mushrooms overnight.

2. Backward Pawn

ADAMS VS. LEVITT
Park Hall, Preston 1989

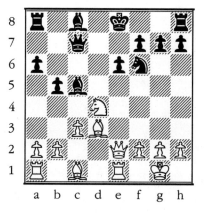

14...Bxd4. Black surrenders the bishop pair but, in compensation, he reduces White's attacking potential. **15.cxd4 0-0; 16.Bg5 Nd5; 17.Rac1 Qd6; 18.Qh5 f5.** After this move, Black's pawn on e6 becomes 'backward'. **19.Qh4 Bb7; 20.Re5.** Typically occupying the weak outpost in front of the backward pawn.

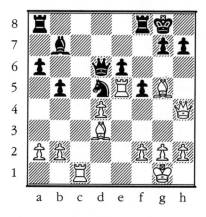

20...h6. Here we see White's isolated queen pawn as an attacking weapon, not a weakness, since it helps to support White's powerful rook on the outpost square e5. **21.Bd2 Rf6; 22.a3 Rd8; 23.Rce1 Nb6.**

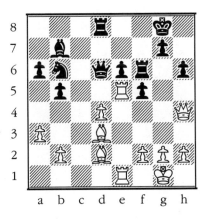

Black accompanied this incautious retreat with a draw offer, but White now has the chance for a sudden tactical coup.

24.Rxe6 Qxd4. If 24...Rxe6; 25.Rxe6 Qxe6; 26.Qxd8+ wins material, or 24...Rxe6; 25.Rxe6 Qxd4; 26.Re8+! Rxe8; 27.Qxd4 winning Black's queen. **25.Re8+ Kh7.**

Or 25...Rff8; 26.Rxf8+ Kxf8; 27.Qe7+ Kg8; 28.Qxb7 Qxd3; 29.Ba5 winning material like clockwork. **26.Qxd4.** Not 26.Bxf5+? Rxf5; 27.Qxd8 Qxf2+ and Black has turned the tables. Adams' move wins rook for knight, after which his masterly technique makes short work of winning the game. 26...Rxd4; 27.Bc3 Rxd3; 28.Bxf6 gxf6; 29.R8e7+ Kg6; 30.Rxb7 Nc4 and Black, material down, resigned on move 42.

3. Doubled Pawns

KASPAROV VS. SOKOLOV
Erevan Olympiad 1996
Scotch Opening

1 e4 e5; 2.Nf3 Nc6; 3.d4. The Scotch is Kasparov's second string weapon when he does not resort to the Ruy Lopez with 3.Bb5. **3...exd4; 4.Nxd4 Nf6.** Black permits White to double his c-file pawns, hoping that they will bolster up his center.

5.Nxc6 bxc6; 6.e5 Qe7; 7.Qe2 Nd5; 8.c4 Ba6; 9.g3. In game eight of his world championship match against Anand in 1995 Kasparov here played 9.b3 which was met by the shocking 9...g5. In this game Kasparov somewhat refines his move order.

9...g6; 10.b3. It is essential to be able to play Bb2 to defend the pawn on e5. **10...Bg7; 11.Bb2 0-0; 12.Bg2 Rfe8; 13.0-0 Nb6.** Of course not 13...Bxe5; 14.Qxe5 Qxe5; 15.Bxe5 Rxe5; 16.cxd5 when White wins material. **14.Re1 d5.**

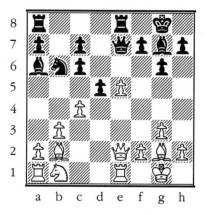

At first sight Black has successfully solved the problems of the opening. His pieces are all developed and his center pawns are active. The problem with Black's position is that his pawns on c7 and c6 remain doubled, and therefore a long term weakness.

15.Qc2. Black cannot now play 15...dxc4 on account of 16.Bxc6 forking his rooks. **15...Qc5; 16.Nd2 Rad8.** Again after 16...dxc4 White has a pleasant choice between augmenting the strategic pressure by 17.Rac1 or going for an immediate attack with 17.Ne4.

17.Rac1 d4. A committal decision but White was threatening cxd5. Black speculates on creating a strong passed d-pawn, even though his doubled c-pawns are now condemned as a permanent weakness. **18.Nf3 d3; 19.Qd2 Bc8; 20.h3 h5; 21.Rcd1 Bf5.**

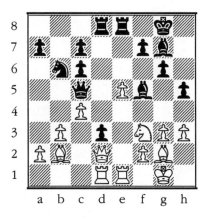

If Black can maintain his bishop on f5 he will have sufficient counterplay. Kasparov now cuts across this plan with an inspired pawn sacrifice.

22.e6 Rxe6. If 22...Bxb2 the interposition 23.exf7+ is highly unpleasant. **23.Rxe6 Bxe6.** Or 23...fxe6; 24.Bxg7 Kxg7; 25.Qg5 (threatening both 26.Qxd8 and 26.g4) 25...Qf8; 26.g4 hxg4; 27.hxg4 Be4; 28.Qe5+ winning a piece.

24.Bxg7 Kxg7; 25.Qc3+ Kg8; 26.Rxd3 Rxd3; 27.Qxd3 Nd7. The upshot of Kasparov's brilliant move 22.e6 is that simplification has arisen, in which Black's queenside pawns now represent a decisive weakness.

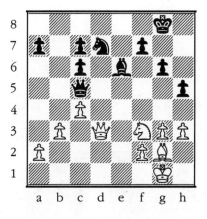

28.Qc3 Bf5; 29.Nd4 Qe5; 30.Qd2 c5; 31.Nxf5 Qxf5; 32.Qa5.

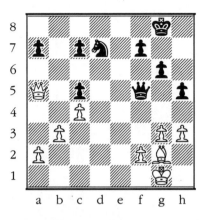

Black can no longer defend his pawns. His only hope is a last ditch attack against White's king, angling for a draw by perpetual check.

32...Ne5; 33.Qxa7 h4; 34.Qa8+ Kg7; 35.Qe4 Qf6. Black could not contemplate the trade of queens, since White's passed a-pawn would prove immediately decisive. But now he loses a second pawn and the game is over. **36.Qxh4. Black resigns.** Better structure was converted here into a winning material edge.

In certain cases, though, doubled pawns can be used to strengthen a central pawn mass, as in this example.

KEENE VS. KERR
Sydney 1979
Nimzo-Indian Defense

1.d4 Nf6; 2.c4 e6; 3.Nc3 Bb4; 4.e3 b6; 5.Nge2 Ba6; 6.Ng3 0-0; 7.e4 Nc6. White has a huge pawn center and Black tries to snipe at it with his pieces. **8.Bd3.**

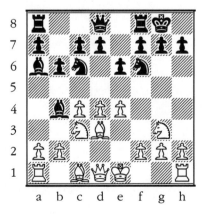

8...e5. Not 8...Nxd4? falling into the trap 9.Qa4! winning material. **9.a3.** To force the doubled pawn issue. This move was a new idea at the time, with 9.d5 being more common. However, not 9.0-0 Nxd4!; 10.Qa4 Bxc3; 11.bxc3 Ne6!; 12.Qxa6 Nc5 and, due to the fork, Black wins.

9...Bxc3+; 10.bxc3 d6. Or 10...exd4; 11.cxd4 Nxd4; 12.Bb2 when White's powerful bishops give him good compensation for the pawn. **11.Bg5!** With the threat of Nh5, to double and smash Black's pawns in front of his king. This bishop move provokes ...h6, which is a weakness and future target.

11...h6; 12.Be3 Na5; 13.Qe2 Qd7; 14.Nf5 Qa4? Overlooking disaster in his haste to concentrate his attack against White's c4-pawn, the front doubled pawn.

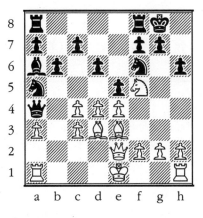

15.Bxh6!! This wins in all variations.

15...gxh6; 16.Qe3 Ne8; 17.Qxh6 Qd7. If 17...f6; 18.Qg6+ Kh8; 19.Ne7 threatening Qh6 mate. But now White has a decisive zigzag maneuver.

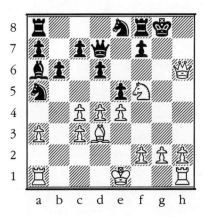

18.Qg5+ Kh7; 19.Qh4+ Kg8; 20.Qg3+ Kh7; 21.Qh3+ Kg8; 22.Nh6+. Black resigns. He loses his queen.

4. The Passed Pawn

ALEKHINE VS. KERES
Munich 1942

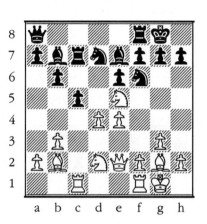

16.b4. The key to White's advantage. Black's pawn on c5 is pinned, hence White not only gains control of the important square c4 by means of this thrust, he also establishes a blockade over Black's entire queenside army and prepares to convert his nascent queenside pawn majority into a dangerous passed pawn on the b-file.

16...Rfc8; 17.dxc5 bxc5. Now White's brand new passed pawn takes an important step forwards. **18.b5 a6.** Keres has conceived a plan for counterattacking on the queen's flank, but it turns out to be mistaken and only increases White's advantage.

19.a4 axb5; 20.axb5 Qa2. The point of Black's play, but after White's reply the threat of Ra1 obliges Black's queen to beat a hasty retreat. **21.Nec4 Qa8; 22.Bxf6.** This move wins material and breaks up Black's kingside-inflicting doubled pawns. **22...gxf6.** If 22...Nxf6; 23.Nb6 or 22...Bxf6; 23.b6 Rc6; 24.e5.

23.b6.

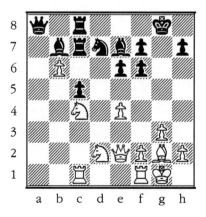

The advance of White's passed pawn is the logical outcome of his previous fine strategic play. It is fascinating that so strong a player as Keres should have been reduced to utter help-lessness with almost all the pieces still on the board, and only three pawns exchanged on each side.

23...Rc6; 24.e5. Winning rook for knight. Quite often, after a material gain, the side that has come off worse in this respect gains counterplay but here, if anything, Alekhine's expert play actually increases his possibilities of attack.

24...Rxb6; 25.Nxb6 Nxb6; 26.Bxb7 Qxb7; 27.exf6 Bxf6; 28.Ne4 Be7; 29.Qg4+ Kh8; 30.Qf4 Bf8; 31.Nxc5.

If now 31...Bxc5; 32.Rxc5 Rxc5; 33.Qd4+ or 31...Rxc5; 32.Rxc5 Bxc5; 33.Qe5+, when Black's position collapses. **31...Qc7; 32.Nxe6.**

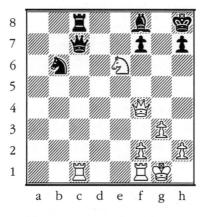

A final tactical blow crushes Black's resistance. **32...Qxf4; 33.Nxf4. Black resigns.** A fine example - passed pawn, doubled pawns, time and material - a full chess lesson in itself.

MOBILITY - WHOLE BOARD VISION

In the next game, Black's attention is diverted to the queenside, where his queen is snatch-ing pawns. Meanwhile, White concentrates his forces for a decisive blow on the opposite wing.

CAPABLANCA VS. BERNSTEIN
San Sebastian 1911
Ruy Lopez

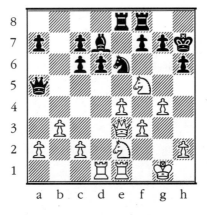

White offers up almost all of his queenside pawns to the marauding black queen in the interests of concentrating his forces against the black king.

22...Qxa2; 23.Neg3 Qxc2; 24.Rc1 Qb2; 25.Nh5 Rh8; 26.Re2 Qe5; 27.f4 Qb5; 28.Nfxg7. The brilliant point of Capablanca's play. If Black accepts the sacrifice with 28...Nxg7 then 29.Nf6+ Kg6; 30.Nxd7 f6; 31.e5 Kf7; 32.Nxf6 Re7; 33.Ne4 gives White an overwhelming attack.

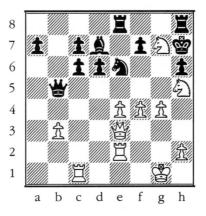

28...Nc5. Instead, Black sacrifices his rook on e8, in a forlorn gesture to stem White's attack. **29.Nxe8 Bxe8; 30.Qc3 f6; 31.Nxf6+ Kg6; 32.Nh5 Rg8; 33.f5+ Kg5; 34.Qe3+. Black resigns.**

KING SAFETY - PROTECTION AND PREVENTION

A very good piece of strategic advice is to castle early, move your king into security and simultaneously mobilize a rook to the all important central files. Conversely, try to avoid having your king pinned down, or driven back to the center; and, if you have castled, try to maintain your pawn wall in front of your king reasonably intact.

The next game exemplifies the dangers inherent in inadequate king safety.

KAMSKY VS. SALOV
FIDE Candidates (Game 4), Sanghi Nagar 1995

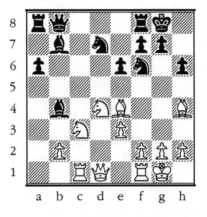

This position had already occurred in the 12th match game between Fischer and Spassky at Reykjavik 1972. At that time Fischer continued with 20 Bg3, which permitted Black eventually to make a draw. Kamsky is ready with an improvement on that game but, as we shall see, White's 20th move is by no means the last of his theoretical refinements.

20.Nc6 Bxc6; 21.Bxc6 Ra7; 22.Bg3 Ne5; 23.Qd4. Considerably more aggressive than 23.Qe2 Bd6; 24.Rfd1 Bc7; 25.Ne4 Neg4 with equality. **23...Bd6; 24.Ne4.** A further vigorous stroke. The interpolation 24.Rfd1 Bc7 and only now 25.Ne4 is rendered harmless by 25...Nh5. **24...Nxc6; 25.Nxf6+ gxf6.** The doubled pawns come into being. Black's king is beginning to look exposed.

26.Rxc6 Be5; 27.Qg4+. Amazingly, this is the first new move of the game and it is a finesse which gives White a virtually overwhelming position. Salov had been relying on an old analysis by the Georgian Grandmaster Georgadze which only gave 27.Bxe5 fxe5; 28.Qh4 Kh7; 29.Qe4+ Kg7; 30.f4 exf4; 31.Rxf4 Qxb2 when Black can defend himself. By retaining bishops on the board Kamsky dramatically increases his chances of attack.

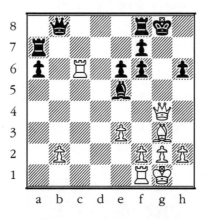

27...Kh7; 28.Qe4+ Kg7; 29.f4 Bc7. If 29...Bxb2 both 30.f5 or 30.Rb1 retain White's initiative. **30.Be1 Qb5.** It is always dangerous to take the b-pawn with the queen but in this case it would be fatal, e.g. 30...Qxb2; 31.Bc3 Qb5; 32.Rf3 Bd8; 33.Rg3+ Kh8; 34.Rc8 e5; 35.Rh3 Kg7; 36.Qf5 exf4; 37.Rc5 Qe2; 38.Qg5+ and wins.

31.Rf3 Rd8; 32.Rg3+ Kh8; 33.h3 Qd5; 34.Qc2 Bd6. Black's case is hopeless for if 34...Bb8; 35.Bc3 Be5; 36.Bxe5 fxe5; 37.Qf5 and White wins.

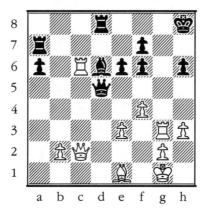

35.e4. Black resigns. After 35...Qd4+; 36.Bf2 wins material while any other move with the queen on move 35 allows Rxd6 followed by Qc8+.

Black never recovered from the doubling of the pawns in front of his king. Once a secure shield, the pawn wall visibly crumbled.

CLERGY & CHIVALRY: GOOD KNIGHTS, BAD BISHOPS & VICE VERSA

Bishops can be particularly deadly on an open board, where blocked pawn formations do not obstruct their movements. Two bishops operating together under such circumstances can be outstandingly lethal.

In the following game, Kasparov quickly obtains the massive advantage of two bishops versus bishop and knight in an open position. He spurns material gain on move 22, simply to retain his task force of bishops. Only on move 24 does he allow one bishop to be traded off but, in return, he has so undermined Anand's pawns that they are soon ripe for harvesting.

KASPAROV VS. ANAND
Immopar 1992

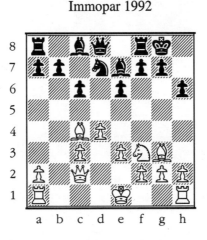

Kasparov has emerged from the opening with a superb position. His pieces are more active and his central pawn structure more compact and dynamic.

12...c5; 13.0-0 Nb6; 14.Bd3 Bd7; 15.Bh7+ Kh8; 16.Be4 Qc8; 17.Ne5 Ba4; 18.Qe2 Nd7; 19.Rab1 Bc6. Allowing Kasparov to trade knight for bishop, which he is delighted to do. **20.Nxc6 bxc6; 21.Qf3 Nb8.** White's bishops rake the board. In order to confront their joint ecclesiastical power, Black is forced into horrible contortions with his knight.

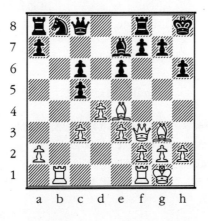

22.Be5. Here Kasparov could have played 22.Bxb8 Rxb8; 23.Bxc6 netting a pawn, but permitting Black the luxury of opposite colored bishops. Since such positions are notoriously hard to win, Kasparov prefers to maintain the pressure.

22...f5; 23.Qg3 Bf6; 24.Bd3 Bxe5. Now Kasparov does permit the exchange of one bishop, but in compensation, White's queen takes up a dominating and voracious post. 25.Qxe5 cxd4; 26.cxd4 Rf6; 27.Rfc1 Nd7; 28.Qa5 f4; 29.Be4 fxe3; 30.fxe3 Rb8; 31.Qxa7.

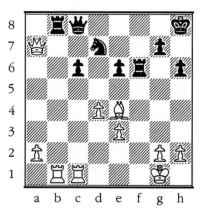

Kasparov at last reaps the fruits of his fine strategy. From now on Anand's pawns are subtly detached from his position. 31...Rxb1; 32.Rxb1 Rf8; 33.Qb7 Qd8; 34.Bxc6 Nf6; 35.Bf3 Nd5; 36.Bxd5 exd5; 37.Rf1.

And, with the world champion two pawns ahead, Anand soon resigned.

Tal, the player of the Black pieces in the game which follows, was a former world champion, best known for his fiery combinative play. No one, however, can become world champion without being a first rate positional player as well as a tactician, and in the following encounter we see his exemplary exploitation of superior pawn structure and better placed pieces. In particular, White is saddled with a bishop stuck on the same color squares as most of his pawns, a so-called 'bad bishop'. Meanwhile, Black's knight is free to wreak havoc on the light squares, over which White has little influence.

SZABO VS. TAL
Portoroz 1958
Sicilian Defense

1.e4 c5; 2.Nf3 d6; 3.Bb5+ Bd7; 4.Bxd7+ Qxd7; 5.0-0 Nc6; 6.c3 Nf6; 7.Re1 e6; 8.d4 cxd4; 9.cxd4 d5; 10.e5. The alternatives 10.exd5 and 10.Nc3 dxe4 both saddle White with a potentially weak isolated d-pawn, so this advance is virtually forced. In any case, White is quite happy to play this move since it leaves him with a modest but lasting spatial advantage.

10...Ne4; 11.Nc3 Nxc3; 12.bxc3 Be7; 13.Ng5 h6; 14.Qh5 Bxg5. Of course not 14...hxg5; 15.Qxh8+. White's kingside attack has started to look slightly menacing, so Black relieves some of the pressure by an exchange. **15.Bxg5 Ne7; 16.Bd2 0-0**.

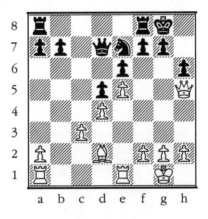

17.a4. According to Tal the sacrifice 17.Bxh6!? was dangerous and would probably have led to a draw. One variation is 17...gxh6; 18.Qxh6 Qd8; 19.Re3 Nf5; 20.Qh5 Nxe3; 21.fxe3 Qe7; 22.Qg4+ Kh7; 23.Qh5+ Kg7; 24.Qg4+ Kh6; 25.Rf1 f5; 26.exf6 Rxf6; 27.Qh4+ with perpetual check.

17...f5; 18.f4. A serious error. It is true that after 18.exf6 Rxf6 it is Black who has the better prospects on the kingside, but the text merely completes the incarceration of White's prelate.

18...Rac8; 19.Reb1 Rc4; 20.Qd1 Rfc8; 21.a5 Nc6; 22.Qb3 Rc7; 23.Rb2.

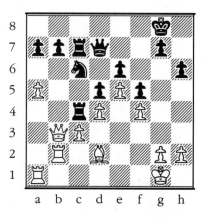

This is a good time to take stock of the position. White's game has several glaring defects: a grotesquely bad bishop and two pawn weaknesses, the isolated pawn on a5 and the backward pawn on c3. Tal now finds a subtle winning plan: the maneuver of his knight to b5. Once the knight reaches this square White's game will be untenable, for Black's constant pressure against a5 and c3 will soon force the win of a pawn at the very least.

23...Kh7; 24.h3 a6; 25.Qb6 Ne7. Intending ...Nc8, dislodging White's queen. **26.Qd6 Qe8; 27.Rb6 R4c6; 28.Rxc6 Qxc6; 29.Rb1 Rd7; 30.Qb4**. The endgame after 30.Qxc6 Nxc6 is quite hopeless. Black would maneuver his knight to b5 and his rook to c4 and one of the White pawns would disappear.

30...Nc8; 31.g4.

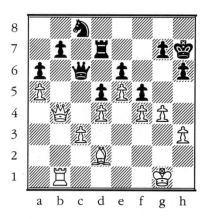

White realizes that he is positionally lost and tries in desperation to conjure up some sort of counterattacking chances on the kingside.

31...g6; 32.Qf8 Rg7; 33.Kf2 Qc4. Preparing a decisive queen penetration now that White's queen is offside. The threat is 34...Qa2. **34.Rb2 Na7; 35.Rb6 Nc6**. Not 35...Nb5; 36.Rxe6. There is no need to allow White any counterplay.

36.Ke1 Qd3; 37.g5 hxg5; 38.fxg5 Nxa5.

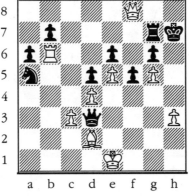

Now that White's army has deserted its monarch, Black can afford to let his e-pawn go. Black's queen and knight charge in to harry him. The rest of the game requires little comment. **39.Rxe6 Nc4; 40.Bc1 Qxc3+; 41.Kd1 Qxd4+; 42.Ke2 Qe4+; 43.Kd1 Qf3+; 44.Kc2 Qe2+; 45.Kc3 d4+; 46.Kb4 a5+; 47.Kc5 Rc7+; 48.Kb5 Nxe5+; 49.Kb6 Rc6+. White resigns.**

The lesson of how to maneuver with a good knight against a restricted bishop is one of the most valuable in the entire chess canon. This theme will be amplified in the next section.

OUTPOST SQUARES - THE HIGH TERRAIN OF THE CHESSBOARD

A common strategic motif sees a White knight planted securely on e4, with no Black f-pawn or d-pawn able to drive it away, and no Black knight able to challenge it and no Black queen bishop able to trade the knight off.

This scenario becomes an automatic strategic win for White if Black's sole remaining minor piece is a dark-squared bishop hemmed in by its own pawns.

Watch out for this and particularly try to steer towards this type of position against the King's Indian Defense. It will win many games for you!

KEENE VS. PENROSE
English Counties Championship 1970
King's Indian Defense

1.Nf3 g6; 2.c4 Bg7; 3.d4 Nf6; 4.g3 0-0; 5.Bg2 d6; 6.0-0 Nbd7; 7.Nc3 e5. A common variation of the popular King's Indian Defense. **8.e4 c6; 9.h3 Qb6; 10.d5 Nc5.**

In my opinion, it is more advisable to block the position with 10...c5. White would retain a useful space advantage, but Black's queen's wing would be less exposed to invasion than after the text move.

11.Re1 Bd7; 12.Rb1.

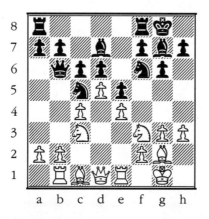

12...cxd5. Black cannot maintain the central tension indefinitely. A time will come when White can capture on c6. Furthermore, Black must use the open c-file to hinder White's intended b4 which would drive away Black's well-placed knight. **13.cxd5 a5; 14.Bf1 Rfc8; 15.Be3 Qd8; 16.Nd2 Ne8.** It might be better to play 16...a4 which, at least, retains a measure of white square control.

17.a4 f5; 18.Nc4.

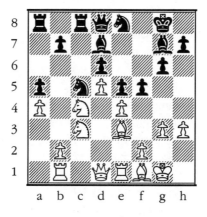

Now the crisis has been reached and Black must take a decision; the move played leads to disaster, but if Black temporizes with ...b6, ...Rab8, ...Kh8 etc, White will capture on f5, weakening Black's king's position and then follow up with Nb5 and a felicitous blend of the breaks b4 and f4, undermining Black's structure in all sectors of the board.

18...fxe4; 19.Bxc5 Rxc5; 20.Nxe4 Rc7; 21.Nb6. Not 21.Ncxd6 Nxd6; 22.Nxd6 Bxa4 with equality. **21...Rb8; 22.Nxd7.**

White exchanges his active minor pieces for Black's inactive ones, which might develop some activity. At the close of this maneuver White has a technically won position, with the traditional 'good' white-squared knight, versus the 'bad' black-squared bishop.

22...Rxd7; 23.Bb5 Re7; 24.Bxe8 Rxe8; 25.b4 axb4; 26.Rxb4.

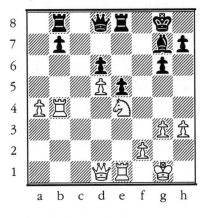

Black is hopelessly lost. He has too many weaknesses and his minor piece is useless.

26...Re7; 27.Qb3 Rd7; 28.Rb6 Qe7; 29.Rb1. A gross winning plan, but the most effective. I wanted to play the aesthetically pleasing h4, Kg2, Rh1 and swing the rook on b4 across to the kingside, but I was worried that my opponent might fight back in the complications.

29...Ra8; 30.Rxb7 Rxb7; 31.Qxb7 Qxb7; 32.Rxb7 Rxa4; 33.Rb8+ Bf8. Or 33...Kf7; 34.Nxd6+ Ke7; 35.Nb5.

34.Ng5 Ra7; 35.Ne6 Rf7; 36.Kf1 Rf6; 37.Ke2 Rf7; 38.Rd8 Rf6; 39.Ke3 Rf7; 40.f3 Rf6; 41.Ke4 h5; 42.h4 Rf7; 43.Ke3. Black resigns.

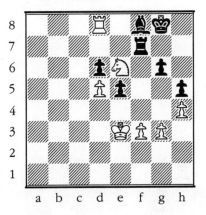

Black has been reduced to paralysis and White has two clear winning methods:

a) Nxf8, Rxd6, Re6 and Rxe5 with two extra pawns, or

b) f4, followed by a king march to c6 and liquidation to a won king and pawn endgame. White's blockading knight left Black utterly strangled throughout.

CASTLES AND TOWERS - ROOKS ON THE SEVENTH

White rooks invading on the seventh rank spell trouble! Conversely, black rooks are dangerous if they penetrate White's position along the second rank.

All Grandmasters are delighted when they can achieve the long range goal of infiltrating the hostile fortress in this fashion. On the seventh (second) rank, the rook may cut off the opposing king, is well placed to scythe through unmoved pawns and is also ready to carry out dangerous tactical blows.

Here is an example of successful planning leading to a victorious rook invasion.

KARPOV VS. KHALIFMAN
Reykjavik 1991

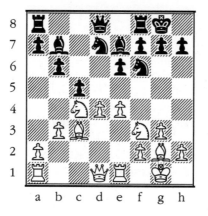

White has a slight space advantage and somewhat greater development and mobility.

14.Qd3. This is a new move. 14.Nfe5 cxd4; 15.Bxd4 b5 was played in Cvitan-Stempin, Warsaw 1990. **14...cxd4; 15.Nxd4 Nc5; 16.Qc2 a6; 17.Rad1 Qc7; 18.Bd2 Ncd7; 19.Bf4 Qc5.** Black avoids the apparently tempting fork 19...e5 on account of 20.Nf5 with a counterattack against Black's bishop on e7.

20.Bc1 Qc7.

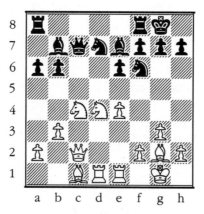

21.e5. The point of White's play. White now carries out this important central advance with his queen's bishop on the safe square c1, rather than exposed on c3 or d2.

21...Nd5; 22.Ne3 Qxc2; 23.Ndxc2 Rac8. Black cannot defend his knight on d5 but this counterattack on the c-file appears adequate for the moment.

24.Bxd5 exd5; 25.Nxd5 Bxd5; 26.Rxd5 Rxc2; 27.Rxd7 Bb4; 28.Red1 Rxa2.

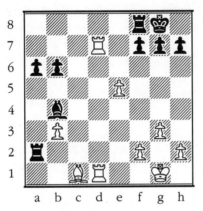

29.Be3. Black must now play 29...b5 in order to defend his queenside pawns. In striving to liquidate to a more obviously drawn endgame, Khalifman overlooks a devilish device.

29...Bc5; 30.Bxc5 bxc5; 31.Rc7 Ra3. Still oblivious to the dangers which are hanging over his head. **32.e6.** The moment of truth. The threat is 33.e7, so Black's hand is forced.

32...fxe6; 33.Rdd7. Black resigns.

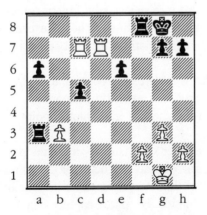

If one rook on the seventh is bad, doubled rooks on the seventh represent a hurricane force tempest! Black must lose both of his kingside pawns since 33...g6 fails to 34.Rg7+ Kh8; 35.Rxh7+ Kg8; 36.Rcg7 checkmate.

With this superb example of strategic foresight from one of the all-time greats, I conclude this overview of Grandmaster strategy.

THE HEROES OF CHESS
Learn from the Champions and Win

"Alekhine's games and writings exerted a great influence on me from a very early age. I fell in love with the rich complexity of his ideas at the chessboard. Alekhine's attacks came suddenly, like destructive thunderstorms from a clear sky. I wished to emulate the dynamic style of this great Russian-born world champion."

World champion Garry Kasparov, on his hero, Alexander Alekhine, who was world champion from 1927-1935 and 1937-1946.

ADOPT A HERO

For years I have been advocating an effective method for players to improve their results - adopt a personal hero and study that player's games in depth. Such a study will provide a ready-made repertoire and a systematic, coherent method of playing. If your chosen model is still active, this procedure will also furnish a steady flow of combative opening innovations - a vital ingredient of success in modern tournament chess - especially junior chess, where profound study of fashionable openings variations is widely perceived (correctly or otherwise) as an infallible key to success.

If a young player's style tends towards the positional or strategic vein, then Botvinnik or Karpov would be the person to choose. If a pupil's inclinations lead towards volatile tactics and ingenious attacking ideas, then the chess teacher should point him or her in the direction of Alekhine or Fischer.

The clearest example of the latter style is the world champion, Garry Kasparov. His very youthfulness makes him a naturally attractive focus for the admiration and attention of other young players. He is living proof that the young can attain the highest pinnacles in chess by sheer force of talent and determination. Kasparov captured the imagination of chess lovers all over the world by his brilliant victory over Anatoly Karpov in the 1985 world title match.

Garry, at 22, thus became the youngest world champion in the history of the game. His dynamic, sacrificial and revolutionary style of play is certain to provide thrills and excitement for those content just to sit back and play over his outstanding games and notes, but it will also furnish red-hot inspiration for everyone who wishes to emulate his style and engage in competitive chess themselves.

First, a classic attacking game by Kasparov featuring a singular sacrifice of a knight on the e5 square. Here is a striking example of how Kasparov's brilliant play could influence and inspire your play.

KORCHNOI VS. KASPAROV
Lucerne Olympiad 1982
King's Indian Defense

1.d4 Nf6; 2.c4 g6; 3.g3 Bg7; 4.Bg2 c5; 5.d5 d6; 6.Nc3 0-0; 7.Nf3 e6. Transposing into the Benoni, ideally suited to Kasparov's uncompromising style.

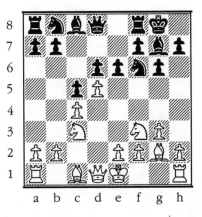

8.0-0 exd5; 9.cxd5 a6; 10.a4 Re8; 11.Nd2 Nbd7; 12.h3 Rb8; 13.Nc4. Black has a weak pawn at d6, and White also enjoys a potentially mobile mass of pawns on the kingside and in the center. Many Black players would be crushed by just such disadvantages, but Kasparov has detected hidden dynamic possibilities for sacrificial counterplay.

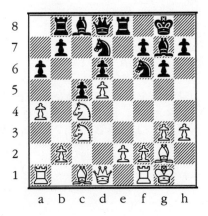

13...Ne5; 14.Na3 Nh5; 15.e4 Rf8; 16.Kh2. Safer was 16.Qe2, discouraging ...b5 but White has a very ambitious plan in mind, to drive Black back on all fronts.

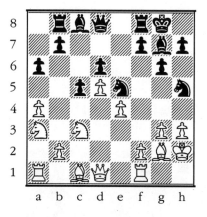

16...f5; 17.f4. Not 17.exf5 Bxf5; 18.g4? Bxg4; 19.hxg4 Qh4+ winning. But now if Black's knight retreats 18 exf4 really is strong. However...

17...b5!! A magnificent conception, whether or not it is completely sound. Black leaves his knight to its fate for seven moves and relies on diversionary tactics.

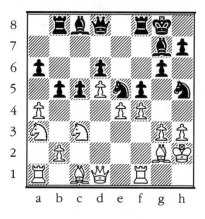

18.axb5 axb5; 19.Naxb5. If 19.fxe5 Bxe5! (threatening both 20...b4 and 20...Nxg3) is very strong. **19...fxe4; 20.Bxe4.**

Now if 20.fxe5 Bxe5; 21.Bf4 Nxf4; 22.gxf4 Bxf4+; 23.Kh1 Qh4 gives Black a murderous attack.

20...Bd7; 21.Qe2 Qb6; 22.Na3 Rbe8.

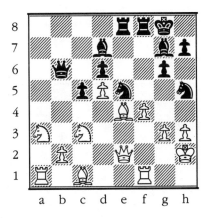

At this moment I decided to watch the Korchnoi-Kasparov game. Of course, it was impossible to see anything. Hundreds of spectators had crowded around the game and people were standing on chairs to get a better view. I glanced up at the manual demonstration board perched above the players' heads, and saw the position in the diagram. My immediate reaction was, Garry's a pawn down, and when he retreats his attacked knight on e5, then White can play the strong Nc4. Then I realized it was Korchnoi's move! This is, in fact, the most critical moment.

Over to Kasparov himself for his explanation: "Now what is to be done if Korchnoi takes the knight? After 23.fxe5 one can look into 23...Bxe5 (23...Rxf1 is also possible) 24.Bf4 Nxf4; 25.gxf4 Bxf4+! 26.Kg2 Qd8 when White has an extra piece but some are poorly placed, e.g. the a3-knight, while Black has many advantages on the king's wing: if 24.Nc4 Bxg3+; 25.Kg1 Qd8 I think this line is playable for Black. At this moment my opponent made a serious error. He could have played 23.Qg2 to consolidate by taking the e5 knight and following with Ne2. According to some critics this would have refuted 16...f5. Surely after 23...Nf7; 24.Nc4 Qb8 the battle is still ahead? White's extra pawn has to be balanced by his weaknesses on central squares and poorly coordinated pieces. After 23.Be3 Nf7; 24.Nc4 Qd8 White is congested."

23.Bd2? Qxb2; 24.fxe5. At last White accepts the bait and his position rapidly disintegrates. **24...Bxe5; 25.Nc4 Nxg3; 26.Rxf8+ Rxf8; 27.Qe1.** An admission of defeat, but there was no adequate alternative.

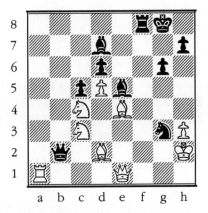

27...Nxe4+; 28.Kg2 Qc2; 29.Nxe5. Or 29.Rc1 Qd3 threatening 30...Qxh3+. Now 29...Nxd2 wins. **29...Rf2+?** Kasparov: "This spoils the game and makes the win uncertain. I had prepared for 30.Kg1, but..."
30.Qxf2!

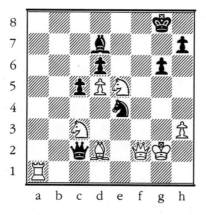

30...Nxf2; 31.Ra2! Qf5!; 32.Nxd7 Nd3. Kasparov: "After the game I devoted an enormous amount of time to analyzing this position. In severe time-trouble, Korchnoi played poorly..." **33.Bh6?** White should play 33.Ra8+ Kf7; 34.Ra7! as Korchnoi pointed out immediately after the game.
33...Qxd7; 34.Ra8+ Kf7; 35.Rh8? Kf6; 36.Kf3?? Qxh3+. White lost on time. An exciting, flawed but inspiring battle!

David Norwood was, at age 17, one of England's brightest hopes. Already an International Master, David tied in 1985 for the bronze medal position in the very strong Commonwealth Championship. Later he went on to earn the Grandmaster title and become captain of the English Chess Olympics team.

Norwood was heavily influenced, as a young player, by Kasparov's ideas, particularly in the Benoni-style formation Kasparov used against Korchnoi. Watch how, in the following game, Norwood suddenly leaps out of a strategically inferior position, to crush his opponent with a Kasparovian knight sacrifice on e5.

RACHELS VS. NORWOOD
London Match 1983
King's Indian Defense

1.d4 Nf6; 2.c4 g6; 3.Nc3 Bg7; 4.Nf3 d6; 5.g3 Nbd7; 6.Bg2 0-0; 7.0-0 c6; 8.e4 e5; 9.h3 a6; 10.d5 cxd5; 11.cxd5 b5; 12.Ne1 b4; 13.Na4 Ne8; 14.Nd3 a5; 15.Be3 Ba6; 16.Re1 f5; 17.exf5 gxf5; 18.f4 e4; 19.Nf2 Bb5; 20.Rb1 Nef6; 21.Bf1 Qb8; 22.Qb3 Kh8; 23.Rbc1 Bxf1; 24.Rxf1 Rg8; 25.Rfd1 Qb7; 26.Rc6 Ra6; 27.Rdc1 h6; 28.Qc4 Raa8; 29.Kh2 Qb8; 30.Bd4 Qf8; 31.Nd1 Nh5; 32.Bf2 Ne5!!

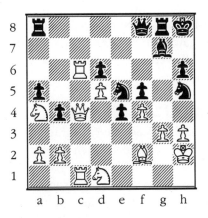

Black's pieces spring to life with this striking echo of Kasparov's sacrifice.
33.fxe5 Bxe5; 34.Qf1 Nxg3. Breaking through on the same square as Kasparov did!

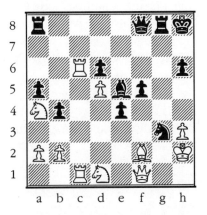

35.Bxg3 Rxg3; 36.Kh1 Rf3; 37.Qg2 Qg8!; 38.R6c2 Rg3; 39.Qf1 Bd4; 40.Nf2 e3; 41.Nd3 e2; 42.Rxe2 Qxd5+.

Now Black is two pawns up, though a knight down. However, he threatens not just ...Rxd3, but also the devastating ...Rxh3+. White has been crushed by Black's flow of tactics.

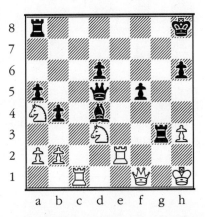

Black went on to win.

This game indicates strongly that pattern recognition of difficult maneuvers is one of the specific benefits which can be gained from the proper study of games by particular leading players. And that is the theme of this chapter, which may be summarized by the acronym VIE -Veneration, Inspiration, Emulation!

PAUL MORPHY THE AMERICAN GENIUS

The great Bobby Fischer consciously adopted Paul Morphy as his role model. When asked to star in an instructional film about the game which had influenced him most, he chose the following masterpiece of dynamic piece play.

The game I present to you now was played in Paris in 1858. White was Paul Morphy, the enigmatic American genius who burst upon the chess scene in 1857. Morphy quickly established a reputation as the world's leading player by defeating several prominent European masters in matches, only to retire completely from serious chess in 1860. The Black pieces were conducted by two noble amateurs, the Duke of Brunswick and Count Isouard de Vauvenargue, acting in consultation. Playing conditions were less than ideal, for the game took place in the Duke's box at the Paris Opera during a performance of Bellini's 'Norma'.

MORPHY VS. DUKE OF BRUNSWICK AND COUNT ISOUARD
Paris 1858
Philidor Defense

1.e4 e5; 2.Nf3 d6; 3.d4 Bg4? Already a serious error, for this move involves loss of time. **4.dxe5 Bxf3; 5.Qxf3 dxe5.**

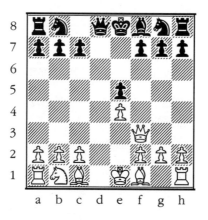

White now has one developed piece, Black none, and it is White's move. We can rightly conclude that White has gained a tempo. In addition White has the two bishops in an open position where, the bishops are better than knights.

6.Bc4. Developing another piece and threatening mate on f7. **6...Nf6; 7.Qb3.**

A non-developing move, it is true, but one which exposes several defects in Black's position. There is a revived threat to f7 and a new threat against b7 which has become weak, since the exchange of Black's queen's bishop.

7...Qe7?!

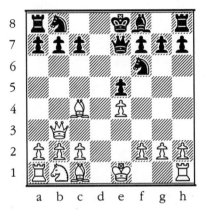

Black already has a lost position. Of course, 7...Nxe4; 8.Bxf7+ leaves Black's king hopelessly exposed. The text shuts in Black's king's bishop and snuffs out hope that Black can get his monarch to relative safety by castling in the near future.

8.Nc3!? An illustration of my earlier remarks about style in chess. White could have played instead 8.Qxb7 Qb4+; 9.Qxb4 Bxb4+; 10.Bd2 winning a pawn or, even better, 8.Bxf7+ Qxf7; 9.Qxb7 winning the exchange since the Black rook on a8 cannot be defended. The existence of this latter continuation provoked Dr. Lasker to remark, "That would have been a butcher's method, not an artist's". True to his combinative nature, Morphy spurns all thoughts of crude material gain, simply develops another piece, and plays for a mating attack. In this instance, perhaps, not only style but also circumstance was involved in his decision. After Black loses the exchange he could still resist for quite a time, although defeat is fairly certain in the long run. Morphy, who loved opera, no doubt wanted the game to end quickly so that he would be left to watch the second act in peace! The result is a memorable finish.

8...c6. Protecting b7, but again this is a non-developing move. **9.Bg5.**

And now poor Black has his one usefully developed piece immobilized by a pin - the knight cannot move, without exposing the queen to capture.

9...b5. After this move Morphy produces a sparkling conclusion. 9...Qc7 was the only way to prolong the game, although Black would still be losing.

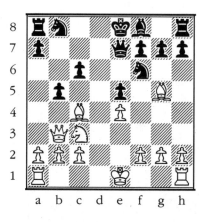

Before we savour the last few moves, take a close look at the diagram. White's final combination is not just an accident of the position, but rather the logical culmination of his previous play. All of White's forces are already, or soon will be, in active service: Black, on the other hand, has moved only two of his pieces off the back rank and, of these, one is pinned and the other is ineffectual. In such situations combinations arise as naturally as ants on a picnic. We should be more surprised if there was *not* a combination available to exploit White's immense positional advantage.

10.Nxb5! The correct method of capitalising on a lead in development is usually to clear new avenues of attack. Every additional open line increases the advantage of the better developed side. In this case White sacrifices a knight in order to free the a4-e8 diagonal for occupation by his bishop - with fatal consequences for Black's king. **10...cxb5; 11.Bxb5+ Nbd7.** 11...Kd8; 12.0-0-0+ is no better. **12.0-0-0.** Rooks love open files and the d-file could hardly be more inviting. White is threatening 13.Rxd7 winning Black's queen.

12...Rd8; 13.Rxd7! Rxd7; 14.Rd1. Bringing the last piece into play with renewed threats against d7. **14...Qe6.**

Now White delivers the coup de grace: **15.Bxd7+ Nxd7; 16.Qb8+!! Nxb8; 17.Rd8 mate.**

ADOLPH ANDERSSEN - EMPEROR OF ATTACK

Aron Nimzowitsch, himself a contender for the world championship, and author of the massively influential book on chess strategy, *My System,* singled out the next game as a particularly formative influence on his early career. Nimzowitsch wrote: "When I was 9 years old, 6 months after I had first learned the moves of chess, my Father, as a reward for my progress at school, demonstrated to me Anderssen's Immortal game. *I not only understood it, but at once fell passionately in love with it!*"

So, as a fitting curtain-raiser to this section I should now like to present one of the most famous combinative masterpieces ever played: the 'Immortal Game' between Anderssen and Kieseritsky. Adolph Anderssen, the victor, was one of the great masters of the mid-nineteenth century. Perhaps his most notable success was winning first prize in the great London tournament of 1851, in which most of the leading players of the day participated.

Some of Anderssen's combinations still rank among the most brilliant on record, and the game which follows, displays a high degree of imagination from start to finish:

ANDERSSEN VS. KIESERITSKY
London 1851
King's Gambit

1.e4 e5; 2.f4 exf4; 3.Bc4!? Usual here is 3.Nf3 developing a piece and preventing 3...Qh4+. The move chosen by Anderssen is more speculative.

3...Qh4+; 4.Kf1 b5?! Black replies to White's aggressive choice of opening with a counter-gambit of his own. By playing 3...b5 Black hopes to entice White's bishop away from c4 (where it attacks f7) and at the same time to clear the a8-h1 diagonal for occupation by his own queen's bishop. Actually, though, the idea has little merit.

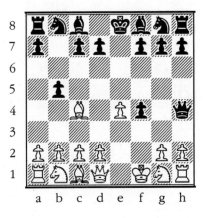

5.Bxb5 Nf6; 6.Nf3. Gaining another useful tempo by developing a piece with an attack against Black's queen. **6...Qh6; 7.d3 Nh5?**

More consistent would have been 7...Bb7, the text (i.e. the move that Black actually played in the game) is inferior. Black now threatens 8...Ng3+; 9.hxg3 Qxh1+ but White's next move constitutes a more than adequate reply.

8.Nh4! Heading for the dominating outpost square f5 - and, of course, preventing 8...Ng3+.

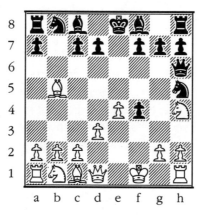

8...Qg5; 9.Nf5 c6; 10.g4 Nf6? Better would have been 10...cxb5; 11.gxh5 but Black gets greedy and plays to win White's g-pawn. No doubt Black expected the game to continue 11.Bc4 Qxg4, but instead Anderssen decides to sacrifice his bishop for a pawn and a raging attack.

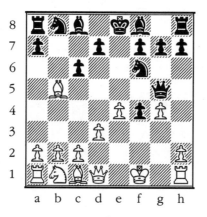

11.Rg1! cxb5; 12.h4 Qg6; 13.h5 Qg5; 14.Qf3! With the terrible threat of 15.Bxf4 winning Black's queen. In order to gain some mobility for his consort, Black is forced to 'undevelop' his only active minor piece.

14...Ng8; 15.Bxf4 Qf6; 16.Nc3 Bc5.

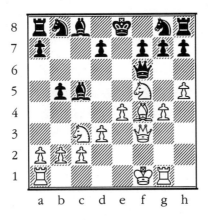

17.Nd5!!? A more prosaic but more effective alternative was 17.d4! after which White's position is overwhelming. If 17...Bxd4; 18.Nd5 wins easily. The text plans an amazing sacrificial continuation and deserves '!!' for the brilliance of the conception. Unfortunately, we are compelled to add a '?' since the idea contains a flaw.

17...Qxb2; 18.Bd6 Qxa1+; 19.Ke2 Bxg1? A double rook sacrifice! Alas the outcome would have remained totally obscure, if Black had refrained from snatching the second rook, and instead played 19...Qb2! Much analysis has been devoted to this variation, but no one has yet shown that White has a forced win. After the gluttonous text, Anderssen brings matters to a sparkling conclusion. Note, in passing, that 19...Qxg1 allows 20.Nxg7+ Kd8; 21.Bc7 mate.

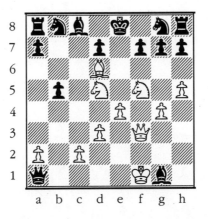

20.e5!! A quiet move which is, nonetheless, completely decisive. The threat, once again, is 21.Nxg7+ Kd8; 22.Bc7 mate. **20...Na6**; 20...Ba6; 21.Nc7+ Kd8; 22.Nxa6 would have allowed Black to resist a bit longer but the outcome would have been the same.

21.Nxg7+ Kd8; 22.Qf6+! A final queen sacrifice to top off the combination! **22...Nxf6; 23.Be7 mate.**

Adolph Anderssen was the greatest exponent of an opening called the Evans Gambit, which often led to fierce attacks, at the cost of material. After Anderssen's time, the Evans lay neglected for almost a century, but Garry Kasparov, as we shall see, studied Anderssen's attacks, and revived it with great force in the 1990s.

ANDERSSEN VS. STEINITZ
London 1866 Match
Evans Gambit

1.e4 e5; 2.Nf3 Nc6; 3.Bc4 Bc5; 4.b4.

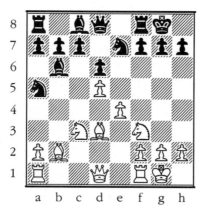

The Evans Gambit, introduced with this move, is a rare guest in modern tournaments but in 1866, as we shall see, it was one of the great highways of chess theory. For his pawn, White gains faster mobilization and greater control of the center. It is one of the most thrilling of the chess openings.

4...Bxb4; 5.c3 Bc5; 6.0-0 d6; 7.d4 exd4; 8.cxd4 Bb6; 9.d5 Na5; 10.Bd3 Ne7; 11.Bb2 0-0; 12.Nc3.

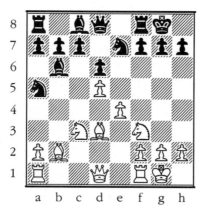

12...Ng6. This was one of the most commonly tested positions in the match, with Anderssen repeatedly stressing his faith in White's initiative, while Steinitz believed in the extra black pawn. The first game, also the fifth and the eleventh of the same match saw Steinitz varying from this with 12...c6.

13.Ne2. In game 7 Anderssen had tried 13.Qd2. **13...c5; 14.Qd2 Bc7; 15.Rac1 Rb8; 16.Ng3 f6; 17.Nf5 b5; 18.Kh1 b4; 19.Rg1.**

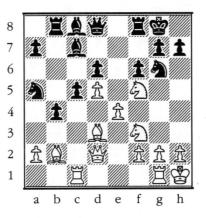

19...Bxf5. This exchange seems natural enough, at first sight, but was condemned by analysts of the day, since White, virtually by force, can now transfer his remaining knight to the dangerous attacking square e6.

20.exf5 Ne5; 21.Bxe5 fxe5; 22.Ng5 Qd7; 23.Ne6 Rfc8. Steinitz masses his entire army on the queen's flank with the intention of smashing through in that sector with his pawns. In fact, it would have been more circumspect to play 23...Rf6 in order to maintain reserves in the vicinity of his king. Steinitz had evidently underestimated the energy White can now develop by charging forward with his own g-pawn, a harbinger of the aggressive White forces lurking in the rear.

24.g4 b3; 25.g5 bxa2; 26.g6. The key move of the decisive combination, full of ingenious points, the first being that 26...h6 would be instantly obliterated by 27.f6.

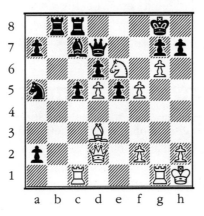

26...Nb3; 27.gxh7+ Kh8; 28.Qg5 Bd8. The only move to avoid the immediate defeat threatened by White's f6. **29.Nxd8 Nxc1.** If instead 29...Rxd8 then 30.f6, always the leitmotiv of White's attack, e.g. 30...Rb7; 31.fxg7+ Qxg7; 32.Qxd8+ winning.

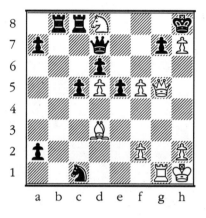

30.f6 Rc7; 31.f7 Qxf7; 32.Nxf7+ Rxf7; 33.Rxc1 Rxf2; 34.Qe7 Rbf8; 35.Qxa7.

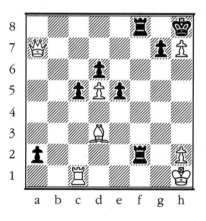

It is clear that White has won. Steinitz drags out his resistance rather superfluously for the next seven moves, but he can never make anything of his far flung pawns.

35...R8f7; 36.Qb8+ Rf8; 37.Qxd6 e4; 38.Bxe4 c4; 39.Qb4 c3; 40.Rg1 R2f7; 41.Qxc3 Rf6; 42.d6. Black resigns.

EMANUEL LASKER - SURVIVAL OF THE FITTEST

Over 100 years ago Emanuel Lasker (born 24th December 1868 in Brandenburg, Germany) wrested the world chess championship from the aging Wilhelm Steinitz. The match took place in New York, Philadelphia and Montreal over the months of March, April and May 1894. Lasker went on to hold the world title for a record near 27 years, winning virtually all of the important tournaments in which he participated.

He did not confine his talents solely to chess, he was also a writer of verse dramas, a philosopher and a mathematician of some note.

When his biography appeared, the foreword was written by Albert Einstein, who wrote of Lasker: 'Emanuel Lasker was undoubtedly one of the most interesting people I came to know in my later life. Few, indeed, can have combined such a unique independence of personality with so eager an interest in all the great problems of mankind. I met Emanuel Lasker in the house of a mutual friend and I came to know him well during the many walks we took together, discussing ideas on a variety of subjects. It was a somewhat unilateral discussion in which, almost invariably, I was in the position of listener, for it seemed to be the natural thing for this eminently creative man to generate his own ideas, rather than adjust himself to those of some-one else.'

St. Petersburg has a great name in chess. This city proved a particular hunting ground for Lasker, with three of the most celebrated tournaments being held there in 1896, 1909 and 1914. Lasker won all three, though he had to share first place with Rubinstein in 1909. In 1896, Lasker outmatched Steinitz, Pillsbury and Chigorin, with only Tarrasch of his main rivals re-fusing his invitation. In 1914 Lasker headed a field which included Capablanca, Alekhine, Tarrasch and Marshall. To have maintained his dominance over an 18 year period in this fash-ion argues that Lasker was a truly special champion.

LASKER VS. CAPABLANCA
St. Petersburg 1914
Ruy Lopez

1.e4 e5; 2.Nf3 Nc6; 3.Bb5 a6; 4.Bxc6 dxc6.

The Exchange Variation of the Ruy Lopez was responsible for many of Lasker's victories. Black is quickly saddled with doubled pawns, and an inferior pawn structure. As we shall see, it has also become a major favorite with Bobby Fischer.

5.d4 exd4; 6.Qxd4 Qxd4; 7.Nxd4 Bd6; 8.Nc3 Ne7; 9.0-0 0-0; 10.f4. This is very risky since it weakens White's center, but Lasker absolutely had to win this game to take first prize in the tournament, and he was never averse to risk in such situations. Black's correct response is 10...Bc5.

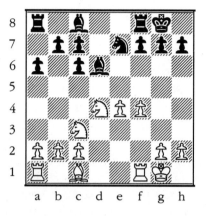

10...Re8; 11.Nb3 f6; 12.f5 b6; 13.Bf4.

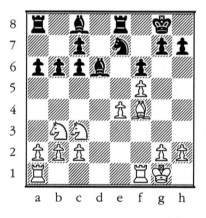

13...Bb7. Capablanca succumbs to the lure of having his doubled queenside pawns straightened out but, in fact, this leaves him with a passive position. Necessary, as Nimzowitsch pointed out, was 13...Bxf4; 14.Rxf4 c5; 15.Rd1 Bb7; 16.Rf2 Rac8 with the plan of ... Nc6 - e5. **14.Bxd6 cxd6; 15.Nd4 Rad8.** Now, as in the previous game, White establishes a knight on the powerful square, e6.

16.Ne6 Rd7; 17.Rad1 Nc8; 18.Rf2 b5; 19.Rfd2 Rde7; 20.b4 Kf7; 21.a3 Ba8; 22.Kf2 Ra7; 23.g4 h6; 24.Rd3 a5; 25.h4 axb4. Black has been outplayed but can still probably draw by sacrificing the exchange (rook for knight) at the appropriate moment to eliminate White's powerful knight hence, 25...Rxe6 is necessary.

26.axb4 Rae7; 27.Kf3 Rg8.

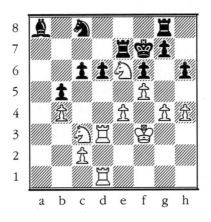

Having unwisely opened the a-file, the sacrifice of the exchange on e6 is no longer so attractive. From now on Black is strangled. Capablanca himself said that Lasker's play after move 28 was probably perfect.

28.Kf4 g6; 29.Rg3 g5+; 30.Kf3 Nb6; 31.hxg5 hxg5; 32.Rh3 Rd7; 33.Kg3 Ke8; 34.Rdh1 Bb7; 35.e5. A dramatic vacating sacrifice, which enables White's second knight to charge into the black position.

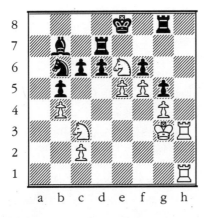

35...dxe5; 36.Ne4 Nd5; 37.N6c5 Bc8. Forced. If 37...Rc7; 38.Nxb7 Rxb7; 39.Nd6+. **38.Nxd7 Bxd7; 39.Rh7 Rf8; 40.Ra1 Kd8; 41.Ra8+ Bc8; 42.Nc5. Black resigned.**

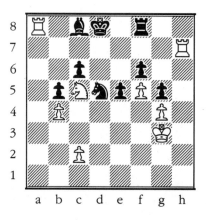

There is nothing to be done against the three threats: Rd7+, Nb7+ and Ne6+.

Lasker described the conclusion of this memorable sporting contest as follows: 'The spectators had followed the final moves breathlessly. That Black's position was in ruins was obvious to the veriest tyro. And now Capablanca turned over his king. From the several hundred spectators there came such applause as I have never experienced in all my life as a chessplayer. It was like a wholly spontaneous applause which thunders forth in the theatre, of which the individual is almost unconscious.'

JOSE CAPABLANCA - PERFECT TECHNIQUE

The legendary iron man of chess, Jose Raoul Capablanca, was born in Havana in 1888. Capablanca seemed destined for the chess purple from an early age, and when he did take the supreme title from Emanuel Lasker in 1921, the Cuban maestro did so without the loss of a game, a feat which has never since been repeated.

At the chess board Capa, as he was affectionately known, was razor sharp, but he also had a keen appreciation of his own tremendous strength and the wit to trumpet this should aspersions be cast on his genius. When the Russian master, Eugene Alexandrovich Znosko-Borovsky, published a booklet entitled *Capablanca's Mistakes*, Capa was not slow to announce that he had tried to write a book called *Znosko-Borovsky's Good Moves*, but had renounced the project in despair at the lack of material.

Of Capablanca's own games it has been written, with justice, that they breathe a serenity, a lucid crystal clarity, a type of model perfection. Indeed, that they are the product of supreme chessboard art.

When Capablanca died, on March 8, 1942, his great rival Alexander Alekhine wrote: "Capablanca was snatched from the chess world much too soon. With his death we have lost a very great chess genius, whose like we shall never see again." The following game helps to explain Alekhine's admiration for the Cuban.

ALEKHINE VS. CAPABLANCA
St Petersburg 1914
Ruy Lopez

1.e4 e5; 2.Nf3 Nc6; 3.Bb5 d6; 4.d4 exd4; 5.Nxd4 Bd7; 6.Nc3 Nf6; 7.0-0 Be7; 8.Nf5. White's sally with his knight is soon revealed as an overoptimistic advance which achieves little more than the weakening of his own pawn structure.

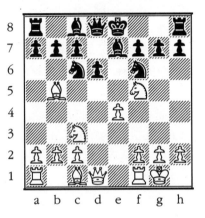

8...Bxf5; 9.exf5 0-0. We have already seen a similar operation in the game Anderssen-Steinitz. There White also played Nf5, parried by ...Bxf5. Here, though, White has none of Anderssen's pre requisites for an attack on the Black king. On the contrary, it is Black's mobilization which is more efficient.

10.Re1 Nd7; 11.Nd5 Bf6; 12.c3 Nb6; 13.Nxf6+ Qxf6; 14.Bxc6 bxc6. Alekhine's exchange of bishop for knight on move 14 was aimless. He merely strengthens the Black center thereby. Correct would have been 14.Qf3.

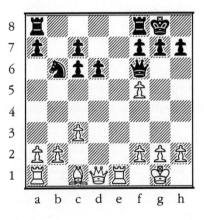

15.Qf3 Rfe8; 16.Be3 c5; 17.Re2 Re5; 18.Rae1 Rae8.

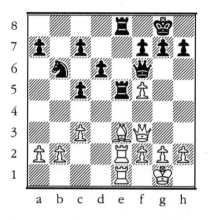

Alekhine was notorious for his tactical traps, and here the ever-alert Capa sidesteps two particularly devilish variations. Thus 18...Rxf5 would fail to 19.Bg5 exploiting the vulnerability of Black's back rank. Alternatively, 18...Qxf5; 19.Qxf5 Rxf5 and now 20.Bxc5! returning to the same motif.

19.Qb7 Qxf5; 20.Qxc7 Qe6.

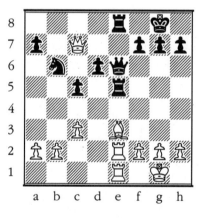

While Capablanca masses his pieces in the center Alekhine has erroneously despatched his queen to hunt down a few harmless pawns on a remote perimeter of the battlefield. It is, therefore, hardly a surprise that Capablanca's concentrated legions can now launch the decisive onslaught against White's denuded king's field.

21.Qxa7 Nd5; 22.Kf1 Nf4; 23.Rd2. With his forces poised, Capablanca now has the choice between the prosaic 23...Qg4; 24.f3 Qe6 or the key sacrifice. He prefers to play to the gallery.

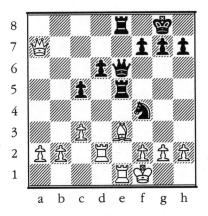

23...Nxg2!! 24.Kxg2 Qg4+.

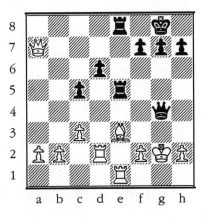

The knight sacrifice wins by driving White's king into the open, where it soon succumbs to the action of the Black pieces. White's passed a-pawn is only a minor distraction.

25.Kf1 Qh3+; 26.Ke2 Rxe3+; 27.fxe3 Qxe3+; 28.Kd1 Qxe1+; 29.Kc2 Qe4+; 30.Kb3 Qc6; 31.a4 d5. As so often, the element of the initiative has translated into advantages of material and structure. White is now a pawn down, his king is exposed, and Black threatens ...Ra8.

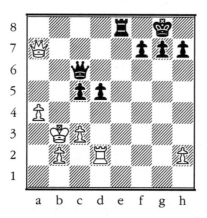

32.a5 Qb5+; 33.Ka3 Rb8; 34.Ka2 h6; 35.a6 Qb3+. White resigns. After 36.Kb1 Re8; 37.Rc2 Re1+; 38.Rc1 Re2 mate is forced. A wonderfully energetic game.

ALEXANDER ALEKHINE - BLITZKRIEG BRILLIANCE

In this section, I salute the great world champion and brilliant master of attack, Alexander Alekhine, who was born in Moscow in 1892. Alekhine led one of the most turbulent careers of any chess professional. The first world war, in which he served during the hostilities between Russia and Austro-Hungary, followed by the Russian Revolution, almost wrecked him. As an aristocrat, his very survival was in question, but he escaped to Paris, where he established himself during the 1920s as the leading contender for Capablanca's world crown.

Alekhine scoured the world to find financial backers for a match against Capablanca, and ultimately he found them in Buenos Aires. In 1927, Alekhine achieved the virtually impossible. He defeated Capablanca in a match. This was the high point of Alekhine's career. If one examines the statistics, Capablanca lost fewer games than any other great master, and to beat him six times in one contest, as Alekhine did, bordered on the miraculous.

Alekhine held the world championship until 1935, en route dominating tournaments such as San Remo 1930 and Bled 1931, in a way that few champions have done, before or since. Alekhine lost the title to Euwe in 1935, only to regain it two years later. His latter years were marred, once more, by turbulent world events as Alekhine was sucked into the sphere of Nazi influence during the second world war. To complete the picture of the bohemian, romantic artist, the genius buffeted by the cruel reality of the world, Alekhine died, impoverished and intoxicated in a Lisbon hotel, still in possession of the title in 1946. His was one of the most glorious and one of the most tragic careers on the chequered board.

I have devoted much effort to analyzing Alekhine's games and have come to the somewhat paradoxical conclusion that his most brilliant and profound masterpieces were actually produced during the opening shots of the match he lost to Euwe in 1935. The following is a case in point and the notes are based on Alekhine's own.

EUWE VS. ALEKHINE
World Championship Match 1935
Gruenfeld Defense

1.d4 Nf6; 2.c4 g6; 3.Nc3 d5. Alekhine was a pioneer of the Gruenfeld Defense, which later became a favorite of Kasparov. **4.Qb3 dxc4; 5.Qxc4 Bg7; 6.Bf4 c6; 7.Rd1.** An artificial and unnecessary move, instead of which 7.Nf3 was indicated. Black can now obtain at least an equal game.

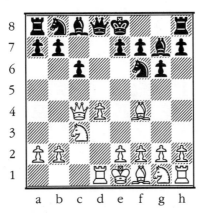

7...Qa5; 8.Bd2 b5. Very risky but quite in Alekhine's stormy style. The simple 8...Qb6 would have secured Black an advantage in development. **9.Qb3 b4.** Black prevents e4, but at a price!

10.Na4 Na6; 11.e3 Be6; 12.Qc2 0-0; 13.b3 Rab8; 14.Bd3 Rfc8; 15.Ne2. White underestimates the value of the following pawn sacrifice. He should have stifled Black's counterplay with 15.Bxa6 Qxa6; 16.Nc5.

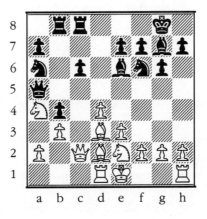

15...c5! Now Alekhine is in his element and the storm bursts. **16.Bxa6 Qxa6; 17.Nxc5 Qb5; 18.Nf4?** This allows Black to open the center and destroy White's position. The correct defense was 18.e4 Nd7; 19.Be3 with a probable draw as the result.

18...Bg4; 19.f3 e5; 20.Nfd3 exd4! An attractive and exactly calculated piece offer, which White is practically forced to accept, since both 21.exd4 Nd5 and 21.e4 Nd7 would leave him with even fewer chances of salvation.

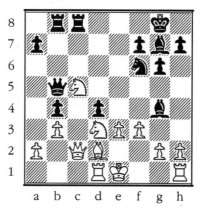

21.fxg4 dxe3; 22.Bxe3 Nxg4; 23.Bf4 Bc3+; 24.Rd2 Rxc5; 25.Nxc5 Qxc5. A deluge of sacrifices has guaranteed Alekhine an unstoppable attack.

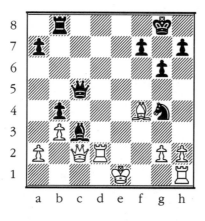

26.Bxb8 Qe7+; 27.Kd1 Ne3+; 28.Kc1 Nxc2; 29.Rxc2 h5. A necessary preparation for ...Bg7.

30.Rd1 Bg7; 31.h3 a5. Black's chief trumps, which must eventually guarantee the win, consist of the permanent insecurity of the White king and the unprotected position of the bishop, whose efforts to find a safe square are bound to fail. The game remains lively and instructive until the very end.

32.Bf4 Qe4; 33.Bc7 Qe3+; 34.Kb1 a4. This break-up, which could not, in the long run, be prevented, wins Black the exchange.

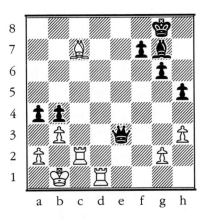

35.bxa4 b3; 36.axb3 Qxb3+; 37.Kc1 Bh6+; 38.Rdd2 Qxa4; 39.Be5 Kh7; 40.Bc3 Qb5; 41.Bd4 Qe2; 42.g4 Qe1+; 43.Kb2 Bxd2; 44.Rc8 Bc1+. White resigns.

For devotees of Alekhine's games, I strongly recommend the classic *Alekhine's Greatest Games* published by Batsford.

Alexander Alekhine is regarded as one of the great tactical geniuses of the chessboard. Garry Kasparov, an ardent devotee of the great man, records his own admiration: "Alekhine's attacks came suddenly, like destructive thunderstorms that erupted from a clear blue sky. This style of Alekhine's was what I admired and what I wanted to develop in my own games."

Here are some more flashes of Alekhine's stormy genius, which explain Kasparov's adulation:

ALEKHINE VS. FLOHR
Bled 1931

White to Play

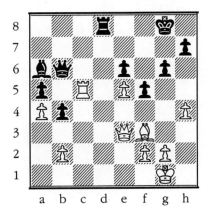

Alekhine struck down his unsuspecting opponent with **1.Rc8!!** and Black resigned. 1...Rxc8; 2.Qxb6 wins Black's queen or 1...Qxe3; 2.Rxd8+ Kg7; 3.fxe3 and White wins a rook. White's second move is a fine example of a zwischenzug.

ALEKHINE VS. LASKER
Zurich 1934

White to Play

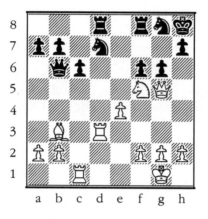

Alekhine destroyed his opponent, world champion from 1894-1921 with the thunderbolt **1.Qxg6!!** when Black resigned on the spot, since 1...hxg6; 2.Rh3+ forces mate.

MIKHAIL BOTVINNIK - THE SOVIET JUGGERNAUT

Mikhail Botvinnik, who died in Moscow in mid 1995 at the age of 83, was the last link with the old generation of greats. Botvinnik played against, defeated, or taught every single world champion, apart from the very first one, Wilhelm Steinitz. Botvinnik won one of the most brilliant games on record against the mighty Capablanca, and he had a plus score against Lasker, Alekhine, Spassky and Smyslov. Both Karpov and Kasparov were his pupils, with Botvinnik famously saying of the latter in his early days: 'In the hands of this young man lies the future of chess.'

What fascinated me about Botvinnik was the way in which his play seemed to become deeper, richer and more aggressive, and certainly more experimental, in the mid to late 1960s. It seemed to me that Botvinnik saved his best until last and the games he played between the ages of 53 and 59 were his finest legacy. Here are two samples of the peaks of creative artistry he was able to achieve in his final years. His victims in the two following positions were both Candidates for the world championship.

BOTVINNIK VS. KERES
USSR Team Championship Moscow 1966

White to Play

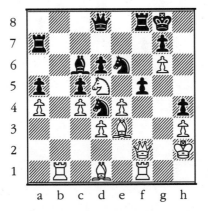

In this seemingly complex situation, in which both sides have attacks in train and where both kings seem somewhat exposed, Botvinnik suddenly brought down the curtain with **1.Rb8!!** After this coup, Black resigned, since his queen has been wrenched by force from its defense of the pawn on h4. After, for example,

1...Qxb8; 2.Qxh4. Black has no defense to mate starting with Qh7.

BOTVINNIK VS. PORTISCH
Monaco 1968

White to Play

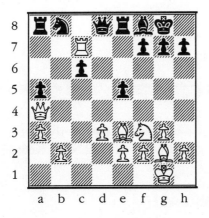

Here, White has already sacrificed rook for bishop but the question remains, is White's

remaining rook on c7 a source of aggression, or is it trapped? Botvinnik immediately provides the answer, tearing into Black's position with volcanic force.

1.Rxf7!!

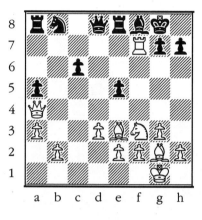

1...h6. Black cannot play 1...Kxf7 on account of 2.Qc4+ Kg6 (if 2...Qd5; 3.Ng5+) 3.Qg4+ Kf7; 4.Ng5+ Kg8; 5.Qc4+ Kh8; 6.Nf7+. **2.Rb7 Qc8; 3.Qc4+ Kh8; 4.Nh4.**

A fantastic move, leaving the other rook to its fate in the interests of hounding the black king. If White took off time to retreat his rook Black might have been able to consolidate with a move like ... Qe6.

4...Qxb7; 5.Ng6+ Kh7; 6.Be4 Bd6; 7.Nxe5+ g6; 8.Bxg6+ Kg7; 9.Bxh6+.

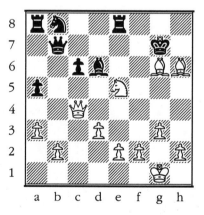

Black resigns. Botvinnik's final sacrifice has utterly destroyed the Black position. For example 9...Kxh6; 10.Qh4+ Kg7; 11.Qh7+ Kf6; 12.Ng4+ Ke6; 13.Qxb7 when Black's position is laid waste.

PRACTISING WHAT I PREACH

My rook sacrifice on f7 in the following game - to smoke the Black king out of hiding - was directly inspired by the amazing rook sacrifice of my hero, Botvinnik, which we have just witnessed!

KEENE VS. ROBATSCH
Madrid 1971

White to Play

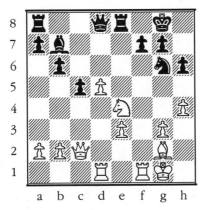

21.Rxf7!! The decisive sacrifice which hunts Black's king to its doom. **21...Kxf7; 22.Rf1+ Ke7.** If 22...Kg8; 23.Nf6+ gxf6; 24.Qxg6+ Kh8; 25.Qxh6+ Kg8; 26.Qg6+ Kh8; 27.Rxf6 Re7; 28.Be4 wins.

23.d6+ Kd7; 24.Rf7+ Ne7. If instead 24...Kc8; 25.Rc7+ Kb8; 26.Rxb7+ Kxb7; 27.Nxc5+ Kb8; 28.Na6 checkmate. **25.Qa4+ Kc8.** The king tries to hide on his own back rank. If 25...Bc6; 26.Bh3 is checkmate.

26.d7+ Qxd7.

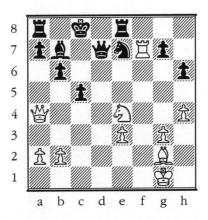

27.Bh3. Black resigns. If 27...Qxh3; 28.Qxe8+ Kc7; 29.Rxe7+ is terminal.

BOBBY FISCHER - REVOLUTIONARY AMERICAN

American Grandmaster Bobby Fischer set the chess world alight with his world championship victory over Boris Spassky in 1972. By ending decades of Soviet domination, Fischer inspired a host of aspiring champions and Grandmasters outside the USSR.

Bobby Fischer had never been particularly complimentary about Emanuel Lasker, once dismissing him in an infamous article as a 'coffee-house player'. However, if one looks more deeply, one sees that one of Fischer's all-time favorite openings was a leaf taken directly out of Lasker's book!

FISCHER VS. SPASSKY
World Championship Match, Sveti Stefan 1992
Ruy Lopez

1.e4 e5; 2.Nf3 Nc6; 3.Bb5 a6; 4.Bxc6. The exchange variation was a favorite of the great Emanuel Lasker, who used it, for example, as we have seen, to win the deciding game against Capablanca at St. Petersburg 1914. It had been considered harmless for many years since then, because it was regarded as excessively simplifying, but in 1966, at the Havana Olympics, Fischer reintroduced it to great effect in three games against Portisch, Gligoric, and Jimenez.

4...dxc6; 5.0-0 f6; 6.d4 exd4. The main alternative is 6...Bg4, for example:

a) 7.c3 exd4; 8.cxd4 Qd7; 9.h3 Be6 (9...Bh5; 10.Ne5 Bxd1; 11.Nxd7 Kxd7; 12.Rxd1 Re8; 13.f3 Ne7; 14.Nc3 with advantage to White, Fischer-Jimenez, Havana Olympiad,1966) 10.Nc3 0-0-0; 11.Bf4 Ne7; 12.Rc1 also with advantage to White, Fischer-Gligoric, Havana Olympiad, 1966; b) 7.dxe5 Qxd1; 8.Rxd1 fxe5; 9.Rd3 Bd6; 10.Nbd2 Nf6; 11.Nc4 0-0; 12.Nfxe5 Be2; 13.Re3 Bxc4; 14.Nxc4 with advantage to White, Fritz4-Beliavsky, Bled 1996. It seems that even computers learn from Fischer!

7.Nxd4 c5; 8.Nb3 Qxd1; 9.Rxd1 Bg4. Now 9...Bd6; 10.Na5 b5; 11.c4 Ne7; 12.Be3 f5; 13.Nc3 f4; 14.e5! Bxe5; 15.Bxc5 with advantage was seen in Fischer-Portisch, also from the Havana Olympiad 1966.

10.f3 Be6; 11.Nc3 Bd6.

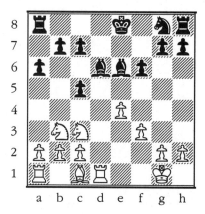

This is the kind of position which established the reputation of the Exchange variation as being harmless. White enjoys the better pawn structure, due to Black's doubled pawns and White's kingside pawn majority, while in addition White has a slight lead in development. On the other hand, Black's position is extraordinarily solid and he has the bishop pair. Such positions tended nearly always to be drawn. But in this game Fischer has other ideas.

12.Be3 b6; 13.a4. This advance is the only way to put pressure on Black's position.

13...0-0-0; 14.a5 Kb7. A startling blow, but it is, in fact, known theory. 15.e5 is a sophisticated way of emphasizing the mobility of White's kingside pawn mass. If now 15...fxe5 (15...Bxe5?? is ruled out on account of 16.Rxd8) then 16.axb6 cxb6; 17.Ne4 threatening Nxd6+ and if the bishop moves to e7 then 18.Rxd8 followed by Nbxc5+.

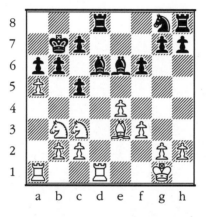

15.e5 Be7; 16.Rxd8 Bxd8; 17.Ne4. This is Fischer's real innovation. Instead the immediate 17.axb6 led to equality and a swift draw in the game Adorjan-Ivkov, Skopje, 1976; 17...cxb6; 18.Ne4 Bxb3; 19.Nd6+ Kc6; 20.cxb3 Ne7; 21.Rxa6 Nd5. Draw agreed.

17...Kc6? White's threat had been 18.Nexc5+ sacrificing a piece temporarily to win the Black bishop on e6. Faced with a novel situation, Spassky's protective king move seems a sensible way of deflecting this menace, but, in fact, it is a terrible blunder which Fischer punishes in devastating fashion. Black had to play 17...Bxb3; 18.cxb3 f5 though 19.Rd1 still leaves White with a substantial advantage. The plausible 17...Bxb3; 18.cxb3 fxe5 fails to 19.axb6 when 19...Kxb6; 20.Nxc5 is clearly unacceptable, as is 19...cxb6; 20.Nd6+ followed by Nf7.

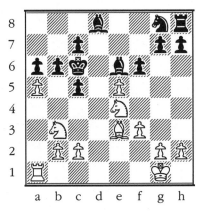

18.axb6 cxb6; 19.Nbxc5! Absolutely crushing. If now 19...bxc5; 20.Rxa6+ Kd7; 21.Nxc5+ wins, or 20...Kd5; 21.Rd6+ followed by Rxd8 when Black is paralysed.

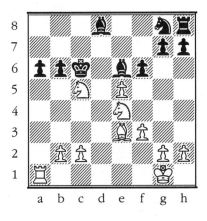

19...Bc8; 20.Nxa6 fxe5; 21.Nb4+. Black resigns.

ANATOLY KARPOV - UNDER LOCK AND KEY

Karpov enjoys a justified and outstanding reputation as a squeeze player, one able to drain the life from his opponent's position with the subtlest of means. The slightest domination of an important square, or the most refined control of a color complex on the board, can be quite sufficient for Karpov to score a victory. However, Karpov is also quite capable of producing the most slashing sacrificial attacks based on deep analysis of complicated opening variations. The following fine game is a case in point.

TIMMAN VS. KARPOV
Montreal 1979
English Opening

1.c4 Nf6; 2.Nc3 e5; 3.Nf3 Nc6; 4.e3 Be7; 5.d4 exd4; 6.Nxd4 0-0; 7.Nxc6 bxc6; 8.Be2 d5; 9.0-0 Bd6; 10.b3 Qe7; 11.Bb2.

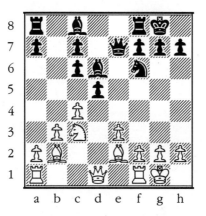

This variation had become popular at the time. Originally employed by the great chess thinker Aron Nimzowitsch in the 1920s, I had revived it in my game as White against the Swedish master Jansson at the Haifa Olympiad of 1976. In that encounter Jansson had continued against me with 11...Rd8; 12.cxd5 Qe5; 13.g3 Bh3; 14.Re1 Bb4; 15.Qc2 Bf5; 16.Qc1 cxd5; 17.Bf3 Qe7; 18.a3 Ba5; 19.b4 Bb6 and now 20.Nxd5 introduced tactical complications which were favorable to White. Karpov had seen this game and had prepared a remarkable surprise.

11...dxc4. By giving up the center, and leaving his doubled c-pawns shattered and isolated, Karpov appears to be breaking all the strategic rules. However, this seemingly anti-positional capture reveals Karpov's true genius. Although the move shatters Black's pawns, thus rendering it unthinkable for most players, Karpov has seen that Black gains a variety of tactical counterchances, which more than outweigh his strategic disadvantage.

12.bxc4. If 12.Bxc4 Ng4; 13.g3 Nxh2; 14.Kxh2 Qh4+ is one way for Black to gain a fierce attack. Even 12...Bxh2+ comes into consideration.

12...Rb8; 13.Qc1 Ng4. This looks like a naive sortie, but White is curiously powerless to drive away the black knight.

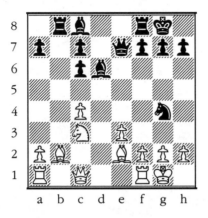

14.g3 Re8; 15.Nd1 Nxh2. If now 16.Kxh2 Qh4+; 17.Kg2 Qh3+; 18.Kg1 Bxg3; 19.fxg3 Qxg3+; 20.Kh1 Re4; 21.Rf4 Bh3 and Black wins. Timman finds an ingenious counter, but Karpov had also taken this into account.

16.c5 Nxf1; 17.cxd6.

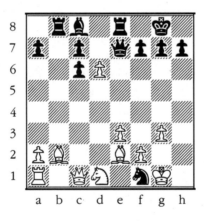

Timman doubtless believed that Black now had to recapture on d6 with either the pawn or the queen. In that case, White could calmly recapture Black's knight on f1 with the better chances, but Karpov had calculated all this in advance and now comes up with a thunderbolt of a zwischenzug which leaves White's king entirely without shelter.

17...Nxg3!! If now 18.dxe7 Nxe2+; 19.Kf1 Nxc1 winning easily on material. **18.fxg3 Qxd6; 19.Kf2 Qh6; 20.Bd4 Qh2+.**

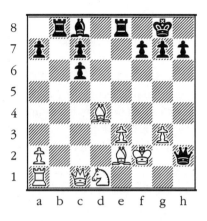

The upshot of Karpov's combination is that White's king has become hopelessly exposed and is rapidly pummelled to death by Black's massive and well coordinated central army. The square h2 has definitely been White's nemesis, or Achilles Heel, in this game.

21.Ke1 Qxg3+; 22.Kd2 Qg2; 23.Nb2 Ba6; 24.Nd3 Bxd3; 25.Kxd3 Rbd8; 26.Bf1 Qe4+; 27.Kc3 c5. The final key to Black's attack, displacing the bishop and opening more lines for Black's major pieces to hound White's king to its destruction.

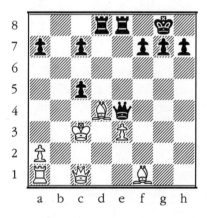

28.Bxc5 Qc6; 29.Kb3 Rb8+; 30.Ka3 Re5; 31.Bb4 Qb6. White resigns.

In his best games it is remarkable how Karpov's opponents always seem to be utterly deprived of counterplay. In this sense, he is very much a disciple of Capablanca. The next game is a fine example. When Black (Leko) does stir up a counterattack, it is already an act of pure desperation.

KARPOV VS. LEKO
Tilburg 1996
Gruenfeld Defense

1.d4 Nf6; 2.c4 g6; 3.Nc3 d5; 4.Nf3 Bg7; 5.Qb3. One of Karpov's favorites. By pressuring d5 he hopes to persuade Black to surrender the center by capturing White's pawn.

5...dxc4; 6.Qxc4 0-0; 7.e4 a6. Although this move was invented by Alekhine in the 1930s, it has only really gained respectability after adoption by Hungarian Grandmasters. Popular alternatives are 7...Bg4 and 7...Na6, both of which have been played by Kasparov.

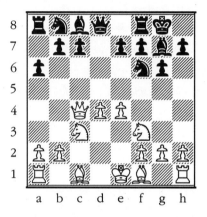

8.e5. The point of Black's opening is that after the natural 8.Bf4, as played by Dr Max Euwe in one of his world championship games against Alekhine in 1935, Black can resort to the dangerous strategic pawn sacrifice 8...b5; 8.Qxc7 Qxc7 (Alekhine played the inferior 8...Qe8) 9.Bxc7 Bb7, with plenty of counterplay against White's unwieldy pawn center.

8...Nfd7. Leko varies from two games in the Karpov-Kamsky FIDE world championship match played earlier in 1996 in Elista, where Black did not fare particularly well with the immediate 8...b5. **9.Be3 Nb6; 10.Qc5 Be6.** Leko's attempt to improve on 10...f6; 11.Rd1 which led to a White win in the game Niedhardt-Koerner, Hessen 1992.

11.Ng5 Bf5; 12.Be2 Kh8; 13.g4 Bc8; 14.0-0-0 f6.

The board is in flames, as is so often the case when the players castle on opposite wings. White's target is clearly the Black king.

15.Nge4 f5; 16.gxf5 Bxf5; 17.h4 N8d7; 18.Qa3 Nd5; 19.Ng5. Avoiding 19.Nxd5 Bxe4 forking two white pieces. **19...N7b6; 20.h5 Nxe3; 21.fxe3 Bh6; 22.Nce4 Qd7; 23.hxg6 Qc6+; 24.Kd2.**

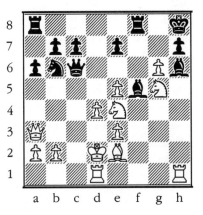

White's king marches towards the sound of gunfire but 24.Kb1 is clearly out of the question on account of 24...Bxe4+.

24...Qxg6; 25.Rdg1 Rad8. If 25...Bxe4; 26.Nxe4 Qxe4; 27.Rxh6 leaves Black very badly placed. **26.e6.** Threatening Nf7+ winning Black's queen. Black also has to contend with the threat of Bh5. Leko, therefore, takes drastic countermeasures, but he has overlooked a neat tactical trick.

26...Rxd4+; 27.exd4 Bxe4.

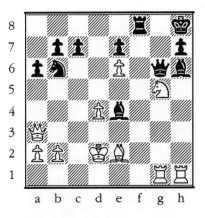

With his pin against White's knight Black appears to have confused the issue, but Karpov now deals the death blow.

28.Rxh6 Qxh6; 29.Qe3. Black resigns. White threatens both to capture the Black bishop on e4 and to win Black's queen with Nf7+ and if 29...Rg8; 30.Nf7 is checkmate.

Karpov is an ideal champion to study, for those who wish to hone their strategic, structural and schematic skills.

GARRY KASPAROV - THE NAPOLEON OF CHESS

Who is the greatest player in the history of chess? In my opinion, the choice must either be Fischer or Garry Kasparov. Sadly, these two giants have never met head-on. Fischer, both in the past and in the mid 1990's, has made his name with a titanic series of duels with Boris Spassky. Kasparov, on the other hand, has established his position in the pantheon of greats with his marathon contests against Anatoly Karpov.

So, the comparison between Kasparov and Fischer must be made through surrogates, not directly. What I have noticed is that Fischer's attacks tend to brook no opposition. Once he gains the initiative, they are clear-cut and forceful. The opponent never seems to get any kind of counterplay. In sharp contradistinction, Kasparov always seems to be attacking from the knife-edge of defeat. More often than not, while Kasparov is hunting the enemy king, some portion of his own position is under heavy fire and on the verge of collapse.

To me, Kasparov's attacks seem more complex and less inevitable than those of Fischer. It is the contrast between Capablanca and Alekhine or Mozart and Beethoven. Whose style is superior? This must remain a matter of taste, unless the longed-for match between Fischer and Kasparov ever takes place. This dramatic finale points up the difference.

KASPAROV VS. KARPOV
New York World Championship 1990

White to Play

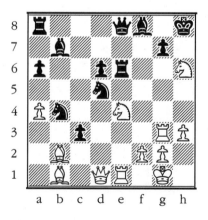

In the diagram, Kasparov is launching a do-or-die, death or glory attack against Black's king. Meanwhile, though, the rest of White's position is collapsing around him. White will not only be a piece down, but Black is also about to obtain a passed pawn on the seventh rank, one square away from queening. One small error in the conduct of White's attack will spell certain doom for him.

27.Nf5 cxb2; 28.Qg4 Bc8; 29.Qh4+ Rh6; 30.Nxh6 gxh6; 31.Kh2. A typical Kasparov quiet move, tucking his king away from possible checks, in the middle of his attack.

31...Qe5; 32.Ng5 Qf6; 33.Re8 Bf5. Simultaneously protecting his king, and trying to destroy White's blockader on b1, so that Black's b2-pawn can promote. But Kasparov has the perfect response.

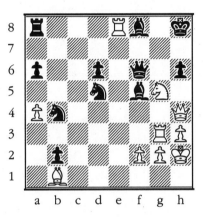

34.Qxh6+!! This spectacular queen sacrifice is the culmination of White's onslaught.

34...Qxh6; 35.Nf7+ Kh7; 36.Bxf5+ Qg6; 37.Bxg6+ Kg7; 38.Rxa8 Be7; 39.Rb8 a5; 40.Be4+ Kxf7; 41.Bxd5+. Black resigns.

I am constantly struck by the similarity between the play of Kasparov and that of his own chosen hero Alexander Alekhine. Alekhine's two greatest tournament victories, San Remo 1930 and Bled 1931, were based on shock tactics, terrifying opening innovations, unexpected gambits and the taking of terrible risks, especially with Black. His Grandmaster opponents were bowled over. They did not know what had hit them. So it is with Kasparov.

In the tournament of Riga 1995, it looked as if the spirit of Alekhine had been re-born. Once again, we were seeing barely credible, quick victories against the world's top players, combined with a love of risk which only succeeds because the complications, thereby conjured-up annihilate the opposition's powers of mental resistance.

KASPAROV VS. ANAND
Tal Memorial, Riga 1995
Evans Gambit

1.e4 e5; 2.Nf3 Nc6; 3.Bc4 Bc5; 4.b4.

A champion can create fashion overnight. This gambit had been neglected for about a century, since the days of Anderssen and Chigorin, but now its analysis is all the rage.

4...Bxb4; 5.c3 Be7; 6.d4 Na5; 7.Be2 exd4; 8.Qxd4 Nf6; 9.e5 Nc6.

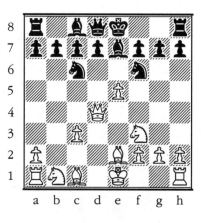

10.Qh4. This is Kasparov's prepared improvement on published play, namely a game between two obscure Russians, Melts and Gajewski, played in the USSR in 1981 where 10.Qf4 Nh5; 11.Qg4 g6 got White nowhere. **10...Nd5; 11.Qg3 g6.** Black would like to castle but if 11...0-0; 12.Bh6 wins material. **12.0–0 Nb6.** In view of what follows Black should have castled here.

13.c4. Kasparov prepares to sacrifice yet another pawn, but here the simple 13.Bh6 d6; 14.Bb5, designed to prevent Black from castling, might have been objectively superior. **13...d6; 14.Rd1 Nd7; 15.Bh6.** Investing another pawn for the attack and definitively preventing Black from castling.

15...Ncxe5; 16.Nxe5 Nxe5. Anand is happy to meet 17.Bg7 with 17...Bf6; 18.Bxh8 Bxh8 when Black's position is solid. Kasparov prefers to stoke up the attack.

17.Nc3 f6; 18.c5.

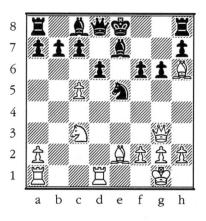

18...Nf7. The onus of defending against Kasparov's onslaught finally takes its toll and Black commits an inaccuracy which allows an elegant and speedy, yet quite unexpected, finish. The best defense would have been 18...Bd7 when subsequent analysis revealed that Black would have been fine. It is easy to say this after the game, but in the heat of battle, especially against Kasparov, such finesses are readily overlooked.

19.cxd6 cxd6; 20.Qe3 Nxh6; 21.Qxh6 Bf8; 22.Qe3+ Kf7; 23.Nd5 Be6; 24.Nf4 Qe7; 25.Re1. Black resigns.

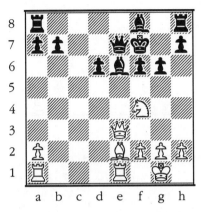

Black's resignation is perfectly justified as can be seen from the variations:

a) 25...Re8; 26.Qxe6+ Qxe6; 27.Nxe6 Rxe6; 28.Bc4 or 27...Kxe6; 28.Bb5+.

b) 25...Bh6; 26.Bc4 Bxf4; 27.Bxe6+ Kg7; 28.Qxf4 winning.

c) 25...d5; 26.Bf3 Re8; 27.Nxe6 Qxe6; 28.Qxe6+ Rxe6; 29.Bxd5.

d) 25...Bd7; 26.Bc4+ Ke8; 27.Qd2 winning Black's queen.

e) 25...Qd7; 26.Bb5 Qxb5; 27.Qxe6+ Kg7; 28.Nd5 Qb2; 29.Rb1 with a devastating attack; or 28...Re8; 29.Qxe8 Qxd5; 30.Rac1 when Black can only survive for a couple of moves.

Once again, Kasparov revives Adolph Anderssen's most feared weapon.

KASPAROV VS. PIKET
Amsterdam 1995
Evans Gambit

1.e4 e5; 2.Nf3 Nc6; 3.Bc4 Bc5; 4.b4 Bb6. As we have seen, Anand tried 4...Bxb4 at Riga but lost quickly.

5.a4 a5. Seems to be playing into White's hands, since he now gains time by attacking Black's knight. 5...a6 is more circumspect, since White does not gain anything by immediately pushing on with b5 in that case.

6.b5 Nd4; 7.Nxd4 Bxd4; 8.c3 Bb6; 9.d4 exd4; 10.0–0. A further gambit, typical of the way in which Kasparov handles this opening. **10...Ne7; 11.Bg5 h6; 12.Bxe7 Qxe7; 13.cxd4 Qd6.** Playing with fire, but if Black castles then 14.Nc3 gives White an obvious plus, control of the center and a clear lead in development. **14.Nc3.**

14...Bxd4. Black's greed meets with a crushing refutation, but also if 14...Qxd4, trying to exchange queens, Kasparov gleefully pointed out this brilliant line after the game: 14...Qxd4; 15.Nd5 Qxc4; 16.Nxb6 cxb6; 17.Qd6 Qe6; 18.e5 Qxd6; 19.exd6 Kd8; 20.Rfe1 Re8; 21.Rxe8+ Kxe8; 22.Re1+ Kf8; 23.Re7. In this situation, although bishop and pawn ahead, Black is utterly helpless against a mass advance of White's kingside pawns. This would eventually break open an avenue for the white king, when Black would certainly lose at least one kingside pawn, while White would promote one of his own to become a queen.

15.Nd5. Sacrificing rook for bishop, but Black's position is so underdeveloped that White's attack is bound to succeed. **15...Bxa1; 16.Qxa1 0–0; 17.e5 Qc5.**

Black's queen is extraordinarily short of squares. **18.Rc1.** The threat is now 19.Nxc7 Qxc7; 20.Bxf7+ netting Black's queen. **18...c6; 19.Ba2 Qa3.** If 19...Qa7; 20.b6 Qb8; 21.Nc7 and

Black is paralyzed.

20.Nb6. The dual threats of Nxa8 and Bxf7+ now lead to the win of a piece, after which Black might as well resign.

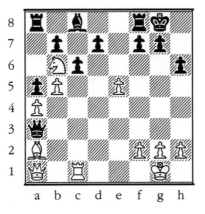

20...d5; 21.Nxa8 Kh8; 22.Nb6 Be6; 23.h3 Rd8; 24.bxc6 bxc6; 25.Rc3 Qb4; 26.Rxc6 Rb8; 27.Nxd5 Qxa4; 28.Rc1 Qa3; 29.Bc4. Black resigns. A wonderfully energetic game by Kasparov.

JUDIT POLGAR - BEATING THE BOYS

The world champion and his main challengers all conform to a certain profile - males between the ages of 20 and 50. Perhaps the greatest future threat to their collective supremacy is posed by a player who does not fit the standard image of a professional master at all, the Hungarian girl, Judit Polgar.

Judit Polgar continues to savage male Grandmasters, one of her exploits being a sharp annihilation of Nigel Short in the 1995 Madrid tournament. The evidence now is that the old prejudices about chess being a game exclusively for boys are way out of date. Indeed, chess places in school and national teams are now selected entirely on merit with no regard to the sex of the players. For example, in the 1996 international chess team championship held in Armenia, Judit Polgar led the Hungarian team ahead of five male Grandmasters. Here is her demolition of Nigel Short.

SHORT VS. JUDIT POLGAR
Madrid 1995
Sicilian Defense

1.e4 c5; 2.Nf3 d6; 3.d4 cxd4; 4.Nxd4 Nf6; 5.Nc3 e6; 6.Be2. The most aggressive course here is the Keres Attack 6.g4. However, Short prefers a more strategic approach.

6...Be7; 7.0-0 0-0; 8.f4 Nc6; 9.Be3 e5; 10.Nb3 a5; 11.a3. Slightly unusual, with 11.a4 being the more normal course, but Short wishes to explore a new idea.

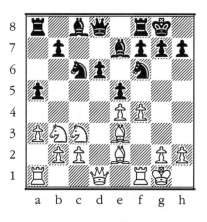

11...a4; 12.Nd2. This seemingly retrograde step is Short's novel ploy. Previous theory recognised the move 12.Nc1, keeping the d-file open for White's queen. **12...exf4; 13.Rxf4 Be6; 14.Nc4 Nd7; 15.Rf1.** Short avoids the trap 15.Nxd6 Bg5; 16.Rf3 Bxe3+; 17.Rxe3 Qb6 when Black has too much counterplay.

15...Qb8; 16.Nd5 Bd8; 17.Nxd6. This capture of a key pawn appears decisive since if 17...Qxd6 the discovery 18.Nf6+ Bxf6; 19.Qxd6 leaves Black with insufficient compensation for her queen. Nevertheless, Black's position is still full of resources.

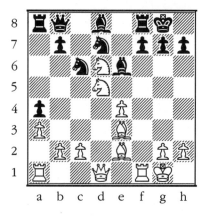

17...Bxd5; 18.Qxd5. This is the moment where Short overestimates his chances. Simply 18 exd5 Qxd6; 19.dxc6 Qxc6; 20.Bf3 gives White a comfortable edge, based on the power of his bishop pair in an open position. **18...Nf6; 19.Qd1 Bc7; 20.Rxf6.** White is already committed to this sacrifice since 20 Nf5 Bxh2+; 21.Kh1 Nxe4 sees Black well in charge. In the further course of play Short hopes to profit from the broken fortifications around Black's king, but as the game develops it turns out that Black's king is, in fact, quite safe.

20...gxf6; 21.Nf5 Kh8; 22.h3 Qe8; 23.Bd3 Qe5; 24.Kf1 Rg8. Short's case is now quite desperate. Apart from the threats to his queenside pawns, Black is also gearing up with moves like ... Rg6, ... Rag8, ... Qh2 and ... Ne5 to follow, engineering a winning attack against the White king.

25.Nh6 Rg7; 26.Ng4 Qxb2; 27.Rb1 Qxa3; 28.Rxb7 Qd6; 29.Qa1 Ne5; 30.Bf4 a3; 31.Rxc7. Short's last throw against the deadly advance of Black's a-pawn. If Black now had to play 31...Qxc7 then both 32.Nxe5 or even 32.Nxf6 would allow White to complicate matters. Unfortunately for Short, Judit is ready with a sharp blow which severs the lines of communication of White's last-ditch attack.

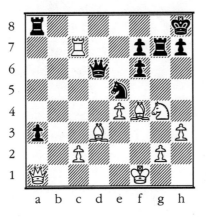

31...Rxg4; 32.hxg4 Qxc7. Now all is clear, although Judit finishes off with the maximum of efficiency.

33.g5 Qc5; 34.Ke2 a2; 35.Be3 Qb4; 36.Bd4 Qxd4. White resigns. Ultimately ensuring the triumph of the a-pawn for if 37.Qxd4 a1/Q there is no fight left.

With this game, in which a brilliant female player defeats a former challenger for the World Championship, I conclude this chapter. The message is clear, chess is for everyone, men, women, boys, girls. In chess, it is your mental aptitude that counts.

THE HISTORY OF CHESS:
Origins, Celebrities, Records

HISTORY

Chess in its various manifestations can rightly be regarded as the king of board games. Millions of people are fascinated by it, or follow the exploits of its leading practitioners. The World Chess Federation, with over 150 member states, is the largest mind sports organization in the world. Chess is capable of making multi-millionaires ot its top champions. The prize, for example, in the 1992 Fischer-Spassky match was a staggering five million dollars. And that contest was not even for the World Championship!

Chess is said to have originated in India around 600 AD under the name Chaturanga. This was a word describing the four traditional army units of Indian military forces, namely foot soldiers (pawns), cavalry (knights), chariots (rooks) and elephants (which have come down as bishops in contemporary chess).

The name "chess" is derived from the Persian word "Shah", meaning a king or ruler. The word is also related to "check" and may even be cognate with the words Caesar, Kaiser and Czar, respectively denoting rulers in the Roman Empire, the German Empire and the Russian Empire.

The earliest written reference is from an ancient Persian poem of the late 6th century AD, the Chatrang Namak. Chess, in its original (rather slow) form flourished during the Baghdad Caliphate in the 10th century AD.

Baghdad was the world capital of chess. In the ninth and tenth centuries AD, Baghdad was to shatranj (the old Arabic form of chess) what Moscow is to the modern game. It was a cultured flourishing center, packed with chess grandmasters and theoreticians who wrote volume after volume on critical positions and opening theory.

Two of the key differences between shatranj and chess as we know it are that a win could be achieved by taking all your opponent's pieces (apart from his king) and some of the pieces moved differently. For example, pawns could only move one square, the bishop could only move two squares, jumping the intermediate one and any piece that was in its path, and the queen moved only one square diagonally. Rook, knight and king were identical to modern chess.

Chess was actually fortunate to have survived at all under Islam, since the game tended to violate two central prohibitions of the prophet, that against the making of images and that against gambling. The first objection was ingeniously circumvented by the adoption of abstract designs by the Arabs for their chess pieces. The problem of gambling, which was rife, was more serious. The solution was a diversionary countergambit. Various chess-loving Caliphs announced that chess was a preparation for war and thus permissible.

The problems concerning Islamic Law are still very real. Only recently has the Rafsanjani regime in Iran revoked the Ayatollah Khomeini's prohibition against playing chess, while Western chess masters travelling to Saudi Arabia are advised against bringing in Western chess sets. The Christian cross surmounting the kings might cause offence to devout customs officials.

The most renowned chess grandmaster in Baghdad was As-Suli (880-946AD). Just like Kasparov, he came from an area bordering the Caspian Sea, and he travelled to the capital from his far-flung outpost of empire to become the chess favorite of the Saddam Hussein of his day, the Caliph Al-Muktafi. In 940AD, according to the *Oxford Companion to Chess*, As-Suli made an indiscreet political comment and had to flee from Baghdad. He died in poverty in Basra. Following is an example of his play.

AS SULI VS. ANONYMOUS
Baghdad circa 940 AD

1.g3 g6; 2.g4. This would have been regarded as an aggressive and dashing opening line in the days when pawns did not have the privilege of advancing two squares on their first move. **2...f6; 3.e3 e6; 4.Ne2 d6; 5.Rg1 c6; 6.f3 b6; 7.f4 a6.**

In modern chess, Black's slow opening would be an invitation to disaster, but given the absence of early contact between the opposing forces in Shatranj, Black's idea of clearing the second rank in order to swing his queen's rook into action towards the center, via a7, is not to be dismissed. Still, Black's decision to postpone development of his pieces does allow White a dangerous temporary sacrifice.

8.f5 gxf5; 9.gxf5 exf5. Black has won a pawn, but White can easily regain it, when Black's pawns on the king's flank become scattered and weak.

10.Bh3 Ne7. Note that Black's bishop on c8 does not defend the pawn on f5.

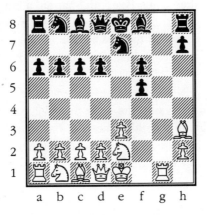

11.Rf1 Rg8; 12.Ng3 Rg5; 13.Bxf5 h6; 14.Bh3 Nd7; 15.d3 d5; 16.c3 Qc7; 17.b3 Ra7; 18.c4 Bd6; 19.Nc3 Be6; 20.cxd5 cxd5; 21.d4 Bf8. Black's long term problem is his isolated f6-pawn, exposed to attack in the open f-file

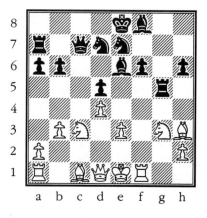

22.Rf2 Qd6; 23.b4 Rc7; 24.Kd2 b5; 25.Ba3. The White bishop is striving for an excellent square on c5. **25...Nb6; 26.Bc5 Nc6.**

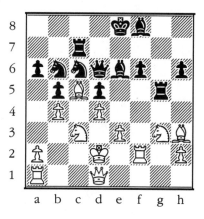

On c5 the White bishop is threatening Bxe7. In Shatranj a knight was worth considerably more than a bishop, hence the decision to remove it. White's next move is a consolidation measure, before returning to his siege of the pawn on f6. It was also possible to play 27.Rxf6 but then 27...Nc4+; 28.Ke2 Bg4+ is complicated. Remember that White's bishop on h3 does not control g4 in this ancient version of chess.

27.a3 Kf7; 28.Qc2 Bc4. 28...Nc4+ would have been better. **29.Raf1 Rg6; 30.Nh5.**

White's concentration of force against the weak f6-pawn is now overwhelming. **30...Ke8; 31.Nxf6+ Kd8; 32.N6xd5.** This is possible since the only black piece defending d5 is the knight on b6. 32...Rb7. There is no good way of defending the bishop on f8 which actually has no move. **33.Rxf8+ Kd7; 34.Bf5+ Ke6; 35.Nf4 mate.**

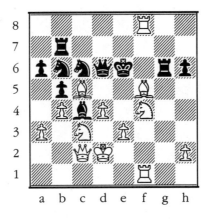

It is mate from the knight on f4. The bishops on c5 and f5 merely serve, respectively, to cut off the escape squares e7 and d7 from the Black king.

THE FIRST MODERN GAME

In the previous section I showed how Baghdad around AD930 was the center of world chess, but, although recognisable to modern eyes as chess, it was a game with certain restrictions concerning the powers of the queen and bishop. In 1475, a mere 22 years after the fall of Constantinople, the last bastion of the Roman empire, to the invading Ottoman Turks, the modern form of chess was introduced.

It was during the 15th century that castling was introduced, pawns gained the privilege of advancing two squares on the first move, and the queen was transformed from a waddling cripple of a piece (the Arabic vizier) to one of devastating mobility. This game, played at a time when the new chess had only been extant for 20 years, was created when Columbus was in the act of discovering America.

Within 20 years, it had obliterated the older version, propelled by the immense cultural influence and widespread dominance of communications exerted by the burgeoning Spanish empire, where the new chess, the variant now played across the planet, had first taken its roots. Here is the very first recorded game of modern chess, played 500 years ago.

FRANCESCO DI CASTELLVI VS. NARCISO VINOLES
Catalonia, circa 1493
Center Counter Defense

1.e4 d5; 2.exd5 Qxd5; 3.Nc3 Qd8; 4.Bc4 Nf6; 5.Nf3 Bg4. At this point Castellvi misses a trick, but it is one often overlooked in modern and social chess, so one should not be too hard on this early pioneer of the game. He could have played 6.Bxf7+ Kxf7; 7.Ne5+ Ke8; 8.Nxg4, winning a pawn and disrupting Black's position.

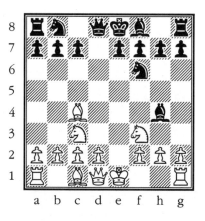

6.h3 Bxf3; 7.Qxf3 e6. But this is a much more serious error. Vinoles had to play 7...c6 to defend his queen's flank. **8.Qxb7.**

This capture is ruinous for Black, whose queen's flank is now decimated without mercy.

8...Nbd7; 9.Nb5 Rc8; 10.Nxa7 Nb6; 11.Nxc8 Nxc8; 12.d4 Nd6; 13.Bb5+ Nxb5; 14.Qxb5+ Nd7; 15.d5 exd5; 16.Be3 Bd6; 17.Rd1 Qf6; 18.Rxd5 Qg6; 19.Bf4. This terminates the game elegantly. White batters a path through Black's column of pieces on the d-file to come directly to grips with the black king. However, objectively speaking Black could now have tried 19...Qe4+ to muddy the waters, hence 19.0-0 would have been better.

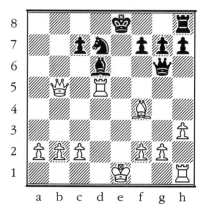

19...Bxf4; 20.Qxd7+ Kf8; 21.Qd8. Checkmate.

ANDRE PHILIDOR

In the 18th century, the great French master Andre Danican Philidor invented a new style of play. Formerly the leading masters had been obsessed with the power of the pieces on the open board, regarding the pawns, in contrast, mainly as cannon fodder to be sacrificed. Philidor revolutionized chess thinking by showing that pawn structure lay at the basis of strategic play.

He stood head and shoulders above his contemporaries in England and France - his only possible rivals in playing strength being the Modenese Masters, Giambattista Lolli, Domenico Ponziani and Ercole del Rio. Sadly, although they indulged in long-range literary polemics, Philidor never met any of these Italian masters face to face across the board.

It was not, however, Philidor's strategic insight which occasioned his renown in London and Paris, it was the Frenchman's extraordinary skill at playing blindfold chess simultaneously against three opponents, all of whom had sight of the board. Philidor seems to have found this feat easy and played with relative speed, usually making each move in less than 30 seconds. His hosts in London were duly amazed.

One report of the day ran:

"It is a phenomenon in the history of man, and so should be hoarded among the best samples of human memory - till memory should be no more. When the intrinsic difficulty of the game is considered, as well as the great skill of his adversaries, who, of course, conducted it with the most subtle complications; this exertion seems absolutely miraculous and certainly deserves to be recorded as a proof, at once interesting and astonishing, of the power of human intelligence."

Here is one of those blindfold games which caused such a stir in the fashionable London of the late 18th century:

COUNT BRUHL VS. PHILIDOR
Blindfold Simultaneous Display 1792
Bishop's Opening

1 e4 e5; 2.Bc4 c6; 3.Qe2 d6; 4.c3 f5; 5.d3 Nf6; 6.exf5 Bxf5; 7.d4 e4. Philidor's favorite strategem, establishing a pawn wedge in the center.

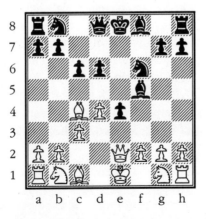

8.Bg5 d5; 9.Bb3 Bd6; 10.Nd2 Nbd7; 11.h3 h6; 12.Be3 Qe7; 13.f4 h5; 14.c4 a6; 15.cxd5 cxd5; 16.Qf2 0-0; 17.Ne2 b5. Preparing to occupy the outpost on c4.

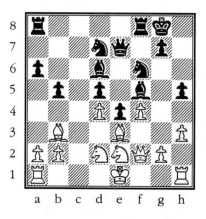

18.0-0 Nb6; 19.Ng3 g6; 20.Rac1 Nc4; 21.Nxf5 gxf5; 22.Qg3+ Qg7; 23.Qxg7+ Kxg7.

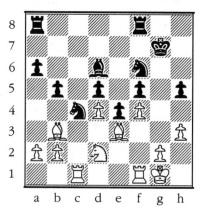

24.Bxc4 bxc4. Philidor is here let down by his penchant for capturing towards the center with his pawns. Instead, the divergent capture 24...dxc4! would lead to an overwhelming Black advantage, since the crushing ... Nd5 is coming.

25.g3 Rab8; 26.b3 Ba3; 27.Rc2 cxb3; 28.axb3 Rfc8; 29.Rxc8 Rxc8; 30.Ra1 Bb4; 31.Rxa6 Rc3. White has almost regained his balance, though Black's center pawns still give him the edge. **32.Kf2 Rd3; 33.Ra2 Bxd2; 34.Rxd2 Rxb3; 35.Rc2 h4; 36.Rc7+ Kg6; 37.gxh4 Nh5.**

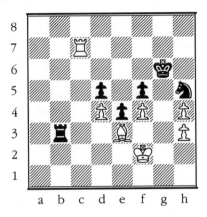

If now 38 Ke2 Rb2+ and ... Rh2. **38.Rd7 Nxf4; 39.Bxf4 Rf3+.** Now White should fight on with 40 Ke2! After the text, his king is temporarily cut off. **40.Kg2 Rxf4; 41.Rxd5 Rf3; 42.Rd8 Rd3; 43.d5 f4; 44.d6 Rd2+; 45.Kf1 Kf7; 46.h5 e3; 47.h6 f3. White resigns.**

The final avalanche of Black pawns is typical of a Philidor win.

PHILIDOR VS. COTTER
London, 1792

This extract shows that Philidor also had a fine sense for attacking combinations. Black is material ahead, but has neglected his development (neither Black rook has moved) and his king is stuck in the center. Philidor finished him off with elan:

1 Bxc6! If 1.Qd6, which is superficially attractive, then 1...0-0 allows Black to resist. **1...Bxc6.** Black should still castle, even though he would then be at a material disadvantage. Now, though, he is mated. **2.Rxe7+ Kxe7; 3.Qd6+ Ke8; 4.Qxc6+ Ke7; 5.Bd6+ Kd8; 6.Qc7+ Ke8; 7.Qe7. Checkmate.**

HOWARD STAUNTON

Staunton is a name known to every chessplayer throughout the English speaking world. He was a typical product of the self-confident Victorian age. By beating the French player Saint Amant he made himself the effective, though unofficial, champion of his day.

In 1851, Staunton organized a chess competition to coincide with the great London Exhibition, the imperial showcase of Queen Victoria's all-powerful Empire. Such was his energy and enthusiasm that he managed to persuade London's chess enthusiasts to subscribe a prize of £500, an enormous sum for the time.

His book on the event, *The Chess Tournament*, published in 1852, ushered in a new era of international competitive chess. The tournament was the pre-cursor of modern grandmaster tournaments, and of the World Championship cycle itself.

The first match which closely resembled a modern world championship was the Staunton-St. Amant contest in Paris in 1843, which established an Englishman, Howard Staunton, as the foremost player in the world. Twenty-one games were played and Staunton scored eleven wins to his opponent's six. We'll look at the first of those games now.

ST. AMANT VS. STAUNTON
Paris, 1st Match Game 1843
Sicilian Defense

1.e4 c5; 2.f4 e6; 3.Nf3 Nc6; 4.c3. White prepares to transpose into a variation of the French Defense one, however, in which he has taken on too many obligations. For instance, the early f4 does not fit in to the pure advanced variation. A more flexible alternative, and one favored by modern grandmasters is 4.Bb5 Nge7; 5.0-0 as in Larsen-Kavalek, Las Palmas 1974.

4...d5; 5.e5. Now we have the advance French, but White has difficulty in defending his broad center. **5...Nh6; 6.Na3 Be7; 7.Nc2 f5; 8.d4.** This is the kind of position in which Nigel Short would tend to play 8.exf6 en passant in order to open the e-file and somewhat weaken Black's kingside.

8...0-0; 9.Be2 Bd7; 10.0-0 Rc8; 11.Kh1 cxd4; 12.cxd4 Nf7; 13.Rg1. The commencement of a faulty plan. St Amant believes that the central battlefield is quiet, therefore he can open up a second front in safety. This turns out not to be the case. **13...Kh8; 14.g4.**

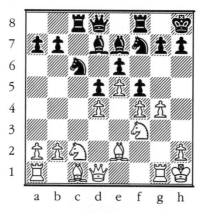

This is a capital error. If White wished to achieve the advance g4 he should, at least, have prefaced it with h3. As played the open g-file provides few benefits but the exchange of pawns which immediately ensues leaves White's kingside full of holes.

14...fxg4; 15.Rxg4 Nh6; 16.Rg3 Be8. As a natural consequence of White's misguided 14th move, Black's pieces begin to pour into the gaps that have appeared in White's pawn structure. The rerouting of Black's queen's bishop towards the kingside light squares is particularly dangerous for White. **17.Bd3 Bh5; 18.Qg1 Bh4; 19.Nxh4 Qxh4; 20.Ne1.**

Naturally not 20.Rxg7? which is immediately refuted by 20...Bf3+.

20...Nb4; 21.Bd2. If 21.Bf1 Black wins with 21...Rxc1; 22.Rxc1 Qxf4; 23.Nd3 Nxd3; 24.Bxd3 Bf3+; 25.Rg2 Bxg2+; 26.Qxg2 Qxc1+. **21...Nxd3; 22.Rxd3 Bg6; 23.Qg3 Qh5.**

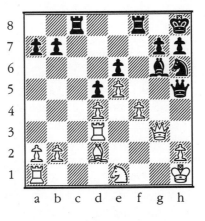

Black's concentration of force has reached decisive proportions. What follows might be termed a study, Black to play and win on the light squares. **24.Rb3 Qe2; 25.Qe3 Qf1+; 26.Qg1 Be4+.** The game is up. The Frenchman could have resigned but was probably reluctant to face his Waterloo so quickly in the first game of the contest.

27.Rf3 Bxf3+; 28.Nxf3 Qxf3+; 29.Qg2 Qxg2+; 30.Kxg2 Rc2; 31.Rd1 Rxf4; 32.Kg3 Rxd4; 33.Bxh6 Rxd1. White resigns

Staunton was a noted denizen of Simpson's-in-the-Strand, the Mecca for the masters and grandmasters of 19th century chess. For an entrance fee, gentlemen were allowed to congregate in the Grand Divan, play chess, drink coffee, smoke cigars, discuss the politics of the day and read the newly published journals. During the 1993 Kasparov-Short world championship, Simpson's once again became the great social focus for chess for the two-month period September and October. The championship press center was located there and chess enthusiasts were able to rub shoulders every day with their heroes and the notables of the game.

PAUL MORPHY - THE "INVENTOR" OF MODERN CHESS STYLE

Paul Morphy, one of the great chess champions, was born in New Orleans in 1837 and developed an exceptional talent from an early age. At the age of 13, he was already established as one of America's leading players. He came to Europe in 1858 and, to everyone's surprise, defeated the cream of European chess: Lowenthal, Harrwitz and Anderssen were all overwhelmed in matches over a six-month period.

Morphy was able to reach these astronomical heights in chess with relatively little traditional-style study of the game because he could depend upon a naturally studied and developed ability to make images and to translate this into an astonishingly powerful memory. Like Bidder, Heinecken, Magliabechi, and others before him, Morphy used the base of his knowledge to extend himself into other fields, acquiring on his way to chess mastery, four different languages and a degree in law.

Morphy also distinguished himself in another extraordinary mental memory field: blindfold chess. Morphy developed this skill to play many simultaneous games blindfolded - a mental test which requires a perfect recall of every new position in every simultaneous game. He also applied his memory to law and could recite verbatim most of the Civil Law Code of Louisiana.

Morphy certainly holds a high place in the all time pantheon of chess greats. In fact, he virtually invented the modern style of play. Morphy was well versed in the contemporary theory of the day - he made the theory. He had a perfect sight of the board, he played rapidly, he never blundered, he was ingenious, resourceful and possessed an outstanding endgame technique.

At the age of twelve in his home town of New Orleans, Morphy defeated the visiting European Master Lowenthal. This amazing feat established Morphy as a chess prodigy, a curious precursor of his compatriot Bobby Fischer. Seven years later in 1857 Morphy was invited to the first American Chess Congress held in New York. There he swept the field and defeated another outstanding European Master, Louis Paulsen, in the finals of the competition. The crushing margin of Morphy's victory five wins, two draws and just one loss, combined with the coruscating brilliance of his play left no doubt he was a star of the very first magnitude in the chess world firmament.

The way he played was staggering. It had a million dollar PR effect when he sacrificed his queen to force checkmate against Paulsen and the Americans went wild with enthusiasm. Encouraged by triumph on his home territory, Morphy left the US in 1858 for a grand European tour. In a series of set matches in London and Paris, he again overwhelmed Lowenthal, he beat Harrwitz and finally he destroyed the great Adolf Anderssen himself, the man who had been regarded as the de facto Chess Champion ever since the tournament in London in 1851. The margins of Morphy's superiority were astonishing, namely the opponents won one or two games but Morphy won games in droves. Had anyone thought of creating the official World Chess Championship at that time, Morphy would have been the laureate.

However, after beating Anderssen, Morphy played no more chess matches or indeed games against first class opponents. He confined himself to simultaneous displays, playing 20, 30, and even 40 people at once and casual games against inferior opponents where he habitually gave heavy odds, such as an extra rook, or an extra knight, at the start of the game. Morphy, in fact, issued a challenge to the world to play him at the odds of a pawn but no one took it up. In effect, Morphy was announcing that he was the world's greatest player and nobody could face him over the chess board. Thereafter, through the rest of his life, Morphy withdrew from chess.

Morphy only played two consultation games against Staunton, triumphing in both; here is the more dramatic of the two.

STAUNTON & PARTNER VS. MORPHY & PARTNER
London 1858
Philidor's Defense

1.e4 e5; 2.Nf3 d6; 3.d4 f5; 4.dxe5 fxe4; 5.Ng5 d5; 6.e6 Nh6; 7.Nc3 c6; 8.Ngxe4 dxe4. Modern theory recommends 8...Nf5 in this position as given by grandmaster Tony Kosten in his book, *Winning with the Philidor.*

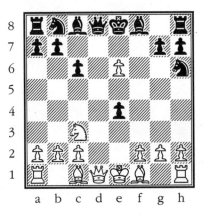

9.Qh5+ g6; 10.Qe5 Rg8. White should now play 11.Bg5! but at the time Staunton's choice was thought to be the best move. **11.Bxh6 Bxh6; 12.Rd1 Qg5.** This move improves on the 12...Qe7 played in the game Atwood-Wilson, London 1798, which proved to be too passive and led to a swift loss for Black. From the 60 years it took for this improvement to be found one can see that opening innovations travelled more slowly in the mid 19th century than they do nowadays, when the trip is sometimes reduced to hours!

13.Qc7. For Black to have permitted this intrusion, which threatens Qxc8+ as well as a mate on the move, is proof of steady nerves or most accurate calculation. **13...Bxe6; 14.Qxb7 e3.** Continuing an active defense. There is a threat of ... exf2+ and ... Qe3 mate.

15.f3 Qe7; 16.Qxa8. The capture of a rook, at the cost of the queen's embarrassment, is a well-known theme of chess tactics.

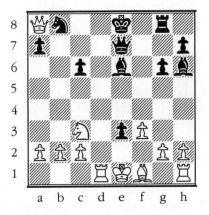

16...Kf7; 17.Ne4 Bf4; 18.Be2 Kg7; 19.0-0; 19.g3 is better, although the White allies wanted to castle as soon as possible. **19...Qc7.** At last the threat of winning the queen becomes effective (20...Nd7) and added to it is a subsidiary threat: 20...Bxh2+.

20.Nc5 Bxh2+; 21.Kh1 Bc8. Preventing 22.Qb7. **22.Rd4 Bg3.** With the threat of 23...Qe5. **23.Re4 Kh8; 24.Rd1 Qg7; 25.Rh4.** Preventing the deadly 25...Qh6+ in an ingenious manner. **25...Bxh4; 26.Qxb8.**

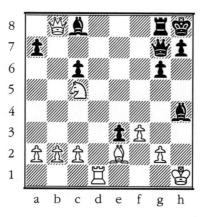

The queen has been saved, but at a disastrous cost. **26...Ba6; 27.Qh2 Bxe2; 28.Rd7 Qh6.** Attack and defense. If now 29.Qe5+, the counter-check 29...Bf6+ would be decisive. A mistake, however, would be 28...Qf6, because of 29.Ne4 Qe6; 30.Rxh7+ Kxh7; 31.Ng5+ followed by Nxe6.

29.Ne4. With the threat of 30.Nf6, which Black, however, parries in a manner as unexpected as it is conclusive. **29...Bc4; 30.Nf6 e2; 31.Re7 Qc1+; 32.Qg1 Qxg1+; 33.Kxg1 e1Q+; 34.Rxe1 Bxe1. White resigns.**

THE ADVENT OF THE OFFICIAL WORLD CHAMPIONSHIP MATCH

During the 1880's, Wilhelm Steinitz and Johannes Zukertort had emerged as clearly superior to all of their contemporaries. Both of them claimed to be the strongest player in the world. After a series of bitter verbal exchanges the two men finally met at the chessboard to resolve their conflict. Steinitz scored a decisive victory with ten wins to Zukertort's five.

The outstanding matches in the history of the World Chess Championship have, by general consent, been those which exhibited a fierce contrast in the playing style of the two protagonists. At the very dawn of recognized world championship play in 1886 the fiery imagination and tactical arsenal of Johannes Zukertort, although meeting with initial resounding successes, ultimately foundered on the rock hard strategic logic of the new scientific school propounded by Wilhelm Steinitz. After a series of fascinating games, Steinitz was declared the first official chess champion of the world.

The new champion held the title until 1894, when he lost a match to the rising German star Emanuel Lasker. A second defeat at Lasker's hands in 1896 was, perhaps, a partial cause of

Steinitz's suffering a nervous breakdown, from which he never fully recovered. He died in a state of poverty as a public ward of the City of New York in 1900.

Steinitz was the chief promoter of the 'Modern' school of chess, a system which rejected the pyrotechnics of sacrifices and combinations, concentrating instead on positional play aimed at the accumulation of small advantages. Yet Steinitz, too, was to meet his master eventually in the shape of Emanuel Lasker. For all his strategic skill Steinitz could not cope with the slippery shifting pragmatism of Lasker's style, a style possessed of such flexibility and resilience that it was to maintain Lasker's grip of the supreme title until 1921, when he was defeated by the Cuban genius Capablanca. However, when Lasker and Capablanca had first clashed at St Petersburg in 1914, Lasker proved the stronger.

Alexander Alekhine

Garry Kasparov has often stated that Alexander Alekhine is his chess hero. Their stylistic resemblance is clear to see. Both love combinations and the attack, though in 1927, when Alekhine had to face the virtually invincible Capablanca for the World Championship, he curbed his natural predilections in order to become a super-strategist. Kasparov had to learn the same lesson when struggling against Karpov six decades later.

From 1927 until 1946 (with a two-year gap after his defeat in the first match against Euwe) the genius Alexander Alekhine held sway over the chess world. Alekhine had a style so multi-faceted that he could outmatch Capablanca in the Cuban champion's own blend of trench warfare and victory by attrition. Nevertheless, Alekhine was far more at home in the confused tactical melées which characterized his four matches from 1929 until 1937 against Bogoljubow and Euwe.

The Soviet Reign

During the 1950's, chess was dominated by the Soviet School, exemplified by Botvinnik and Smyslov, players so close in style that their games were hardly distinguishable from each other. It was not until 1960, when the vibrant young Latvian, Mikhail Tal, inflicted a crushing defeat on Mikhail Botvinnik, that the stylistic clash to be found at the core of great matches once again became truly visible. Botvinnik's Olympian calm was repeatedly shattered by the Napoleonic force of the young Tal: their games were replete with grand strategic designs occasionally triumphing, but more often collapsing under the variegated assault of tempestuous tactical sorties.

For connoisseurs, the two matches between Botvinnik and Tal in 1960 and 1961 represented some of the most bloodthirsty and exciting chess seen at world championship level. Although he was defeated in the first match, Botvinnik, employing subtle psychology, triumphed in the second, exploiting Tal's dislike of simplification and the endgame.

Mikhail Botvinnik had won the World Championship in 1948, finishing ahead of Smyslov, Reshevsky, Keres and Euwe in the quintangular match tournament held to determine the new champion after Alekhine had died in possession of the title. During the 1950's and early 1960's Botvinnik had to fight off challenges from Mikhail Tal, as well as David Bronstein, Vassily

Smyslov and Tigran Petrosian.

Smyslov drew with Botvinnik in 1954, seized the championship in 1957 but a year later succumbed to Botvinnik's revenge match. As we have seen, Tal also briefly deposed Botvinnik, only to lose the title back in a revenge match. It was Petrosian, in 1963, who eventually and definitively unseated Botvinnik from the world throne, and this time Botvinnik did not have the right to a revenge match!

A Western World Champion

Although Petrosian narrowly succeeded in defending the title against Boris Spassky in 1966, he eventually relinquished it to Spassky in 1969. Spassky in turn was usurped by the unpredictable American Bobby Fischer in a titanic match in Reykjavik 1972.

Spassky was an adventurous attacker. His play was very much in the mould of Tal and Alekhine, yet in Fischer he succumbed to the prophet of heroic materialism. Fischer was a chess superman who would snatch material in a fashion that might have seemed sordid in a lesser player, only to release it at the appropriate moment for overwhelming advantages in terms of the initiative, mobility and striking power. It was a tragedy for the world of chess that Fischer ceded the title by default to Anatoly Karpov in 1975 and did not play a single serious tournament or match game for the two decades from 1972 to 1992.

The Greatest Rivalry

After successfully defending the title twice against the Soviet defector Viktor Korchnoi, Karpov had to face a fresh challenge in 1984 from Garry Kasparov, whose rise to challenger status had been nothing less than meteoric. Their first match ended in controversial circumstances when the FIDE President Florencio Campomanes stopped the match after more than five months' play, claiming exhaustion on the part of the contestants and organizers. Kasparov disputed this decision vehemently and accused Campomanes of coming to Karpov's aid, just when Kasparov was looking as if he might snatch victory from the jaws of defeat.

This injustice must have spurred Kasparov to greater efforts in his assault on the crown, for in the return match in 1985, he seized the title in dramatic fashion to become the youngest World Champion in history. Since 1985, Kasparov has successfully defended against Karpov on three occasions, most recently in the 1990 match, split between New York and Lyons. The apparent narrowness of Kasparov's margin of victory is illusory. Kasparov already had the match wrapped up by game 22, but slipped back to lose game 23 after he had already decided the contest in his favor.

After this match Karpov was defeated by Nigel Short in the elimination cycle and the challenger's baton was passed to the young Englishman. Short lost to Kasparov in 1993, and Kasparov successfully defended his title again in 1995 against Anand of India.

Roll of Honor of World Champions and Challengers

The roll of honor of champions reads as follows. In that roll of honor, Kasparov holds a special place, while Nigel Short and Vishy Anand join those illustrious challengers, such as

Johannes Zukertort, Mikhail Chigorin, Siegbert Tarrasch, Karl Schlechter, David Bronstein and Viktor Korchnoi, those immortals of chess, who have given their best, but still failed to wrest the supreme title.

World Champions

1886-1894 W. Steinitz (Austria)
1894-1921 E. Lasker (Germany)
1921-1927 J. Capablanca (Cuba)
1927-1935 A. Alekhine (Russia/France)
1935-1937 M. Euwe (Holland)
1937-1946 A. Alekhine (Russia/France)
1948-1957 M. Botvinnik (USSR)
1957-1958 V. Smyslov (USSR)
1958-1960 M. Botvinnik (USSR)
1960-1961 M. Tal (USSR)
1961-1963 M. Botvinnik (USSR)
1963-1969 T. Petrosian (USSR)
1969-1972 B. Spassky (USSR)
1972-1975 R. Fischer (USA)
1975-1985 A. Karpov (USSR/Russia)
1985-   G. Kasparov (USSR/Russia)

Challengers

1886   Zukertort (Prussia)
1889, 1892 Chigorin (Russia)
1890-91   Gunsberg (Hungary/UK)
1907   Marshall (USA)
1908   Tarrasch (Germany)
1910   Janowsky (Poland)
1910   Schlechter (Austria)
1929, 1934 Bogoljubow (Russia/Germany)
1951   Bronstein (USSR)
1978, 1981 Korchnoi (USSR/Switzerland)
1995   Short (UK)
1996   Anand (India)

The challengers listed are those who failed to go on to claim the ultimate title.

THE GREAT GAMES

This section gives games which have been decisive or important in the history of chess or the development of chess ideas. This game goes further. It was a crunch and grudge match, and pitted those two great rivals, Garry Kasparov and Anatoly Karpov, against each other.

Kasparov was racing ahead in the tournament, but a win by Karpov at this stage, playing with the advantage of White, would have meant that he caught up.

To add fuel to the flames, Kasparov had just declared that he would break away from FIDE, the World Chess Federation, to defend his title against Nigel Short under the auspices of the newly formed Professional Chess Association. Karpov, conversely, was about to announce that he would be prepared to take the FIDE title by default and play a match for the FIDE Championship with Short's vanquished opponent, the Dutchman Jan Timman.

The stage was set for a cliffhanger which could decide the fate of world chess. The notes to this crucial encounter are Kasparov's own.

KARPOV VS. KASPAROV
Linares 1993
King's Indian Defense

1.d4 Nf6; 2.c4 g6; 3.Nc3 Bg7; 4.e4 d6; 5.f3 0-0; 6.Be3 e5; 7.Nge2 c6; 8.Qd2 Nbd7; 9.Rd1 a6; 10.dxe5 Nxe5.

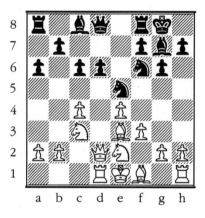

This move dooms the d6-pawn, but what true King's Indian player would be held back by such a trifle? It is much more important to create piece play.

11.b3 b5; 12.cxb5 axb5; 13.Qxd6 Nfd7.

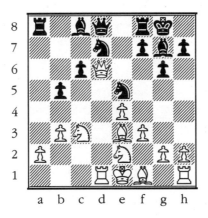

This position is extremely hard to analyze, because both sides have an alternative to almost every move in almost every line.

14.f4. Here, one of Karpov's greatest assets, his sense of danger, lets him down. 14.Bg1 was preferable. **14...b4!** The essence of Black's idea is as simple as it is effective. This is illustrated by the variations 15.Qxb4 c5!; 16.Bxc5 Nxc5; 17.Rxd8 Ned3+ and 15.Na4 Rxa4; 16.bxa4 Nc4; 17.Qd3 Nb2; 18.Qc2 Nxd1; 19.Qxd1 Qa5 with a clear advantage in both cases.

15.Nb1? This move is the decisive mistake. This may seem somewhat radical, but the almost forced variations that follow dispel all doubts. White had to try 15.fxe5 bxc3; 16.Nxc3 but then after 16...Qa5, Black has the better of the complications. **15...Ng4; 16.Bd4 Bxd4; 17.Qxd4 Rxa2; 18.h3 c5; 19.Qg1 Ngf6; 20.e5 Ne4; 21.h4 c4; 22.Nc1.**

How often do you see a sizeable White army huddled on the first rank after only 22 moves? Now I realized it was possible to ignore the attack on the rook.

22...c3!!; 23.Nxa2 c2.

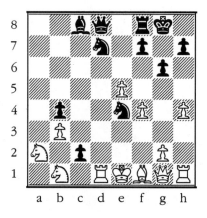

24.Qd4. Karpov avoids the beautiful loss which is inevitable after 24.Rc1 Nxe5!. The following variations are examples, 25.Rxc2 Bg4 and now:

a) 26.Be2 Nd3+; 27.Bxd3 Qxd3.

b) 26.Rd2 Nxd2; 27.Nxd2 Re8; 28.fxe5 Rxe5+; 29.Kf2 Qxd2+; 30.Kg3 Re3+; 31.Kh2 Rh3 mate.

c) 26.Nd2 Nd3+; 27.Bxd3 Qxd3; 28.Nxe4 Qxe4+; 29.Kd2 Qxf4+ with an elementary win in all variations.

24...cxd1Q+; 25.Kxd1 Ndc5; 26.Qxd8 Rxd8+; 27.Kc2 Nf2.

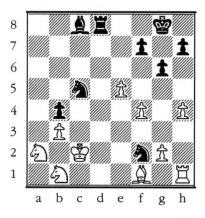

In this position White lost on time, thus saving himself the choice between 28.Rg1 Bf5+; 29.Kb2 Nd1+; 30.Ka1 Nxb3 mate or 30.Kc1 Nxb3 mate.

So, Kasparov had triumphed dramatically and reasserted his right at a most critical moment to be regarded as the strongest chessplayer in the world.

KASPAROV - ANAND

Kasparov obliterated Anand in their 1995 New York world championship match. By early 1999, Kasparov had played seven matches for the world championship and had not yet been defeated. With a reign that exceeds a decade, and having crushed his last two challengers, Kasparov must be considered one of the greatest, if not the greatest champion of all time.

Lasker and Alekhine, it is true, held the title respectively for 27 and 17 years, but in comparison with Kasparov, their title defenses were few and far between, and not always against the best opposition. Lasker, for example, managed to go 11 years without a title match, while Alekhine played frequently against Bogolyubov and Euwe rather than giving the more dangerous Capablanca a return bout.

Five of Kasparov's title matches were against Karpov, and resulted in extremely close outcomes. In comparison, Kasparov has waltzed away with the last two, defeating Nigel Short by a five point margin in London and Anand in New York by three points in a shorter match than had hitherto been the norm. Setting Karpov aside, who was eliminated by Nigel Short in the last cycle and who chose not to compete in this one, how do the performances of Short and Anand compare?

Short was clearly bowled over in the first part of his challenge. Thereafter, he squared up well to the champion and scored 50% over the final ten games. Anand, on the other hand, kept on a level footing with Kasparov, and even moved into the lead after game nine but then suddenly and dramatically collapsed. He was betrayed by his inexperience of match play, notably in repeating a risky opening for game ten and being slaughtered by Kasparov's home analysis. After a severe battering from games 10-14, in which Anand secured one miserable half-point, he more or less lost all stomach for the fight. Thereafter, only game 17 was a real struggle. The remaining games were perfunctory draws, allowing Kasparov to coast home.

Nigel Short was heavily criticized in 1993 for what many condemned as his poor showing. Yet the British grandmaster overperformed in terms of his rating at that time, and Anand's collapse in the latest match puts Short's result in clear perspective. Anand was lauded as a serious contender, yet once Kasparov put his mind to the task he was brushed aside like some minorly irritating bug. What truly distinguishes the two matches, though, was the fighting attitude displayed by Nigel Short, compared with Anand's supine surrender after his match situation became critical. There were some fine games this time, of course, but Anand truly gave up after game 14. Nigel, on the other hand, fought to the bitter end.

Here are three key moments from the New York match.

ANAND VS. KASPAROV
Intel World Championship, Game 9

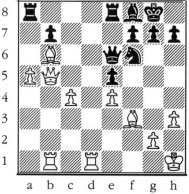

27.Rd5 Nxd5. The losing move. The world champion spent a mere seven minutes over this fateful decision, after which White's king's bishop is permitted to re-enter the fray with a vengeance. Kasparov must have hallucinated or vastly over estimated his own attacking chances against White's king, yet these remain negligable. The key factor is White's passed d-pawn, which now comes into life, and which is promoting on a square controlled by White's bishop, operating from b6. Anand said that Black should have played passively with 27...Rac8, when, according to the challenger, White is only 'slightly better'.

28.exd5 Qg6; 29.c5 e4; 30.Be2 Re5; 31.Qd7. This powerful incursion puts an end to Black's kingside demonstration, while simultaneously threatening to annihilate what remains of Black's queenside with Qxb7. If Black replies 31...Re7, then 32.Qg4 f5; 33.Qxg6 hxg6; 34.d6 with an easy win.

31...Rg5; 32.Rg1 e3; 33.d6 Rg3; 34.Qxb7 Qe6; 35.Kh2. Black resigns.

In game 11, Anand fell into a devilish trap. Thinking to win rook for knight, he unwittingly permitted Kasparov to snatch two pawns.

ANAND VS. KASPAROV
Intel World Championship, Game 11

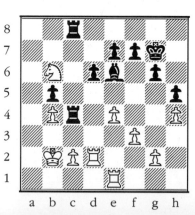

30...Rxb4+; 31.Ka3 Rxc2. This extraordinary tactical trick in a simplified position leaves Black two clear pawns ahead after either 32.Kxb4 Rxd2 or 32.Rxc2 Rb3+; 33.Ka2 Re3+; 34.Kb2 Rxe1.

The game which made it clear that Kasparov would stay on as champion was game 13. Here a hammer blow knight sacrifice on move 25 convinced Anand to resign on the spot.

ANAND VS. KASPAROV
Intel World Championship, Game 13

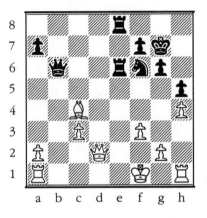

25...Ne4. If the knight is taken with 26.fxe4 then 26...Rf6+; 27.Ke1 Rxe4+; 28.Be2 Qf2+; 29.Kd1 Rxe2; 30.Qxe2 Rd6+. Alternatively, if White spurns Black's offer with 26.Qe1 then 26...Rd6; 27.Rd1 Rxd1; 28.Qxd1 allows a choice of mates by 28...Qf2 or 28...Ng3.

By his overwhelming victory against Anand, Kasparov, at the age of 32, has silenced all those critics who claimed he was past his best. Kasparov has now defeated Karpov, Short and Anand in match play, and must be considered one of the greatest, if not the greatest, champion of all time.

THE GREATEST CHESS PLAYERS OF ALL TIME

Chessplayers love statistics and are particularly fascinated with questions such as who was the greatest player of all time? This love of statistical evaluation can be observed, if by no other means, from the fact that the world chess federation issues a twice yearly mathematical ranking list containing thousands of names, each with a numerical ranking based on the mathematical theories of Professor Arpad Elo. On Elo's scale, 2700 represents world championship level, 2600 world championship candidate standard, 2500 grandmaster and 2400 approximately international master.

The secretary of the world chess federation ratings commission has issued some fascinating figures showing the *peak* ratings throughout the history of chess. Some time ago I collaborated with Professor Nathan Divinsky, the well-known chess statistician from the University of British Columbia, to work on *limetime averages* for the top players. It is interesting to compare the two sets of results for the leading positions in the tables below. In both tables, the top six show a truly remarkable degree of congruence.

Top Elo List	Top Divinsky List
1. Kasparov	Kasparov
2. Fischer	Karpov
3. Karpov	Fischer
4. Capablanca	Botvinnik
5. Botvinnik	Capablanca
6. Lasker	Lasker

WORLD CHESS RECORDS

Longest Reign as World Champion
Dr. Emanuel Lasker: 1894-1921 - a total of 26 years, 337 days.

Youngest World Champion
Garry Kasparov (born April 13, 1963) defeated Anatoly Karpov on November 9, 1985. Kasparov's precise age: 22 years, 210 days.

Oldest Player to hold the Championship
Wilhelm Steinitz (born 1836) who won the title in 1886 and held on to it until losing to Lasker on 26 May 1894. Champion at 58 years and 10 days.

Highest Rating
An Elo rating of 2820 by Garry Kasparov.

Highest Rated Female Player
Judit Polgar with a rating of 2675 in 1996, thus making her overall world number 10 at that time.

Youngest Grandmaster
Ruslan Ponomariev of the Ukraine in 1997, when 13 years old.

Most Invincible Player
Josè Capablanca who lost just 34 games out of 571 during his career as a chessplayer from 1909 to 1939. He established the amazing feat of remaining unbeaten over 63 Master and Grandmaster level games, including a World Championship match - from February 10, 1916 to 21 March 1924. This will be one of the hardest Mental World Records to break.

Judit Polgar Beats Fischer's record

Her last game of the Hungarian Championship won her both national crown and Grandmaster laurels.

Becoming a chess Grandmaster at the age of 15 is the kind of record one does not expect to see broken. Now, however, after a gap of more than 30 years, Bobby Fischer's record as the youngest-ever chess Grandmaster had been well and truly felled.

It was in 1958 at the Portoroz Interzonal leg of the World Championship qualifying tournament that Fischer established his record for becoming the world's youngest Grandmaster.

Fischer was born on March 9th, 1943, and on September 10th, 1958 he qualified from the Interzonal tournament for the World Championship Candidates event. This feat automatically made him a Grandmaster at the age of 15 years, 6 months and 1 day.

Fischer used to boast that he could give the odds of a knight to any woman and still beat her easily. It is, therefore, ironic that Judit Polgar, a teenage girl and the youngest of the three amazing Polgar sisters, had smashed his record. This was a feat, by the way, that had eluded such other modern greats as Kasparov, Karpov, Kamsky, Anand, and Nigel Short.

Judit Polgar confirmed her Grandmaster title in one of the most convincing manners possible. Not for her obscure victories against mediocre players in open tournaments, but a superb and dominating first prize in a super-strong Hungarian Championship. Hungary is well known as a nation with one of the strongest chess traditions, having won Olympic gold on more than one occasion.

Judit Polgar was born on July 23rd, 1976, and achieved Grandmasterdom on December 20th, 1991. Dramatically she saved the best until last, simultaneously earning the title and winning the championship with her victory in the last round. As a result, she became a Grandmaster at the age of 15 years, 4 months and 28 days, and we will be prepared to bet that Fischer could no longer give her any sort of odds and hope to emerge unscathed.

Judit and her two sisters, Zsofia and Zsuzsa (reigning Women's World Champion), are taking the chess world, traditionally a male bastion, by storm. They have all concentrated on chess since the age of four, their talent being fostered by their father Laszlo. He was convinced that conventional educational methods could not bring out the full potential in children. Although the oldest sister, Zsuzsa, at first showed an aptitude for mathematics, she quickly turned to chess as her favorite activity, and the younger siblings, not unnaturally, wanted to follow suit. When I asked Judit how she first began to learn chess she said: "We started with the knight. It has such an interesting move."

Polgar's Record Falls!

In January 1994 another Hungarian, Peter Leko, smashed Polgar's record, knocking more than a year off, when he gained his final norm at the tournament in Wijk aan Zee, Holland. He had already made two of the three required performances the previous year, one in Budapest, and one in Leon, Spain, but Wijk aan Zee was his strongest showing yet. In an international field which included two Candidates for the World Championship (and in which Leko himself was the only non-Grandmaster) he finished in equal third place.

Amazingly, Leko's new record of 14 years, 4 months and 22 days, was demolished by 13 year old Ruslan Ponomariev from the Ukraine who achieved the grandmaster title in 1997.

Records for Youngest Victories Against Grandmasters

1999: (World Record) Murugan Thiruchelvam, aged 10, defeated Levitt, in London.

1922: (Silver Medal Performance and US Record) Sam Reshevsky aged 10 beat Janowsky in New York.

1995: (Third youngest in World) Ganguly aged 11 beat Serper in Calcutta.

Simultaneous Marathon Chess World Record

On April 23-24, 1977, the Czech Grandmaster Vlastimil Hort played against 201 opponents at one and the same time. Venue: Seltjarnes, Iceland.

On January 6, 1996, Grandmaster Ulf Andersson played against 311 opponents simultaneously. He took 15 hours and 23 minutes to win 269 of them, draw 20, and lose just 2. Venue: Alvsjo, Sweden.

Consecutive Marathon Chess World Record

Master player Graham Burgess took 72 hours from Wednesday May 18, 1994, until Saturday May 21, at the London Chess Center, Euston, to win 431 games, draw 25 and lose 54, for an 87% score against opposition rated 1855 on average.

Man vs. Machine World Record

Garry Kasparov lost to the IBM Deep Blue computer in New York 1997 by the score of 3.5-2.5.

Blindfold Chess World Record

On February 1, 1925 in Paris, Alexander Alekhine played 28 boards simultaneously blindfold, scoring 22 wins, 3 losses and 3 draws. Although later players (including Alekhine himself, for example, at Chicago in 1932, where he took on 32 opponents) have slightly surpassed Alekhine's total of opponents, Alekhine's display against top French amateurs is regarded as having provided the greatest strength of opposition for such an exhibition.

Though standard over-the-board play requires a good memory, this is as nothing compared to the demands made by blindfold chess, particularly simultaneous blindfold chess, where a master or grandmaster takes on many opponents at the same time but without being allowed to see the board or pieces at any stage. I have tried this myself, successfully playing five games blindfold at one and the same time, but compared with the greats in the discipline this is mere dilettantism.

For example, Alexander Alekhine played 32 blindfold simultaneous games at Chicago in 1932, while George Koltanowski increased this to 34 at Edinburgh 1937 while at Sao Paulo in 1947 Miguel Najdorf took on 45 opponents.

A particular exponent of blindfold chess and the memory powers associated with it was the

American grandmaster Harry Nelson Pillsbury, and one feat which particularly delighted his audiences was to play, without being able to see any of the boards 12 games of chess and six games of draughts at the same time. While doing this he also conducted a game of duplicate whist.

On one occasion, at such a display, two professors read out to Pillsbury a sequence of 28 words and short phrases, which he only heard once. Pillsbury repeated them in the order given and then in reverse order and had no difficulty repeating them the next day. This randon collection of curious words and phrases is worth repeating for posterity. Perhaps readers would care to try it for themselves: antiphlogistine, periosteum, takadiastase, plasmon, Threlkeld, streptococcus, staphylococcus, micrococcus, plasmodium, Mississippi, Freiheit, Philadelphia, Cincinnatti, athletics, no war, Etchenberg, American, Russian, philosophy, Piet Potgelter's Rost, Sala Magundi, Oomisillecootsi, Bangmamvate, Schlechter's Nek, Manzinyama, theosophy, catechism, Madjescomalops.

What is the prime memory quality required for conducting numerous games of chess at once without the anchor of being able to see the boards and pieces? The suggestion is that it is 'simultaneous alternation', the power to remember every detail and then, as the positions shift to forget, in order to concentrate all one's energy on the next point and so on shifting like a searchlight until the game's end.

Here is a stunning example of blindfold vision.

PILLSBURY VS. HOWELL
12 Board Blindfold Simultaneous Display, Brooklyn 1900
Hampe-Allgaier Gambit

1.e4 e5; 2.Nc3 Nc6; 3.f4 exf4; 4.Nf3 g5; 5.h4 g4; 6.Ng5 h6; 7.Nxf7. White sacrifices a piece to expose the Black king.

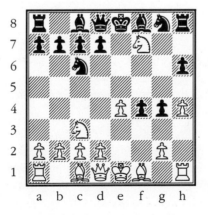

7...Kxf7; 8.d4 d5; 9.Bxf4 Bg7; 10.Be3 Bf6; 11.g3 dxe4; 12.Bc4+ Kg7; 13.0-0 Bxd4. Apparently decisive, but White has a diabolical tactic in his mind's eye.

14.Rf7+ Kg6; 15.h5+ Kxh5; 16.Rg7!! A brilliant coup. The threat is 17.Bf7 mate and if 17...Bxe3+; 18.Kg2 Qxd1; 19.Bf7 still finishes Black off.

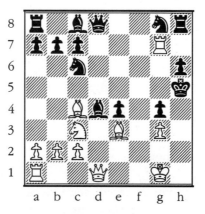

16...Ne5; 17.Bxd4 Ng6; 18.Kg2 Rh7; 19.Qh1+ Nh4+; 20.Qxh4+ Qxh4; 21.Bf7 check-mate. A colossal performance by a blindfold grandmaster against a sighted player.

THE GREATEST TOURNAMENT OF ALL TIME

The AVRO tournament of 1938, can lay claim to being the strongest tournament in the history of the game. It was packed with world champions and title contenders. The Estonian grandmaster Paul Keres tied for first prize with the American, Reuben Fine, but Keres was awarded the Palm on tie-break. It is notable that the AVRO field contained every player who held the world championship from 1921 to 1957. What is more, AVRO produced a huge number of very fine games. Here, for example, is Keres's win against the Cuban genius Capablanca.

KERES VS. CAPABLANCA
AVRO, Holland 1938
French Defense

1.e4 e6; 2.d4 d5; 3.Nd2 c5; 4.exd5 exd5; 5.Ngf3 Nc6; 6.Bb5 Qe7+. This check can be identified as the source of Black's further troubles. Although the move gains a pawn, its retention is merely temporary. Hence, the correct move would have been 6...Bd6, fluently completing his development.

7.Be2 cxd4; 8.0-0 Qc7; 9.Nb3 Bd6; 10.Nbxd4 a6; 11.b3 Nge7; 12.Bb2 0-0; 13.Nxc6 bxc6; 14.c4. A powerful thrust which undermines Black's central pawn structure. Whether Black plays ... dxc4 at some moment, or whether he simply waits for White to play cxd5 himself, Black is always in trouble.

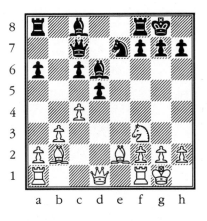

14...Be6; 15.Qc2 dxc4; 16.Bxc4 Bxc4. Capablanca seeks salvation in his time-honored technique of exchanges. In this case, unfortunately for him, the simplification merely serves to accentuate the vulnerability of Black's queenside pawns.

17.Qxc4 Rfb8; 18.h3 Rb5; 19.Rac1 Rc8; 20.Rfd1 Ng6; 21.Nd4 Rb6. As always, Capablanca's defense has been resilient, but now he overlooks a shattering knight sacrifice on an empty square, which brings the Black position to the verge of ruin.

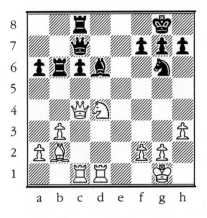

22.Ne6. A supremely elegant stroke, which exploits the superior coordination of White's forces to launch a winning attack. If now 22...fxe6; 23.Qxe6+ forks Black's king and bishop. Alternatively, if 22...Bh2+; 23.Kh1 fxe6; 24.Qxe6+ Kh8; 25.Rd7 and White wins.

22...Qb8; 23.Ng5 Rb7; 24.Qg4 Bf4; 25.Rc4 Rb5; 26.Nxf7 Re8. A miserable necessity, but if 26...Kxf7 White again wins with 27.Rd7+.

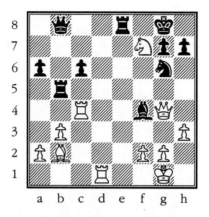

27.g3 Qc8; 28.Rxf4 Qxg4; 29.Rxg4 Kxf7; 30.Rd7+ Re7; 31.Rxe7+ Kxe7; 32.Bxg7 Ra5; 33.a4 Rc5; 34.Rb4 Ke6; 35.Kg2 h5; 36.Rc4 Rxc4; 37.bxc4 Kd6; 38.f4. Black resigns. A wonderful tour de force by Keres against an opponent widely considered to be invincible.

THE BEST GAMES OF CHESS EVER PLAYED
Lessons from the Chess Geniuses

It is commonly said that to watch the best in the world, whatever the activity, is a deeply rewarding experience. In chess we are lucky. Almost nothing that is truly great has been lost to us. Games of football or baseball played before the advent of television and video recording are only available to us in the form of bald statistics or the narration of the commentator. In chess, we actually have written records stretching back to the great civilization of Baghdad in the tenth century AD!

Similarly, we can still follow the moves of the one genuine game of chess played by Napoleon Bonaparte that has come down to posterity. The game is terrible, belying the great tactician's skill on the battlefield, but the moves are still there for all to see.

In this section I eschew such cultural curiosities and concentrate instead on my selection of some of the most dazzling gems in the archives of our game. It is a treasure store of the imagination, as often as not, proof that material sacrifice in chess demonstrates the sheer power of the brain to control and dominate matter.

Learn, but above all, enjoy and marvel at the exploits of the mind which will now unfold.

ANDERSEEN AND ZUKERTORT

In the 19th century, games between the top masters had a social atmosphere to them, which it would no longer be wise to replicate. In one of their world championship matches, for example, Steinitz was supplied with free champagne during the games, while his Russian challenger, Chigorin, had access to an unlimited supply of brandy to oil his cogitation.

The games, too, sometimes resembled the chivalric clash of feudal knights, with one side offering material for the attack, and the other accepting everything, almost as a matter of honor. Relish the wonderful world of the imagination which this game conjures up.

ANDERSSEN VS. ZUKERTORT
Barmen 1869
Evans Gambit

1.e4 e5; 2.Nf3 Nc6; 3.Bc4 Bc5; 4.b4. The Evans Gambit, introduced with this move, was all the rage in the latter half of the 19th century. From the mid-1890s onwards, though, good defensive methods were found and it lay more or less neglected until Kasparov himself revived it in 1995 in two buccaneering games against Anand and Piket.

4...Bxb4; 5.c3 Ba5; 6.d4 exd4; 7.0-0 Bb6. Modern investigation centers on 6...Nge7; 7.cxd4 d5; 8.exd5 Nxd5. Although Black's king is temporarily stuck in the center, his position is solid enough to withstand White's assault. In view of that, White might prefer the speculation 6...Nge7; 7.Ng5 Ne5; 8.Nxf7 Nxf7; 9.Bxf7+ Kxf7; 10.Qh5+ g6; 11.Qxa5, with an obscure situation to compensate for Black's extra pawn.

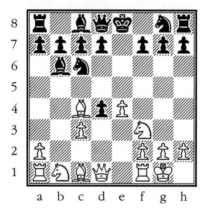

8.cxd4 d6; 9.d5 Na5; 10.Bb2 Ne7. Not 10...Nxc4 allowing 11.Bxg7, transfixing Black's rook in the corner. **11.Bd3.** Now 11.Bxg7 Rg8 is less happy for White.

11...0-0; 12.Nc3 Ng6; 13.Ne2 c5; 14.Qd2 f6. The game has crystallized into a race between Black's massive superiority in pawns on the queen's flank, and White's slow but massive build up of pieces on the other wing. Black's last move is designed to blunt the power of White's queen's bishop operating on the long diagonal.

15.Kh1. The start of a deep attacking plan. White needs the square g1 for his rook. **15...Bc7; 16.Rac1 Rb8; 17.Ng3 b5; 18.Nf5.**

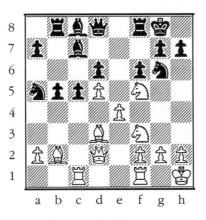

Two days later, in the same tournament, Anderssen, now playing Black, reached substantially the same position against the German master Louis Paulsen. In the later game Anderssen improved Black's play with the immediate 18...c4, which gains a vital tempo to activate Black's pawns by attacking White's bishop. Anderssen, in fact, went on to win that game too.

18...b4; 19.Rg1 Bb6; 20.g4. Now we see the full point of White's king retreat on move 15. White's g-pawn now acts as a battering ram, while its advance also creates the space for White to double his rooks on the g-file. **20...Ne5; 21.Bxe5.** It is better to trade this piece for Black's valuable knight on e5. White needs all of his forces in the vicinity of Black's king to stay at their posts. **21...dxe5.** If 21...fxe5 White can consider both 22.g5 and 22.Ng5. With the recapture in the text, Black hopes to strike directly at White's center with his newly liberated queen.

22.Rg3 Rf7; 23.g5 Bxf5; 24.exf5 Qxd5; 25.gxf6. White avoids the tempting 25.Bc4 Qxd2; 26.Bxf7+ Kxf7; 27.Nd2, when White's attack has vanished and Black's dangerous pawns are more than sufficient compensation for the loss of the exchange.

25...Rd8. Black would like to play 25...Rxf6, to eliminate the dangerous White pawn but then 26.Bc4 does not just win the exchange, it picks off the Black queen. **26.Rcg1.** A brilliant move planning to meet 26...Qxd3 with 27.Qh6 Qxf5; 28.Rxg7+ Kh8; 29.Ng5, exploiting the full murderous concentration of White force in the g-file. **26...Kh8; 27.fxg7+ Kg8; 28.Qh6.** Already threatening 29.Qxh7+ Kxh7; 30.Rh3+ Kg8; 31.Rh8 checkmate. **28...Qd6.**

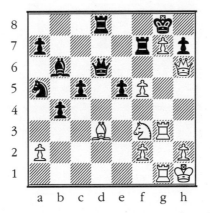

Black hoped with his last move to avoid the queen sacrifice. Here Anderssen announced mate in five moves with **29.Qxh7+ Kxh7; 30.f6+ Kg8.** 30...Qxd3; 31.Rh3+. **31.Bh7+ Kxh7; 32.Rh3+ Kg8; 33.Rh8 checkmate.** A sensational finale.

Lesson One
Learn the power of the queen, pushed right up against the enemy king.

PILLSBURY AND TARRASCH

The famous grandmaster and eloquent chess philospher, Richard Reti, wrote of the following thrilling encounter: 'We are all familiar with the film dramas, in which the hero or the heroine is in imminent danger of death, whilst at the same time other developments are taking place with a view to rescue. The audience follow the action and counteraction in breathless suspense, for to all appearances, the rescuers will arrive on the scene too late. Only at the very last moment, when all hope is abandoned, is the tragic end averted.'

Not just a great and nail-biting game, in terms of its ideas, this win against one of the leading contenders for the World Championship, was instrumental in catapulting the young American genius, Pillsbury, to the forefront of international attention.

PILLSBURY VS. TARRASCH
Hastings 1895
Queen's Gambit Declined

1.d4 d5; 2.c4 e6; 3.Nc3 Nf6; 4.Bg5. This is one of the super highways of modern opening theory, but in 1895 it was still relatively unexplored. Indeed, up until the previous decade, the move 4.e3 was common, locking in the queen's bishop, as often practised by Tarrasch's great German predecessor, Zukertort. The particular nuances and tensions of this bishop pin (quickly broken by Black's 4th move) were a fertile source of investigation for the Hastings masters.

4...Be7; 5.Nf3 Nbd7; 6.Rc1 0-0; 7.e3 b6; 8.cxd5 exd5; 9.Bd3. Pillsbury has a clear idea of attack in mind, based on Ne5 plus f4. Objectively though the right move here is Capablanca's 9.Bb5, exploiting the hole on c6.

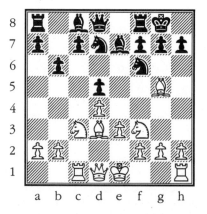

9...Bb7; 10.0-0 c5; 11.Re1 c4. In those early days of the Queen's Gambit Pillsbury was possibly anticipating a double pawn exchange on d4, when his rook on e1 would be well placed on the open file. Instead, Tarrasch proves that he can release the central tension in the interests of establishing an advanced force of pawns on the queen's flank.

12.Bb1 a6; 13.Ne5 b5; 14.f4. The famed Pillsbury Attack, a version of the Stonewall, but with White's queen's bishop outside the pawn chain. If Black plays passively he can be slaughtered by a maneuver such as Qf3-h3. **14...Re8; 15.Qf3 Nf8; 16.Ne2 Ne4.** Excellent decision. At the right moment Tarrasch blots out the attacking activity of White's lurking king's bishop.

17.Bxe7 Rxe7; 18.Bxe4 dxe4; 19.Qg3 f6; 20.Ng4 Kh8; 21.f5 Qd7; 22.Rf1 Rd8; 23.Rf4. Possibly not the correct continuation of the attack. White will not be able to break through against Black's king with pieces alone, he must mobilize his kingside pawns as an attacking force. In this context it is the knight on e2 which belongs on f4, not his rook. I would, therefore, suggest that the right attacking scheme is 23.Qh4 followed by Qh5 and only then Nf4.

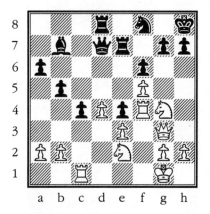

23...Qd6; 24.Qh4 Rde8; 25.Nc3 Bd5. Not 25...b4; 26.Na4 followed by Nc5. **26.Nf2 Qc6; 27.Rf1 b4; 28.Ne2 Qa4; 29.Ng4.** Threatening a sacrifice on f6. **29...Nd7; 30.R4f2.** White's queenside pawns seem to be at Black's mercy but Pillsbury keeps them alive with some elegant tactics. If now 30...Qxa2; 31.Nf4 Bf7; 32.Ng6+ Bxg6; 33.fxg6 h6 and now White can sacrifice on h6 with an ultimate win. **30...Kg8; 31.Nc1 c3.**

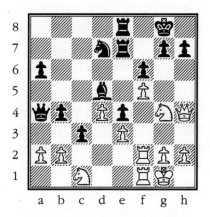

Black's fine strategy has established a passed pawn which will now be a winner for him, unless White can finally get some real action going on the opposite wing.

32.b3 Qc6; 33.h3 a5; 34.Nh2 a4; 35.g4. At long last White gets his pawns moving. His entire attack so far has been based on brilliant, but ephemeral tactical tricks. As I remarked before, the pieces on their own could not break through, he needs a pawn break too. However, it is all painfully slow, and Tarrasch could have made it even slower by now playing 35...h6. Instead, deeming White's late attack, to be desperation, Tarrasch throws caution to the winds and depletes the entire resources of his kingside defenses in order to smash the last vestiges of White's queenside fortifications. It all goes like clockwork, but he has missed a trick.

35...axb3; 36.axb3 Ra8; 37.g5 Ra3; 38.Ng4 Bxb3; 39.Rg2 Kh8; 40.gxf6 gxf6; 41.Nxb3 Rxb3; 42.Nh6 Rg7. Tarrasch had probably calculated up to this point and decided he could beat off the white attack and win with his connected passed pawns on the other flank. But now Pillsbury reveals the true extent of his attacking genius.

43.Rxg7 Kxg7; 44.Qg3+ Kxh6; 45.Kh1. One of the finest attacking moves in chess history and one which makes this game a classic. There is simply no defense to Rg1.

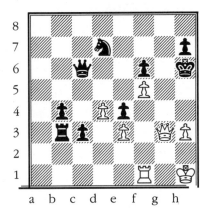

45...Qd5; 46.Rg1 Qxf5; 47.Qh4+ Qh5; 48.Qf4+ Qg5; 49.Rxg5 fxg5; 50.Qd6+ Kh5; 51.Qxd7 c2. He is, in any case, quite lost, for example 51...Rb1+; 52.Kg2 Kg6; 53.d5 Rb2+; 54.Kg3 c2; 55.Qe6+ Kh5 and now 56.h4!! forces mate in four moves. **52.Qxh7 checkmate.**

Lesson Two
The king is vulnerable to attack when cut off on an edge file.

ALEKHINE AND RESHEVSKY

One of my favorite Alekhine games was the turbulent one in which he beat Reshevsky in the Kemeri tournament of 1937. The concluding sacrificial combination to force checkmate is both astounding and beautiful. In the notes which follow I have taken account, both of Alekhine's original comments and the suggested improvements by John Nunn.

ALEKHINE VS. RESHEVSKY
Kemeri 1937
Alekhine's Defense

1.e4 Nf6. An amusing touch, the American grandmaster chooses the defense which Alekhine invented himself to play against its originator. **2.e5 Nd5; 3.Nf3 d6; 4.d4 Bg4; 5.c4 Nb6; 6.Be2 dxe5; 7.Nxe5.** One of Alekhine's specialities was the early pawn sacrifice to energize and complicate situations.

7...Bxe2; 8.Qxe2 Qxd4; 9.0-0. Later Alekhine was to recommend instead of this 9.Na3 N8d7; 10.Nf3, preserving more forces for the attack. **9...N8d7; 10.Nxd7 Nxd7.** Alekhine castigated this move, preferring 10...Qxd7 when the attack would continue by 11.a4 Qc6; 12.Na3 e6; 13.a5 Nd7; 14.Nb5. However, since, according to Dr. Nunn, Black's position remains well playable for some time, Black's tenth move can hardly be blamed.

11.Nc3 c6; 12.Be3 Qe5; 13.Rad1 e6; 14.Qf3 0-0-0. Reshevsky correctly returns material in order to complete his development. If now 15.Qxf7 Bd6; 16.g3 Rhf8 and Black wins. Instead, Alekhine restores the material balance by snatching a wing pawn, one which also happens to be an important defender of the Black king.

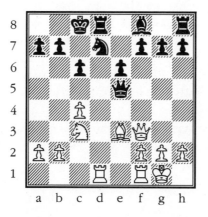

15.Bxa7 Qa5; 16.Bd4 Qf5; 17.Qg3. As Alekhine points out, 17.Qxf5 gives White a favorable endgame. Instead, Alekhine switches to a risky attack. **17...e5; 18.Be3 Bb4; 19.Na4 Ba5; 20.f4 Bc7; 21.b3 f6; 22.fxe5 Qe6; 23.h3 Rhg8; 24.Bd4 Nxe5; 25.Qc3 Nd7; 26.c5 Rge8; 27.b4.**

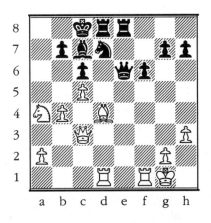

This is a key moment. As Alekhine explains in his notes, he hardly considered either here or at a later stage that Black might consume White's a2-pawn with his queen and thus grant White the open a-file for his own operations against the Black king. However, as Dr. Nunn points out, Black's centralization is so powerful that he can certainly get away with 27...Qxa2; 28.Ra1 Qd5; 29.Rfd1 (thus far Alekhine who stops here) and now the counterattack 29...Re2; 30.Bf2 Qf5, when Black's attack packs greater punch than White's. By postponing this possibility, Reshevsky allows Alekhine's attack against the Black king to gain decisive momentum.

27...Nb8; 28.Nb6+. With Black's knight withdrawn to the back rank, this knight check removes a further key defender of the Black king's field, namely the bishop. **28...Bxb6; 29.cxb6 Qxa2.** Now this pawn snatch really is dangerous for Black and allows White to introduce his rook into the black camp via the a-file.

30.Qg3 Rd7; 31.Bc5. A powerful post for the bishop but Alekhine shows in his notes that 31.Bxf6 gxf6; 32.Rxd7 Kxd7; 33.Qc7+ Ke6; 34.Re1+ would have been even faster. **31...Qf7; 32.Ra1 Qg6; 33.Qh2 Re5; 34.Ra8.**

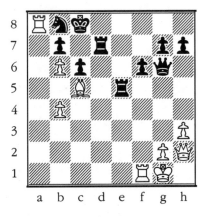

A tense moment with Reshevsky, as usual, in terrible time trouble. The American now lashes out with a seemingly aggressive move which, though, permits Alekhine a stunning sacrificial conclusion leading to checkmate. In his notes, Alekhine states that the alternative 34...Qe8 loses quickly to 35.Qg3 followed by Qa3 and a decisive breakthrough by White's queen in the a-file. Nunn writes, in contrast, in his additional commentary: 'Alekhine only analyzes one alternative to the blunder actually played - the almost equally weak move 34...Qe8, which allows the White queen to enter the attack. Black should have prevented the sacrifice on e5 by 34...Qg5 which both retains the black queen's active position and keeps the White queen in its box.' However after 34...Qg5; 35.h4 Qh5 (or 35...Qd2; 36.Qg3) 36.Qg3 Rd1; 37.Rxd1 Qxd1+; 38.Kh2, White still has plenty to play for. In my opinion the position after 34...Qg5; 35.h4 deserves further analysis and it cannot be said that Black has clearly survived.

34...Rd2; 35.Rxb8+ Kxb8; 36.Qxe5+ fxe5; 37.Rf8+. Black resigns. I give the last word to Alekhine himself: 'I must admit that the final attack gave me much more pleasure that a scientifically correct exploitation. After all, chess is not only knowledge and logic!'

> ## Lesson Three
> Watch out for back rank mates, even in the middlegame.

Bronstein and Keres

Soviet grandmaster David Bronstein first came to prominence in the 1940s, when he won a series of brilliant games with new and dazzling variations of the King's Indian Defense. In 1950 he emerged victorious from the first Candidates' tournament and went on to challenge Botvinnik for the supreme title in 1951. The ultimate score of 12-12 was creditable to Bronstein, but he never quite got over the fact that a drawn result left Botvinnik in possession of the title. Although Bronstein continued to amaze his contemporaries with the depth and sparkle of his ideas for the next decade or so, in sporting terms he was soon to be overshadowed both by Smyslov and Tal. He never challenged for the world title again.

The following game, one of my all-time favorites, is typical of the coruscating fare on offer in Bronstein's games.

BRONSTEIN VS. KERES
Goteborg Interzonal 1955
Nimzo-Indian Defense

1.d4 Nf6; 2.c4 e6; 3.Nc3 Bb4; 4.e3 c5; 5.Bd3 b6. A plausible method of developing his queen's bishop, which would be quite in order if White continued with 6.Nf3 Bb7; 7.0-0 0-0, reaching a normal position. Unfortunately, White has an improvement, which exploits the premature commitment of Black's queen's bishop to the long diagonal. We now know that 5...Nc6 placing immediate pressure on White's center, is more accurate.

6.Nge2. The perfect response. This knight is ultimately heading for g3 and f5 to exploit the fact that Black's queen's bishop will be moving away from its king's defense.

6...Bb7; 7.0-0 cxd4; 8.exd4 0-0; 9.d5. With this move Bronstein advances in the center and simultaneously announces that he will not be afraid of material sacrifice to lure Black's forces away from their king's fortress.

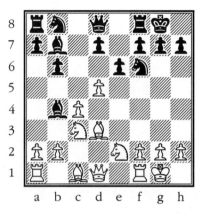

9...h6; 10.Bc2. Building up an ominous battery against the black king. **10...Na6; 11.Nb5 exd5; 12.a3 Be7; 13.Ng3.** White's pieces move in for the kill. The sacrifice of two pawns is well worth the chances White now obtains.

13...dxc4. A move which demonstrates a serious underestimation of White's chances. It was high time to ferry units across to the defense with 13...Nc5.

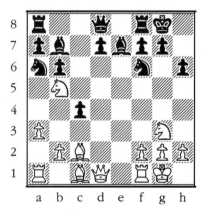

14.Bxh6. In addition to the two pawns, White now sacrifices a piece in order to demolish the barricades around the Black monarch. Black has little choice but to accept.

14...gxh6; 15.Qd2 Nh7. Black has several alternatives here, but all of them leave White with a menacing initiative. For example, 15...Nc5; 16.Qxh6 Nce4; 17.Rae1 d5; 18.Nf5 Ne8; 19.Bxe4 dxe4; 20.Re3 Bg5; 21.Rg3 f6; 22.Qg6+ followed by Rh3+.

16.Qxh6 f5; 17.Nxf5 Rxf5. If 17...Rf7; 18.Nbd6 Qf8; 19.Qg6+ Rg7; 20.Nh6+ Kh8; 21.Ndf7+ Rxf7; 22.Nxf7+ and White wins. Keres, therefore, decides that the time has come to give back some material.

18.Bxf5 Nf8.

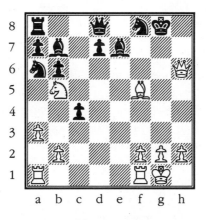

Bronstein now has rook and pawn for two minor pieces, an approximate material equivalent. Nevertheless, the fact that Black's king has been totally stripped of its pawn protection means that White has all the winning chances.

19.Rad1 Bg5; 20.Qh5 Qf6; 21.Nd6 Bc6; 22.Qg4 Kh8; 23.Be4. Evidence of Bronstein's breadth of vision. He now turns his attention to the queen's flank. **23...Bh6; 24.Bxc6 dxc6; 25.Qxc4 Nc5; 26.b4 Nce6; 27.Qxc6 Rb8; 28.Ne4 Qg6; 29.Rd6.**

White's victory is now secure, since the two extra pawns he has garnered even guarantee him a material advantage. The time has come to switch the attack back against the Black king.

29...Bg7; 30.f4 Qg4; 31.h3 Qe2; 32.Ng3 Qe3+; 33.Kh2 Nd4; 34.Qd5 Re8; 35.Nh5. Designed to remove Black's last good defensive piece. **35...Ne2; 36.Nxg7 Qg3+; 37.Kh1 Nxf4.** Black has to lose further material. After 37...Qxg7; 38.Qh5+ or 37...Kxg7; 38.Qe5+ Black loses his knight on e2.

38.Qf3 Ne2; 39.Rh6+ Black resigns. This brilliant performance was awarded the beauty prize in the tournament.

Lesson Four
It is possible to make substantial material sacrifices if you can annihilate
the pawn shelter around the enemy king.

KERES AND PETROSIAN

The best games of Tigran Petrosian, world champion from 1963 to 1969, were supremely instructive. For the student, Petrosian's sublime mastery of chess strategy was profoundly revealing of the correct way to build up an advantage. Petrosian produced more strategic masterpieces, jewels of chessboard art, than any of his predecessors.

When young players mention their chess heroes the names which spring to mind are usually the overtly aggressive and dynamic champions such as Fischer or Tal, Kasparov, Morphy or Alekhine. Nevertheless, the Hungarian prodigy Peter Leko, who briefly became the world's youngest ever grandmaster, admires Petrosian's maneuvering ability and logic.

The following game shows what it was about Petrosian that might have inspired the young grandmaster.

KERES BLACK: PETROSIAN
Candidates Tournament 1959
Sicilian Defense

1.e4 c5; 2.Nf3 Nc6; 3.d4 cxd4; 4.Nxd4 g6; 5.c4 Bg7; 6.Be3 Nf6; 7.Nc3 Ng4; 8.Qxg4 Nxd4; 9.Qd1 Ne6; 10.Qd2 d6; 11.Be2 Bd7.

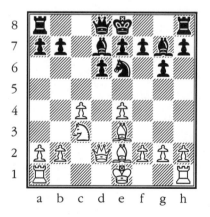

Black has chosen a somewhat passive and cramped opening system, but one that displays immense resilience. In order to break it down, White will have to attempt some extraordinary measure.

12.0-0 0-0; 13.Rac1. Seven years later Petrosian reached this position again as Black against the Danish grandmaster Bent Larsen in the tournament at Santa Monica. There Larsen chose the brutally direct 13.Rad1 and did indeed whip up a deadly attack after 13...Bc6; 14.Nd5 Re8;

15.f4 Nc7; 16.f5. Keres chooses a more placid course which, however, enables Black to consolidate his position.

13...Bc6; 14.Rfd1 Nc5; 15.f3 a5; 16.b3 Qb6; 17.Nb5 Rfc8; 18.Bf1 Qd8; 19.Qf2 Qe8. Black's eel-like defense has so far managed to contain all the dangers. If now, for example, 20.Bxc5 dxc5; 21.Qxc5 Bh6 when White's queen's rook has no truly satisfactory retreat square.

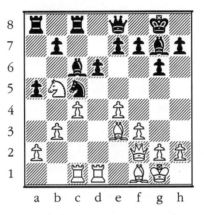

20.Nc3 b6; 21.Rc2 Qf8; 22.Qd2 Bd7; 23.Nd5 Rab8; 24.Bg5 Re8; 25.Re1 Rb7; 26.Qf2 Bc6; 27.Qh4 f6; 28.Be3 e6; 29.Nc3 Rd7; 30.Bd4 f5. After patient defense Petrosian begins to open up the game and to seek the initiative.

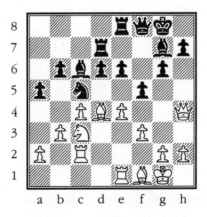

31.exf5 gxf5; 32.Rd2 Bxd4+; 33.Rxd4 Rg7; 34.Kh1 Rg6. It is typical of Petrosian that this rook not only stands ready for aggression in the g-file but also defends laterally the pawns on e6 and d6.

35.Rd2 Rd8. The start of a maneuver to slide this rook along the second rank to its most aggressive post, joining its colleague on the open g-file. **36.Red1 Rd7; 37.Qf2 Qd8; 38.Qe3 e5; 39.f4 e4?** An inexactitude committed under time pressure which allows White to gain the advantage, albeit temporarily. Black should maintain the fluidity of his attack with 39...Qh4.

40.Ne2 Rdg7; 41.Nd4 Bd7; 42.a3. This preparation is too slow and should be replaced with 42 Nb5 placing immediate pressure on the Black d6 pawn.

42...Qa8. Brilliantly blending defense with aggression and intending to meet 43.b4 with 43...axb4; 44.axb4 Nd3.

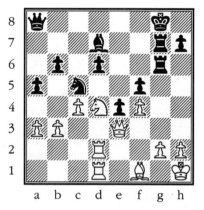

43.Kg1 h5; 44.Rb1 h4; 45.Rbb2 Rg4; 46.Rf2 Qd8; 47.b4 Rg3. An amazing sacrifice of a rook. Petrosian now plays beautifully to extract the utmost from his pressure in the g-file.

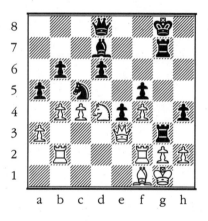

48.hxg3 hxg3; 49.Rfc2 Qh4; 50.Be2 Rh7; 51.Kf1. Keres overlooks a sensational finale. He had to try 51.Bh5 first to make a flight square for his king.

51...Qxf4+.

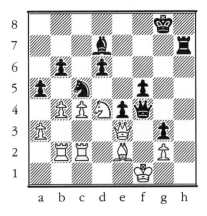

White resigns on account of 52.Qxf4 Rh1 mate.

Lesson Five

It is nearly always a good thing to double rooks on an open file which aims at your opponent's king. Think of the doubled rooks as massed artillery!

FISCHER AND SPASSKY

Boris Spassky, who seized the world title from Tigran Petrosian at Moscow in 1969, was an adventurous attacker. His play was very much in the mould of Tal and Alekhine, yet in Fischer he succumbed to the prophet of heroic materialism. Fischer was a chess superman who would snatch material in a fashion that might have seemed sordid in a lesser player, only to release it at the appropriate moment for overwhelming advantages in terms of the initiative, mobility and striking power. It was a tragedy for the world of chess that Fischer did not play a single serious tournament or match game for the two decades from 1972 to 1992.

The most dramatic game I ever witnessed at Olympic level was the 1970 battle between Boris Spassky, then at the height of his powers and Bobby Fischer. Everyone knew that these were the best two chessplayers in the world and that no mercy would be asked or given in their encounter.

SPASSKY VS. FISCHER
Siegen Olympiad 1970
Gruenfeld Defense

1.d4 Nf6; 2.c4 g6; 3.Nc3 d5; 4.cxd5 Nxd5; 5.e4 Nxc3; 6.bxc3 Bg7; 7.Bc4 c5; 8.Ne2 Nc6; 9.Be3 0-0; 10.0-0 Qc7.

A main line position from the Gruenfeld Defense. This cedes White a gigantic pawn center in return for lateral pressure. It had been one of Fischer's favorite defenses but it is significant that after this game he never repeated it against Spassky in their 1972 world championship match.

11.Rc1 Rd8; 12.h3 b6; 13.f4 e6; 14.Qe1 Na5; 15.Bd3 f5; 16.g4.

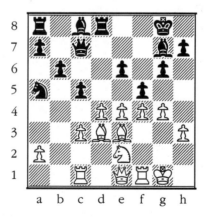

Typical of the aggression displayed by the Spassky of a quarter of a century ago. If White does nothing Black will gradually take over control of the light squares. This move seems to wreck White's pawn cover around his king but the ultimate objective is to blast a path through to the Black monarch.

16...fxe4; 17.Bxe4 Bb7; 18.Ng3 Nc4; 19.Bxb7 Qxb7; 20.Bf2 Qc6; 21.Qe2 cxd4; 22.cxd4 b5; 23.Ne4 Bxd4. Fischer loved taking material but snatching this bait is probably too dangerous. Black could have maintained a very comfortable position with the prophylactic 23...Re8 followed by ... Rad8. The likely outcome would have been a draw.

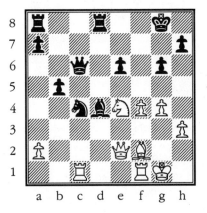

24.Ng5 Bxf2+; 25.Rxf2 Rd6; 26.Re1 Qb6; 27.Ne4 Rd4; 28.Nf6+. The absence of Black's fianchettoed bishop makes this invasion possible. **28...Kh8; 29.Qxe6.**

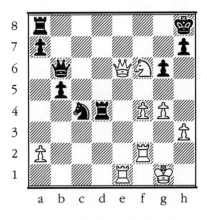

A moment of high drama which had the spectators enthralled. Fischer had initially planned the diabolical refutation of Spassky's play 29...Rd1. At the last minute, though, he recoiled having noticed the even more fiendish response 30.Qf7!! Rxe1+; 31.Kg2 Qc6+; 32.Kg3 Re3+; 33.Kh4 Rxh3+; 34.Kxh3 Qh1+; 35.Rh2 and White wins or 31...Ne3+; 32.Kf3 Qc6+; 33.Kg3 Rg1+; 34.Kh4 Rxg4+; 35.hxg4 Qh1+; 36.Kg5 Rc8; 37.Rd2 Nxg4; 38.Rc2 Rd8; 39.Re2 and White wins.

29...Rd6; 30.Qe4 Rf8; 31.g5 Rd2; 32.Ref1 Qc7; 33.Rxd2 Nxd2; 34.Qd4 Rd8; 35.Nd5+ Kg8; 36.Rf2 Nc4; 37.Re2 Rd6. White's attack has crashed through and this reliance on a flimsy pin to avoid losing his queen is evidently desperate.

38.Re8+ Kf7; 39.Rf8+. Black resigns.

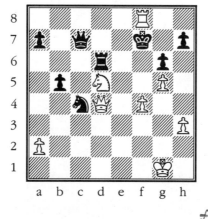

White's final coup has netted Fischer's queen after 39...Kx~~h~~8; 40.Q~~f~~8+.

Lesson Six
Observe the enormous power of a knight established on the sixth rank.

Ivanchuk and Shirov

The Ukranian Grandmaster, Vassily Ivanchuk, has enjoyed an extraordinary run of success, including first prize in three consecutive tournaments. These were at Horgen (Switzerland) 1995, where he bested Kasparov, in the Dutch town of Wijk aan Zee, where he finished ahead of the world championship challenger, Anand, and in the Keres Memorial tournament in Tallinn. In Wijk aan Zee, Ivanchuk revealed a facet of his chess personality which has made him such a feared competitor on the international circuit, colossal creativity allied with in depth research. His 21st move in the game which follows is a fantastic contribution to the theory of the variation, hurling his queen into the vitals of the black position, where it can simply be captured by a bishop.

IVANCHUK VS. SHIROV
Wijk aan Zee 1996
Semi-Slav Defense

1.d4 d5; 2.c4 c6; 3.Nc3 Nf6; 4.Nf3 e6; 5.Bg5 dxc4; 6.e4 b5; 7.e5. Apparently winning a piece, as a result of the pin against Black's knight on f6. However, Black has a resource which staves off immediate material loss.

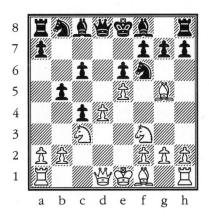

7...h6; 8.Bh4 g5; 9.Nxg5. This temporary piece sacrifice is obligatory, since 9.Bg3 is a feeble retreat. With the knight offer, White is guaranteed to win back his material, since he re-establishes the pin against Black's king's knight. White also decimates the Black kingside, but in compensation Black gains numerous open files, a mass of mobile queenside pawns, and usually manages to castle his king into relative safety on the queenside.

9...hxg5; 10.Bxg5 Nbd7; 11.exf6 Bb7; 12.g3 c5; 13.d5 Qb6.

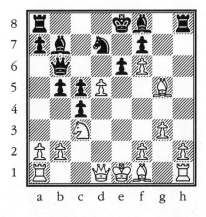

Botvinnik introduced this variation around half a century ago. It is extremely double-edged, with material values changing by the minute. It has become one of the most heavily analyzed in chess theory, with multiple alternatives for each player at almost every move.

14.Bg2 0-0-0; 15.0-0 b4; 16.Na4 Qb5; 17.a3 exd5; 18.axb4 cxb4; 19.Be3 Nc5; 20.Qg4+. The players have reached a key position from this system. Now 20...Kb8; 21.Qd4 Nxa4; 22.Qxa7+ Kc7; 23.Rxa4 Ra8; 24.Qxa8 Bxa8; 25.Rxa8 has been known to be good for White since the game between the Russian Grandmaster Agzamov, and the editor of the British Chess Magazine Murray Chandler, played in the USSR in 1982.

20...Rd7.

A monograph by the Russian Grandmasters Beliavsky and Mikhailcisin claims that White could now gain the better chances with 21.Nxc5 Bxc5; 22.Qg7 Rhd8; 23.Bxc5 Qxc5; 24.Bh3. This pin wins rook for bishop but Black has immense compensation in terms of his mass of center and queenside pawns.

21.Qg7!! Ivanchuk evidently distrusted the published analysis and discovers instead an extraordinary move, sacrificing his queen on one wing to deplete Black's defensive resources on the other.

21...Bxg7; 22.fxg7 Rg8; 23.Nxc5 d4. The best try. If 23...Rxg7; 24.Bh3 Bc6; 25.Rxa7 or 23...Rc7; 24.Nxb7 Rxb7 and now 25.Bd4 gives White a powerful initiative, despite having only two pieces for the queen. **24.Bxb7+ Rxb7; 25.Nxb7 Qb6; 26.Bxd4 Qxd4; 27.Rfd1 Qxb2; 28.Nd6+ Kb8; 29.Rdb1.**

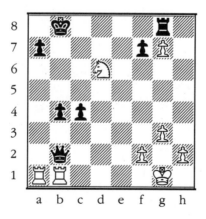

29...Qxg7. Now Black is clearly losing. The best try was 29...Qe5; 30.Rxb4+ Kc7 when one possibility is for White to force a favorable rook endgame with 31.Rb7+ Kxd6; 32.Ra6+ Kd5; 33.Rb5+ Kd4; 34.Rxe5 Kxe5; 35.Rxa7 Rxg7; 36.Rc7 but Black still has drawing chances.

30.Rxb4+ Kc7; 31.Ra6. Another finesse, closing in on the Black king. To prevent 32.Rb7+ Black must jettison material. **31...Rb8; 32.Rxa7+ Kxd6; 33.Rxb8 Qg4; 34.Rd8+ Kc6; 35.Ra1.**

Black resigns. White intends Rc1 and Rd2-c2, cleaning up the c-pawn, a plan against which Black has no reasonable defense.

> ## Lesson Seven
> Combine attacks on both wings.

KASPAROV AND KRAMNIK

There are various permutations of the aspirants for the rival world championship titles, that of the PCA (Professional Chess Association) and of FIDE (World Chess Federation). In 1999, Kasparov was the PCA champion, Karpov was the FIDE champion, and Kamsky had been the FIDE challenger. A fourth K entered the lists in the shape of Vladimir Kramnik. He had no official title or position in the hierarchy of opposing title contests, but his recent results and, in particular, his brilliant play mark him out as a man who is playing like a true world champion. Once the PCA and FIDE sort out their respective cycles, Kramnik may well be the grandmaster most likely to unify the two titles. As Botvinnik once said of Kasparov, the future of chess lies in the hands of this young man.

In the Seville tournament 1996, with an average of 2715 international rating points, the most powerful tournament of the year, Kramnik not only shared first prize with Topalov from Bulgaria but also obliterated Kasparov, Anand and Ivanchuk in brilliant games. Here is how he crushed the PCA world champion.

KASPAROV VS. KRAMNIK
Seville 1996
Semi-Slav Defense

1.d4 d5; 2.c4 c6; 3.Nc3 Nf6; 4.Nf3 e6; 5.e3 Nbd7; 6.Bd3 dxc4; 7.Bxc4 b5; 8.Bd3 Bb7; 9.0-0 a6; 10.e4 c5; 11.d5 c4; 12.Bc2 Qc7.

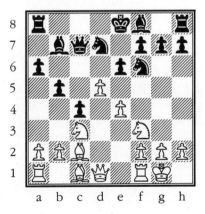

This position has become extremely popular in modern grandmaster circles. The situation is unbalanced, both sides have chances and Black can sometimes inflame matters further by castling queenside. White's normal choice here is 13.dxe6 fxe6 and now there are two possibilities:

a) 14.Ng5 Nc5; 15.e5 Qxe5; 16.Re1 Qd6 (Karpov-Kramnik, Linares 1994). White has sacrificed a pawn for a dangerous initiative and went on to win, though subsequent analysis indicated that Black could have held on.

b) 14.Nd4 Nc5; 15.Be3 0-0-0; 16.Qe2 e5; 17.Nf3 (Lautier-Gelfand, Amsterdam 1996). Now Black snatched the bait of White's e-pawn with 17...Ncxe4 and went on to lose. Instead the defensive 17...Kb8 is a possible improvement. Clearly, Kasparov was not inspired to repeat this variation from White's side.

13.Nd4 Nc5; 14.b4 cxb3; 15.axb3 b4; 16.Na4 Ncxe4.

17.Bxe4. Now is the time to open up the center with 17.dxe6 Rd8; 18.exf7+ Kxf7; 19.Be3 as in the game Yakovich-Sorokin, Calcutta 1991. The text implies that Kasparov had forgotten the main line since it appears illogical to surrender the bishop pair in a fluid position for no obvious compensation. **17...Nxe4; 18.dxe6 Bd6; 19.exf7+ Qxf7; 20.f3 Qh5.**

The threats against h2 give White no time to capture Black's knight. White must now start thinking seriously about defense. **21.g3 0-0.** Adding fuel to the flames. Conversely, White must now capture Black's knight, before it sacrifices itself on g3 and annihilates White's king's protection.

22.fxe4 Qh3; 23.Nf3. For his piece Black has no material compensation whatsoever, but he does possess a raging attack against the White king based on the menacing diagonal on-slaught from his bishop pair. At this moment White should consider 23.Rxf8+ Rxf8; 24.Qe2 Bxg3; 25.Nf5. **23...Bxg3.** Of course 24.hxg3 Qxg3+; 25.Kh1 Bxe4 leads to a deadly pin on the long White diagonal.

24.Nc5 Rxf3.

White's next move appears to be forced and I doubt whether Kasparov took long to play it. Naturally 25.Qxf3 fails to 25...Qxh2 mate but the subtle 25.Ra2!! may still save White. For example, 25...Rxf1+; 26.Qxf1 Qxf1+; 27.Kxf1 Rc8 (forced to save the bishop) 28.Be3 Bf4 (again forced) and now White's best appears to be 29.Nxb7 Bxe3; 30.Rxa6 meeting 30...Rc3 with 31.Nd6 g6; 32.e5 with excellent counterchances. White's b-pawn is doomed but the passed e-pawn could become strong. Having missed this Kasparov is in dire straits.

25.Rxf3 Qxh2+; 26.Kf1 Bc6; 27.Bg5 Bb5+; 28.Nd3 Re8; 29.Ra2.

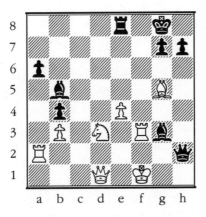

At long last, having rejected the concept on two earlier occasions, Kasparov realizes that the key to defending this position is to erect some kind of defensive system along his second rank. However, by now this palliative measure is really too late to save him.

29...Qh1+. Nevertheless, Kramnik does now become somewhat confused. There was a forced mate by means of 29...Bxd3+; 30.Rxd3 (30 Qxd3 Qh1+ and 31...Qe1) 30...Qh1+; 31.Ke2 Qg2+; 32.Ke3 Rxe4.

30.Ke2 Rxe4+; 31.Kd2 Qg2+; 32.Kc1 Qxa2; 33.Rxg3 Qa1+; 34.Kc2 Qc3+; 35.Kb1 Rd4. White resigns. Black's concentration of force against his king has become too powerful.

For example 36.Bf6 Bxd3+; 37.Ka2 Bb1+; 38.Qxb1 Rd2+; 39.Qb2 Rxb2+ and mate follows. A great win against a great opponent, only slightly marred by Black's failure to locate the faster mate on move 29.

Final Lessons

This game combined many of the elements and lessons we have learned.
To recap the themes present here:

---

a) Black's queen pressed tight up against White's king.
b) Black aimed both of his bishops in unison at the White monarch.
c) Black sacrificed material to annihilate the pawn shelter around White's king.
d) White's king ended up a refugee target in the center, exposed to checkmate.

CONCLUSION

This book has been designed as a general introduction to all the most important facets of playing chess. I have introduced newcomers to the moves and rules, shown you the basic tactics, how to handle the most popular openings, how to approach the middlegame successfully, developing a correct strategy and being aware of the possible winning ploys in common endgames.

Additionally, I have introduced readers to a new theory, following a hero, to help you improve your own results while at all times giving examples of best practice from games by the top grandmasters. I have also taken account some developments in computer chess and advise you to check out the internet (I refer you to Chess City - www.chesscity.com) so that you can gain the maximum advantage from modern technological advances in these areas. As well as this, I have given practical advice on how to achieve the maximum when you play in tournaments, with plenty of practical hints and given you a grounding in the history of chess and the most important champions. Learning about the culture of chess can be just as fascinating as learning how to play.

Finally, I have selected some of the most fantastic games ever played to show you the heights of imagination which the great masters can reach. Having absorbed all this, you will now possess a fully rounded chess education and should be ready to hold your own if you start to enter tournaments, follow chess articles or columns in major papers or, indeed, proceed to study more advanced books in the Cardoza series.

Good luck with your chess careers!

CARDOZA PUBLISHING CHESS BOOKS

- OPENINGS -

WINNING CHESS OPENINGS *by Bill Robertie* - Shows concepts and best opening moves of more than 25 essential openings from Black's and White's perspectives: King's Gambit, Center Game, Scotch Game, Giucco Piano, Vienna Game, Bishop's Opening, Ruy Lopez, French, Caro-Kann, Sicilian, Alekhine, Pirc, Modern, Queen's Gambit, Nimzo-Indian, Queen's Indian, Dutch, King's Indian, Benoni, English, Bird's, Reti's, and King's Indian Attack. Examples from 25 grandmasters and champions including Fischer and Kasparov. 144 pages, $9.95

WORLD CHAMPION OPENINGS *by Eric Schiller* - This serious reference work covers the essential opening theory and moves of every major chess opening and variation as played by *all* the world champions. Reading as much like an encyclopedia of the must-know openings crucial to every chess player's knowledge as a powerful tool showing the insights, concepts and secrets as used by the greatest players of all time, *World Champion Openings (WCO)* covers an astounding 100 crucial openings in full conceptual detail (with 100 actual games from the champions themselves)! *A must-have book for serious chess players.* 384 pages, $18.95

STANDARD CHESS OPENINGS *by Eric Schiller* - The new definitive standard on opening chess play in the 20th century, this comprehensive guide covers every important chess opening and variation ever played and currently in vogue. In all, more than 3,000 opening strategies are presented! Differing from previous opening books which rely almost exclusively on bare notation, *SCO* features substantial discussion and analysis on each opening so that you learn and understand the concepts behind them. Includes more than 250 completely annotated games (including a game representative of each major opening) and more than 1,000 diagrams! For modern players at any level, this is the standard reference book necessary for competitive play. *A must have for serious chess players!!!* 768 pages, $24.95

UNORTHODOX CHESS OPENINGS *by Eric Schiller* - The exciting guide to all the major unorthodox openings used by chess players, contains more than 1,500 weird, contentious, controversial, unconventional, arrogant, and outright strange opening strategies. From their tricky tactical surprises to their bizarre names, these openings fly in the face of tradition. You'll meet such openings as the Orangutang, Raptor Variation, Halloween Gambit, Double Duck, Frankenstein-Dracula Variation, and even the Drunken King! These openings are a sexy and exotic way to spice up a game and a great weapon to spring on unsuspecting and often unprepared opponents. More than 750 diagrams show essential positions. 528 pages, $24.95

GAMBIT OPENING REPERTOIRE FOR WHITE *by Eric Schiller* - Chessplayers who enjoy attacking from the very first move are rewarded here with a powerful repertoire of brilliant gambits. Starting off with 1.e4 or 1.d4 and then using such sharp weapons such as the Göring Gambit (Accepted and Declined), Halasz Gambit, Alapin Gambit, Ulysses Gambit, Short Attack and many more, to put great pressure on opponents, Schiller presents a complete attacking repertoire to use against the most popular defenses, including the Sicilian, French, Scandinavian, Caro-Kann, Pirc, Alekhine, and other Open Game positions. 192 pages, $14.95.

GAMBIT OPENING REPERTOIRE FOR BLACK *by Eric Schiller* - For players that like exciting no-holds-barred chess, this versatile gambit repertoire shows Black how to take charge with aggressive attacking defenses against any orthodox first White opening move; 1.e4, 1.d4 and 1.c4. Learn the Scandinavian Gambit against 1.e4, the Schara Gambit and Queen's Gambit Declined variations against 1.d4, and some flank and unorthodox gambits also. Black learns the secrets of seizing the initiative from White's hands, usually by investing a pawn or two, to begin powerful attacks that can send White to early defeat. 176 pages, $14.95.

COMPLETE DEFENSE TO QUEEN PAWN OPENINGS *by Eric Schiller* - This aggressive counterattacking repertoire covers Black opening systems against virtually every chess opening except for 1.e4 (including most flank games), based on the exciting and powerful Tarrasch Defense, an opening that helped bring Championship titles to Kasparov and Spassky. Black learns to effectively use the Classical Tarrasch, Symmetrical Tarrasch, Asymmetrical Tarrasch, Marshall and Tarrasch Gambits, and Tarrasch without Nc3, to achieve an early equality or even an outright advantage in the first few moves. 288 pages, $16.95.

COMPLETE DEFENSE TO KING PAWN OPENINGS *by Eric Schiller* - Learn a complete defensive system against 1.e4. This powerful repertoire not only limits White's ability to obtain any significant opening advantage but allows Black to adopt the flexible Caro-Kann formation, the favorite weapon of many of the greatest chess players. All White's options are explained in detail, and a plan is given for Black to combat them all. Analysis is up-to-date and backed by examples drawn from games of top stars. Detailed index lets you follow the opening from the point of a specific player, or through its history. 240 pages, $16.95.

SECRETS OF THE SICILIAN DRAGON by *GM Eduard Gufeld and Eric Schiller* - The mighty Dragon Variation of the Sicilian Defense is one of the most exciting openings in chess. Everything from opening piece formation to the endgame, including clear explanations of all the key strategic and tactical ideas, is covered in full conceptual detail. Instead of memorizing a jungle of variations, you learn the really important ideas behind the opening, and how to adapt them at the chessboard. Special sections on the heroes of the Dragon show how the greatest players handle the opening. The most instructive book on the Dragon written! 208 pages, $14.95.

HYPERMODERN OPENING REPERTOIRE FOR WHITE *by Eric Schiller* - Instead of placing pawns in the center of the board as traditional openings advise, this complete opening repertoire for White shows you how to stun opponents by "allowing" Black to occupy the center with its pawns, while building a crushing phalanx from the flanks, ready to smash the center apart with Black's slightest mistake. White's approach is simple to learn–because White almost always develops pieces in the same manner–but can be used against all defenses no matter what Black plays! Plentiful diagrams and explanations illustrate every concept, with games from the greatest players showing the principles in action.The Réti and English openings, which form the basis of the Hypermodern, lead to lively games with brilliant sacrifices and subtle maneuvering. 304 pages, $16.95.

SECRETS OF THE KING'S INDIAN *by Eduard Gufeld and Eric Schiller* - The King's Indian is the single most popular opening and offers great opportunities for spectacular attacks and clever defenses. Readers learn the fundamental concepts, critical ideas, and hidden resources along with the opening traps and typical tactical and strategic mistakes. All major variations are covered, including the Classical, Petrosian, Saemisch, Averbakh, Four Pawns, Fianchetto and unconventional lines. Players learn how the strategies and tactics were applied in the brilliant games of the most famous players, how they can apply them to their own game. 240 pages, $14.95.

- MIDDLEGAME/TACTICS/WINNING CONCEPTS -

WINNING CHESS TACTICS *by Bill Robertie* - 14 chapters of winning ideas show the complete thinking behind every tactical concept: pins, single and double forks, double attacks, skewers, discovered and double checks, multiple threats - and other crushing tactics to gain an immediate edge over opponents. Learn the power tools of tactical play to become a better player. Includes guide to chess notation. 128 pages, $9.95.

303 TRICKY CHESS TACTICS *Fred Wilson and Bruce Alberston* - Both a fascinating challenge and great training tool, this is a fun and entertaining collection of two and three move tactical surprises for the advanced beginner, intermediate, and expert player. Tactics are arranged by difficulty so that a player may measure progress as he advances from simple to the complex positions. The examples, drawn from actual games, illustrate a wide range of chess tactics from old classics right up to the 1990's. 192 pages, $12.95.

10 MOST COMMON CHESS MISTAKES and How to Fix Them *by Larry Evans* - This fascinating collection of 218 errors, oversights, and outright blunders, not only shows the price great players pay for violating basic principles, but how to avoid these mistakes in your own game. You'll be challenged to choose between two moves, the right one, or the one actually played. From neglecting development, king safety, misjudging threats, and premature attacks, to impulsiveness, snatching pawns, and basic inattention, you receive a complete course in where you can go wrong and how to fix it. 256 pages, $14.95.

ENCYCLOPEDIA OF CHESS WISDOM, The Essential Concepts and Strategies of Smart Chess Play *by Eric Schiller* - The most important concepts, strategies, tactics, wisdom, and thinking that every chessplayer must know, plus the gold nuggets of knowledge behind every attack and defense is collected together in one volume. Step-by-step, from opening, middle and endgame strategy, to psychological warfare and tournament tactics, Schiller shows the thinking behind each essential concept, and through examples, diagrams, and discussions, shows its impact on the game. 432 pages, $19.95.

WORLD CHAMPION COMBINATIONS *by Raymond Keene and Eric Schiller* - Learn the insights, concepts, and moves of the greatest combinations ever by the best players of all time. From Morphy to Alekhine, to Fischer to Kasparov, the incredible combinations and brilliant sacrifices of the 13 World Champions are collected here in the most insightful combinations book yet. Packed with fascinating strategems, 50 annotated games, and great practical advice for your own games, this is a great companion guide to *World Champion Openings* and the other titles in the *World Champion* series. 264 pages, $16.95.

WORLD CHAMPION TACTICS *by Leonid Shamkovich and Eric Schiller* - The authors show how the greatest players who ever lived used their entire arsenal of tactical weapons to bring opponents to their knees. Packed with fascinating strategems, 50 fully annotated games, and more than 200 diagrams, players learn not only the thinking and game plan behind the moves of the champions, but the insights that will allow them to use these brilliancies in their own games. Each tactical concept is fully explained with examples and game situations from the champions themselves. 304 pages, $18.95.

WORLD CHAMPION CHESS MATCHES *by Eduard Gufeld and Efim Lazerev* - The exciting highlights and great games of every World Championship chess match are recounted in Gufeld's lively style, with anecdotes, little-known stories and hundreds of key position diagrams. Gufeld does much more than present the in-depth analysis and thinking behind the moves of the greatest of the greats: Gurus, paraphsycologists, dirty tricks, psychological warfare and all the side shows that have brought worldwide media attention to each contest are brought to life. Gufeld should know these secrets; he has played with the very best for decades, and has to his credit the scalps of three former world champions and eight world championship candidates. 304 pages, $18.95.

- BEGINNING AND GENERAL CHESS BOOKS -

THE BASICS OF WINNING CHESS *by Jacob Cantrell* - A great first book of chess, in one easy reading, beginner's learn the moves, pieces, basic rules and principles of play, standard openings, and both Algebraic and English chess notation. The basic ideas of the winning concepts and strategies of middle and end game play are also shown. Includes example games of champions. 64 pages, $4.95.

BEGINNING CHESS PLAY *by Bill Robertie* - Step-by-step approach uses 113 diagrams to teach the basics of chess: opening, middle and endgame strategies, principles of development, pawn structure, checkmates, openings and defenses, how to write and read chess notation, join a chess club, play in tournaments, use a chess clock, and get rated. Two annotated games illlustrate strategic thinking for easy learning. 144 pages, $9.95

WHIZ KIDS TEACH CHESS *Eric Schiller & the Whiz Kids* - Today's greatest young stars, some perhaps to be future world champions, present a fascinating look at the world of chess. Each tells of their successes, failures, world travels, and love of chess, show off their best moves, and admit to their most embarrassing blunders. This is more than just a fascinating look at prodigies like Vinay Bhat and Irina Krush, it's also a primer featuring diagrams, explanations, and winning ideas for young players. 144 oversized pages, $14.95.

KEENE ON CHESS *by Raymond Keene* - Complete step-by-step course shows how to play and deepen one's understanding of chess while keeping the game fun and exciting. Fascinating chapters on chess heroes and lessons one can learn from these greats, basic chess openings, strategy, tactics, the best games of chess ever played, and the history of chess round out a player's education. Readers also learn how to use chess notation and all the basic concepts of game play – castling, pawn promotion, putting an opponent into check, the five ways of drawing or stalemating games, en passant, actual checkmate, and much more. 320 pages, $18.95.

- MATES & ENDGAMES -

303 TRICKY CHECKMATES *by Fred Wilson and Bruce Alberston* - Both a fascinating challenge and great training tool, this collection of two, three and bonus four move checkmates is great for advanced beginning, intermediate and expert players. Mates are in order of difficulty, from the simple to very complex positions. Learn the standard patterns and stratagems for cornering the king: corridor and support mates, attraction and deflection sacrifices, pins and annihilation, the quiet move, and the dreaded *zugzwang*. Examples, drawn from actual games, illustrate a wide range of chess tactics from classics right up to the 1990's. 192 pages, $12.95.

MASTER CHECKMATE STRATEGY *by Bill Robertie* - Learn the basic combinations, plus advanced, surprising and unconventional mates, the most effective pieces needed to win, and how to mate opponents with just a pawn advantage. also, how to work two rooks into an unstoppable attack; how to wield a queen advantage with deadly intent; how to coordinate pieces of differing strengths into indefensible positions of their opponents; when it's best to have a knight, and when a bishop to win. 144 pages, $9.95

BASIC ENDGAME STRATEGY: Kings, Pawns and Minor Pieces *by Bill Robertie* - Learn the mating principles and combinations needed to finish off opponents. From the four basic checkmates using the King with the queen, rook, two bishops, and bishop/knight combinations, to the King/pawn, King/Knight and King/Bishop endgames, you'll learn the essentials of translating small edges into decisive checkmates. Learn the 50-move rule, and the combinations of pieces that can't force a mate against a lone King. 144 pages, $12.95.

BASIC ENDGAME STRATEGY: Rooks and Queens *by Bill Robertie* - The companion guide to *Basic Endgame : Kings, Pawns and Minor Pieces*, you'll learn the basic mating principles and combinations of the Queen and Rook with King, how to turn middlegame advantages into victories, by creating passed pawns, using the King as a weapon, clearing the way for rook mates, and other endgame combinations. 144 pages, $12.95.

365 ESSENTIAL ENDGAME POSITIONS *by Eric Schiller* - From basic mates to sophisticated double-rook endgames, every essential endgame concept is explained. An enormous 365 positions show endgames of every stripe; from king and pawn and bishops vs. knights, rook and pawn vs. two minor pieces, tricky endgames where no pawns are present, and much more.The thinking behind every position is explained in words (unlike diagram-only books) so that you learn which positions are winning, drawn, or cannot be saved. Frequent diagrams show both starting and target positions, so you can visualize the end goals, and steer the middlegame into a successful endgame mate. 400 pages, $18.95.

NEW - CHESSCITY MAGAZINE
Free Online Chess Magazine

CHESS CITY is a sprawling metropolis of chess information, a magazine with the latest news and analysis, to gossip, trivia, and fun features. Travel around the world to visit the most fascinating chess competitions, preview books long they hit the shelves, and read columns on openings, middlegames, endings, tactics, strategies, mates, and more.

Extensive excerpts from our books are available online. Visit often, because we'll be adding more features for your pleasure! Improve your chess knowledge with our articles and features on the opening, middlegame, endgame, strategy, tactics checkmates and more! Whether you're a beginner or master, you'll be able to improve your results with our tips.

Chess is a serious game, but it is also a lot of fun. Chess City Magazine presents trivia, photos, anecdotes, chess art, strange games, trivia and even a bit of gossip for your amusement and pleasure! Drop by often when you need a break!

Go to www.chesscity.com for details

CARDOZA PUBLISHING ONLINE
www.cardozapub.com

To find out about our latest chess and backgammon publications, see our online catalog (www.cardozapub.com) or visit Chess City, our free chess magazine (www.chesscity.com).

USE THIS ORDER FORM TO GET YOUR CHESS BOOKS!

YES! I want to be a better chess player! Rush me these books: (Write in choices below):

Quantity	Your Book Order	Price	

MAKE CHECKS TO:
Cardoza Publishing
132 Hastings Street
Brooklyn, NY 11235

CHARGE BY PHONE:
Toll-Free: 1-800-577-WINS
Local Phone: 718-743-5229
Fax Orders: 718-743-8284
E-Mail Orders: CardozaPub@aol.com

Subtotal		
Postage/Handling: First Item	$5	00
Additional Postage		
Total Amount Due		

SHIPPING CHARGES: For US orders, include $5.00 postage/handling 1st book ordered; for each additional book, add $1.00. For Canada/Mexico, double above amounts, quadruple (4X) for all other countries. Orders outside U.S., money order payable in U.S. dollars on U.S. bank only.

NAME _____

ADDRESS _____

CITY _____ STATE _____ ZIP _____

30 day money back guarantee!   Keene